DISCRIMINATION
AGAINST
WOMEN
Prevalence,
Consequences,
Remedies

Hope Landrine
Elizabeth A. Klonoff

SAGE Publications
International Educational and Professional Publisher
Thousand Oaks London New Delhi

For information:

SAGE Publications, Inc.
2455 Teller Road
Thousand Oaks, California 91320
E-mail: order@sagepub.com

SAGE Publications Ltd.
6 Bonhill Street
London EC2A 4PU
United Kingdom

SAGE Publications India Pvt. Ltd.
M-32 Market
Greater Kailash I
New Delhi 110 048 India

HQ
1237.5
.U6
D57
1997

Printed in the United States of America

Library of Congress Cataloging-in-Publication Data

Main entry under title:

Discrimination against women: prevalence, consequences, remedies/
    edited by Hope Landrine and Elizabeth A. Klonoff.
       p. cm.
    Includes bibliographical references (p.) and index.
    ISBN 0-7619-0954-0 (cloth: acid-free paper).—ISBN 0-7619-0955-9
(pbk.: acid-free paper)
    1. Sex discrimination against women—United States. 2. Sex discrimination against women—Health aspects—United States. 3. Sex discrimination against women—United States—Prevention. 4. Stress (Psychology) I. Landrine, Hope, 1954- .
II. Klonoff, Elizabeth A.
HQ1237.5.U6D57 1997
305.42'0973—dc21
                                   97-4766

97 98 99 00 01 02 03 10 9 8 7 6 5 4 3 2 1

Acquiring Editor: Jim Nageotte
Editorial Assistant: Kathleen Derby
Production Editor: Michele Lingre
Production Assistant: Denise Santoyo
Typesetter/Designer: Marion Warren
Indexer: Cristina Haley
Cover Designer: Candice Harman
Print Buyer: Anna Chin

*For our mothers and
for women everywhere*

Contents

Part I

Prevalence and Consequences of Sexist Discrimination

Foreword

Discrimination is a major challenge to our contemporary society as well as to our global village. Embedded in economic, political, social, and psychological contexts, discrimination becomes an issue of survival. Hope Landrine and Elizabeth A. Klonoff advance the empirical study of discrimination to a higher echelon, documenting the detrimental effects of discrimination on women. Like modern Cassandras, they prophesize within the illustrious confines of research methods. Their predictions are not in vain, their compelling findings persuade those who would listen: Discrimination harms women.

This book offers a format to be used as a model in addressing women's issues. By focusing on sexist discrimination, it discusses its prevalence and consequences while offering remedies. In a truly empowering manner, the authors make the statistical analyses available to non-statisticians, by adding book appendices with lay explanations. Landrine and Klonoff provide a theoretical model of how sexist discrimination causes symptoms in women. Their empirical analyses effectively document the existence of discrimination and its effect on women. Sexist discrimination is insidiously present in the health care system through diagnosis, treatment, insurance benefits, and research. It is also alive and well in the workplace through the devaluation of women's competence and discrimination in salaries, as well as in schools, colleges, and other higher education institutions.

Acknowledging that discrimination is rampant, the researchers concentrate on nonviolent and subtle types of sexist discrimination. Such focus aims to address a gap in the literature because subtle discrimination has been neglected by the research. Thus a major contribution of this book is the empirical documentation of the presence of subtle but pervasive discrimination in women's daily lives. Instances of subtle discrimination involve being ignored, excluded, ridiculed, and treated in an unfair manner. Landrine and Klonoff assert that this subtle level is the level at which most discrimination occurs in women's daily lives. The results discussed in this book suggest that the presence and exposure to sexist acts, rather than women's subjective appraisals of those acts, predict women's symptoms.

The research findings also speak of women's diversity in their experiences of discrimination. By attending to the interaction of gender, ethnicity, and other variables, the researchers found that women of color reported more frequent sexist discrimination than White women in certain domains. As an illustration, Latinas and Asian Americans reported more frequent sexist treatment in their personal realtionships than did White women. Similarly, sexist events contribute even more to the symptoms of non-feminist women than of feminist women.

What can women do about discrimination? Landrine and Klonoff enlist the help of experts who contribute to the volume. These experts conclude that women can use diverse individual and collective strategies to combat sexist discrimination. In addition, they provide basic information on the legal status of discrimination suits and this serves as a valuable resource for women considering legal action. Based on their own data analysis, Landrine and Klonoff add that endorsing a feminist perspective is another remedy against discrimination. Similar to strong social support networks, which can protect women from the deleterious consequences of sexism, a feminist perspective appears to be a powerful resource against discrimination. The researchers also advocate self-empowerment by suggesting calling attention to sexist behavior as a means of extinguishing it.

Please join me in celebrating the publication of this book. Hope Landrine's and Elizabeth Klonoff's voices echo in the desert of a backlash against women's rights. Although this volume comes at a critical time when affirmative action programs are being dismantled due to accusations of reverse discrimination, it is an occasion for a joyous commemoration. As a feminist effort, the authors present valuable information in a collaborative manner. If we pay careful attention, we can try to emulate their inspiring example. Their systemic model involves informing themselves about a deleterious problem, using an armamentum of research methods, providing effective remedies, and power-sharing. Moreover, their major contribution is the empirically based conclusion that as women, we have to develop self empowerment against all odds by being vocal, expressing our concerns, and taking action.

Lillian Comas-Díaz, PhD
Editor in Chief,
Cultural Diversity and Mental Health
and Executive Director,
Transcultural Mental Health Institute

Preface

In this book, we report a set of scientific studies that we conducted in 1995 to assess the frequency of discrimination against women and to examine the physical and mental health impact of that discrimination. We conducted these studies by surveying 1,279 women who were diverse in their education, ethnicity, age, and income and were therefore representative of women in the nation. Our two major findings were

1. Discrimination against women is rampant in America, insofar as 99% of women reported being discriminated against in some form or another. This discrimination ranged from subtle acts, such as being told sexist jokes, being called sexist names (e.g., "bitch"), and being treated as if they were stupid, to discrimination in salaries and promotion, to being physically harmed.

2. We found that this discrimination not only contributed to physical and psychiatric symptoms among women **but also was the single best predictor of those symptoms.** In other words, we found that sexist discrimination—even subtle discrimination, such as being called names—harms women.

Because we believe that these results are important to all women, we have taken two steps in addition to reporting these scientific findings in detail. First, we have tried to make this research accessible to all women by explaining the scientific terminology and statistical analyses. The terminology and the statistics in this book are necessary and indeed essential to a clear scientific proof of the frequency and impact of sexism on women and so must remain. However, we have included an appendix ("Understanding the Statistics Used in This Book"), which explains the scientific terminology and the statistics in simple, nonmathematical terms. We suggest that readers unfamiliar with scientific research or with statistics read this appendix before reading the chapters and consult the appendix while reading the chapters. Readers will find that even the most complex statistics are not difficult to understand and that statistics are an extraordinarily powerful tool for testing and proving a point.

In addition to this effort to make the scientific findings more accessible, we have included a section on what women can do about the discrimination in their lives. These two chapters constitute Part II of the book and were contributed by well-known psychologists, who provide information and specific suggestions on steps that women can take to understand and address the discrimination that they face and to decrease its negative impact. Our hope is that women who read this book will find that they are not alone in facing and struggling with discrimination and that there are things that can be done about it. Finally, in Part III of the book, we have included a review of the laws regarding discrimination against women and of the major court cases of this type, in a chapter written by two prominent attorneys. The purpose of this chapter is to provide women with basic information on the legal status of discrimination suits. We hope that this information can serve as a valuable resource for women who are considering legal action.

Last, we want to acknowledge that race and ethnic discrimination are equally important problems, which no doubt pose a threat to the health of minorities and interact with sexism to pose double threats to the health of minority women. Indeed, one of the only studies of the negative health impact of race discrimination is our own article, "The Schedule of Racist Events: A Measure of Racial Discrimination and a Study of Its Negative Physical and Mental Health Consequences," which was published in the *Journal of Black Psychology* in 1996 (Volume 22, No. 2, 144-168. Also, see the chapter on racism in our book *African American Acculturation: Deconstructing Race and Reviving Culture,* published by Sage, 1996). Likewise, one of the only studies of how race, sex, and class discrimination interact is our own study, "Multiple Variables in Discrimination," published in B. Lott and D. Maluso's 1995 book *The Social Psychology of Interpersonal Discrimination.* Although discrimination based on ethnicity and social class are equally important threats to health, we cannot cover them in this book. That is, in **the first book to ever explore the health impact of sex discrimination,** we cannot examine the health impact of other kinds of discrimination as well. We do, however, carefully examine the differential impact of sex discrimination on women of color versus White women in this book and leave the topic of the interactions of various kinds of discrimination and their effects on women's health for another book.

Hope Landrine and
Elizabeth A. Klonoff

Acknowledgments

We are grateful to the following for assistance in collecting and keypunching the data reported in this book: Jeannine Gibbs, Vickie Manning, Marlene Lund, Robin Campbell, Roxanna Alcaraz, M. Barrientos-Lewis, Stephanie Callahan, Nicole Coulte, Joyce Daniels, Sherry Ellison, Linda Emerson, Martha Esparza, Monica Fuller, Laura LaFerr, Michael Landsman, Susan Loring, Tracy Macz, Cynthia Olivo, Brent Palmer, Barbara Saucedo, Timothy Short, Yolanda Tamayo, Dawn Tomlinson, Branda Wood, and Shannon Wylie.

PART I

Prevalence and Consequences
of Sexist Discrimination

Introduction

Discrimination Against Women

THE SCIENTIFIC EVIDENCE

Numerous scientific studies have demonstrated that discrimination against women in America persists, despite the law, and is widespread. Such discrimination has been documented unambiguously in most arenas of life, ranging from how women versus men are treated in face-to-face interactions (Lott, 1987, 1989) to the sexual harassment of women students and faculty (Paludi, 1990); to the unequal treatment of women in employment, housing, and health and social services (Feagin & Feagin, 1978; Krieger, 1990). For example, consider the following.

Discrimination in Health Care

Many studies have shown that women are discriminated against in health care. For example, coronary heart disease (CHD) occurs in women and in men, and it is the leading cause of death among both (Klonoff, Landrine, & Scott, 1995). Nonetheless, when women and men both present similar cardiac symptoms, physicians are more likely to attribute women's symptoms than men's to psychiatric and other noncardiac causes (Council on Ethical and Judicial Affairs of the American Medical Association, 1991;

3

Tobin et al., 1987). Physicians are also significantly more likely to order important procedures for diagnosing heart disease (e.g., thallium stress tests and cardiac catheterization) for men than for women who present the same cardiac symptoms (Wassertheil-Smoller et al., 1987). If women finally receive tests to diagnose heart disease (e.g., an emergency room electrocardiogram), they receive these significantly later than men, and such diagnostic delays then result in a delay in receiving treatment for women—but not for men (Hawthorne, 1993; Heston & Lewis, 1992). In addition, when finally diagnosed with CHD, women are less likely than men with precisely the same disorder to receive life-saving treatments such as coronary artery bypass surgery and coronary angioplasty (Ayanian & Epstein, 1991; Wenger, 1990). Clearly, women can and do die from this discrimination against them in diagnosis and treatment; such discrimination is not limited to CHD.

AIDS Diagnosis. The AIDS epidemic is a frightening example of bias against women in medical diagnosis. Specifically, 10 years of evidence has shown that the major diagnostic signs of AIDS in women are chronic vaginal infections and cervical dysplasia (Smeltzer & Whipple, 1991). Nonetheless, these symptoms have not been added to the nationally referenced lists of symptoms that are distributed by the Centers for Disease Control (CDC; Fogel & Woods, 1995). Thus physicians have not been alerted to the possibly serious (AIDS-related) meaning of these symptoms in women, and no public health education program to date warns women about the possible meaning of these symptoms either. Only in 1992 did the CDC finally propose adding invasive cervical cancer to the list of 23 symptoms (e.g., Kaposi's sarcoma) of AIDS (Fogel & Woods, 1995). Any failure to diagnose AIDS in women due to a sex-biased definition of the disease obviously constitutes a serious threat to women's health, and to the health of their loved ones and children (Fogel & Woods, 1995; Smeltzer & Whipple, 1991).

Drug and Alcohol Treatment. Other studies have shown that women are discriminated against in drug and alcohol treatment. Specifically, more than 75% of all drug and alcohol treatment programs are designed for men, and there are beds held and reserved for men even though women suffer substance use problems of equal severity (Fogel & Woods, 1995; Lex et al., 1990). Treatment programs designed for male substance abusers also are more comprehensive in both treatment provided and facilities than programs designed for women (Lex et al., 1990).

Medical Insurance. Numerous studies have found that middle-aged and older women, compared with men, are twice as likely to have no health insurance, are less likely to have insurance through their jobs, and, if insured, pay significantly higher premiums than men (Clancy & Massion, 1992; Fogel & Woods, 1995). Indeed, Medicare coverage specifically discriminates against women (Clancy & Massion, 1992) in that it provides full coverage for diseases that are common among men (e.g., lung cancer), but inadequate coverage for diseases that are common among women (e.g., breast cancer).

Health Research. Finally, health research also discriminates against women in the sense that women are usually excluded from it. For example, even though women have extraordinarily high rates of CHD, diabetes, and hypertension (minority women in particular), research on the causes of these diseases rarely includes women—even when women have the single highest rate of the disease in question (Klonoff et al., 1995). Similarly, clinical trials (studies designed to test new treatments for a disease) typically exclude women as participants, and hence it is not known if the new treatments would help women (Bennett, 1993). The major study testing the extent to which taking aspirin would help prevent heart disease was based on men alone—*all* of the 22,071 participants in the study were men (Physicians' Health Study Group, 1989). Likewise, even though CHD is the leading cause of death among women, the first study designed to understand and cure this disease by examining a women-only sample was not conducted until late 1992 (Fogel & Woods, 1995). Indeed, only 13% of the National Institutes of Health (NIH) research funds—funds from the tax dollars of women and men—go to study the health problems of women (Litt, 1992).

Such discrimination in medical diagnosis, treatment, and research constitutes a "hidden malpractice" that can and does cost women's lives (for details, see Corea, 1985). Discrimination in health care is merely one of the many types or arenas of discrimination against women.

Discrimination in Salaries

Literally thousands of studies have demonstrated that women are paid less than men, irrespective of their race or ethnic group. Table A displays the average salaries paid in 1989 to women and men 45 to 49 years old. As shown, men in each ethnic group were paid more than the women

TABLE A Average 1989 Salaries by Gender and Ethnicity for Women and Men, Ages 45 to 49 Years

	Men	Women	Salary Difference	
All	38,174	17,370	All men v. All women:	$20,804
Whites	39,992	17,255	White men v. White women:	$22,737
Blacks	22,856	16,541	Black men v. Black Women:	$ 6,315
Latinos/as	27,772	12,329	Latinos v. Latinas:	$15,443

SOURCE: U.S. Bureau of the Census (1991).

TABLE B Average 1989 Salaries by Gender, at Various Ages

Age	Men	Women	Salary Difference
15 to 24	8,875	6,947	1,928
25 to 29	21,650	14,008	7,642
30 to 34	26,803	14,848	11,955
35 to 39	32,199	16,108	16,091
40 to 44	36,387	17,442	18,945
45 to 49	38,174	17,370	20,804
50 to 54	36,942	15,495	21,447
55 to 59	34,005	13,892	20,113
60 to 64	29,716	12,544	17,172
65 to 69	22,288	10,640	11,648
70 to 74	18,737	11,204	7,533
75 & up	15,284	10,491	4,793

SOURCE: U.S. Bureau of the Census (1991).

in their group, with the gender gap in salaries ranging from $6,315 to $22,737. These differences hold irrespective of age, as shown in Table B.

These salary differences, of course, might not reflect discrimination against women; instead, they could be a simple function of the fact that women and men tend to do different kinds of jobs, and the salaries attached to those differ. For example, electricians (usually men) earn about twice as much as secretaries (usually women). Likewise, women and men might differ in their levels of education, which in turn would effect their salaries, and neither job classification nor education is considered in data collected nationally in the U.S. Census. Unfortunately, however, countless well-controlled studies have demonstrated that sex differences in salaries are not an artifact of such factors. Instead, many studies have proven that women are paid less than men even when doing precisely the same type of job (same job classification) and with the same level of education and experience. O'Neill (1985) found that women were paid 72% of what men were paid (72 cents for every dollar) when occupying the same job, with the same job status and title and the same level of education and experience. Idson and Price (1992) found similar results in their study of public workers in Dade County, Florida. The government employees they studied were matched for job title and education: White women were paid 74.8 cents for every dollar paid to White men. Other studies have shown that women are paid less than their male counterparts for the same job, no matter what occupation they are in: Such results have been found for motor vehicle operators (Colatosi, 1992); engineers, doctors, and accountants (Schreiner, 1984); computer software designers (Schmidt, 1985); and even comedians (Leader, 1991). Gender differences in salary vary with the type of job (and are larger in some occupations than in others) but remain nonetheless. As Lott (1994) summarized it,

> For every dollar earned by men, women in the same occupation earned 73 cents as a bookkeeper, 80 cents as a computer programmer, 76 cents as a cook, 75 cents as a lawyer, 61 cents as an office manager, and 80 cents as a social worker. (p. 245)

Hence, male schoolteachers earn $2,000 per year more than their women counterparts, but male school superintendents earn $3,000 more than female counterparts (Kleinman, 1983, 1991). Male lawyers earn $30,000 per year more than women lawyers, whereas male college professors earn $10,000 to $20,000 more than their colleagues (Lott, 1994). At Harvard University in 1993 for example, male (full) professors were paid $93,600 and their women counterparts $79,900 (DePalma, 1993). In fact, the higher the salary of the job, the greater the gender difference in that salary is. In 1991, Jane Pauley of the *Today* show was paid $750,000, whereas her co-anchor, Byrant Gumbel, was paid $2 million for the same job. Likewise, Al Pacino was paid $6 million, but Michelle Pfeiffer $3 million, for their roles in the film *Frankie and Johnny,* although each had about the same number of lines (see Lott, 1994).

Researchers who attempt to carefully control for other possible causes of the gender difference in salaries (causes other than discrimination) have found that the difference remains, no matter what other factors are taken into account. Jagacinski, LeBold, and Linden (1987) reasoned that the breaks some women take from their careers to have children might account for their lower wages. Thus Jagacinski et al. (1987) matched women and men engineers, not only on job title, education, and experience, but also on number of years since they received their engineering degrees and on number and length of breaks in working. Even when controlling for all these factors, the researchers found that the women were paid $4,600 per year less than their male counterparts. Level of education does not change this picture. Many studies have shown that women are paid less than men irrespective of level of education and that the salary gap *increases* as education increases (e.g., Eccles, 1987). Indeed, Eccles (1987) found that men with *high school* diplomas were paid significantly more than women *college* graduates.

These gender differences in salary not only hold across race and ethnicity but also are exacerbated by minority group status; ethnic discrimination interacts with sex discrimination to yield extremely low salaries for minority women (Landrine, Klonoff, Alcaraz, Scott, & Wilkins, 1995). Thus, as shown in Table A, White men were paid $22,737 more than White women, $23,451 more than Black women, and $27,663 more than Latinas in 1989. In a similar study of this issue, Colatosti (1992) found that White women were paid 75 cents for every dollar paid to White men, Black women 61 cents, and Latina women 55 cents (1992 incomes). These differences are major differences that impair women's ability to support themselves and their children. For example, the Colatosti data mean that

- If a job paid White men $20,000, then White women received $15,000, Black women $12,200, and Latinas $11,000 for the same work.
- If a job paid White men $35,000, White women received $26,250, Black women $21,350, and Latinas $19,250 for the same work.
- If a job paid White men $50,000, then White women received $37,500, Black women received $30,500, and Latina women received $27,500 for the same work.

The study by Idson and Price (1992) found results similar to those of Colatosti. Even when matched on job title, job status, and number of years of education and experience, White women's salaries were 74.8% those of White men (74.8 cents per White male dollar), Latinas' salaries 72.8% those *of White women,* and Black women's salaries 61.5% those *of White women.*

Finally, a 1991 report from the United Nations revealed that male-female salary differences cannot be attributed to experience, skill, or even personality differences between women and men. Focusing on 140 people who had sex-change operations, the study found that all women who had changed to men experienced a large increase in their subsequent salaries, whereas (all but two) men who had changed to women experienced a sharp drop in their subsequent salaries ("News from the United Nations," 1991). Based on the results of thousands of careful scientific studies, one must conclude that women continue to be discriminated against in salaries despite the law (e.g., the Civil Rights Act of 1964) prohibiting that. This does not mean that gender differences in wages have not changed over the years. In fact, the gap has narrowed over time: In 1968, White women were paid 58.5 cents for every dollar paid to a White man; in 1976, they were paid 60 cents; in 1986, it was 65 cents, and in 1992, they were paid 75 cents for every dollar (Colatosti, 1992). Despite the changes over the years and the narrowing of the gap, it is clear that women still have a long way to go where equal pay for equal work is concerned. Discrimination in wages is not the only work-related discrimination that women continue to face.

Other Discrimination at Work

In addition to being paid less, women are also more likely than men to be laid off (Greenhouse, 1984) and to be fired (Kleinman, 1988), and they are less likely to have adequate health insurance and other fringe benefits, such as vacations, at work (Perman & Stevens, 1989)—even when factors such as time on the job, number of hours worked, and job title are taken into account. Likewise, women are less likely than their male counterparts to be promoted, even when their job performance evaluations match those of men (Gupta, Jenkins, & Beehr, 1983; Kleinman, 1991). Women also are offered fewer opportunities than men at work, including opportunities to travel and to increase their levels of responsibility and independence at work (see Lott, 1994). Thus, although women constitute 20% of Hollywood's directors, they have directed only 5% of the major films and none of the major television mini-series. When they did, they were paid less than men—an average of $135,000 for men versus $70,000 for women directors. These women reported that this was not due to lack of motivation, experience, hard work, or effort, but rather to blatant discrimination against them—which they reported is the rule in Hollywood (Lott, 1994; Rohter, 1991).

The Devaluation of Women's Competence. One of the reasons that women are paid less than men and offered fewer important job opportunities is that women are seen as, *and are evaluated as,* less competent than men even when their credentials and performance are exactly the same. This phenomenon is called *the devaluation of women's competence,* and evidence for it comes from several sources. For example, in one experiment, an identical math paper was submitted to mathematicians for evaluation of its quality; for half of these evaluators, the paper's author was listed as "John McKay" and for the others, as "Joan McKay." Results revealed that John's paper received a higher evaluation (see Selvin, 1991). This particular experiment has been conducted many times with many different types of people as the evaluators, and the results are consistent. Whether the evaluators are women or men, college students or professionals, Joan McKay's work is evaluated lower than the identical work attributed to a male counterpart (Goldberg, 1968; Paludi & Bauer, 1983; Paludi & Strayer, 1985; Selvin, 1991).

Likewise, in a scientific experiment on sex discrimination in hiring, Fidell (1970) composed the fictitious resume of a psychologist and sent it to the heads of the psychology departments at many U.S. colleges and universities, asking them if they would hire the individual and if so, at what level and salary. For half of the department heads, the psychologist's resume had a woman's name on it, and for the other half, a man's name. Fidell found that the "woman" psychologist was evaluated lower and offered a lower-level job with a lower salary than the "man" psychologist whose resume was precisely the same. This experiment has been repeated many times with similar results: Women's resumes and credentials are rated lower than those of men even when they are precisely identical (as in scientific experiments), and hence women are offered lower-status and lower-paying jobs than men (Betz & Fitzgerald, 1987; Fitzgerald & Betz, 1983; Nieva & Gutek, 1981). Alternatively, in "the real world" of people applying for engineering jobs, Gerdes and Garber (1983) found that women applicants received lower evaluations than men and hence were less likely to be hired, even though their credentials (their actual job applications) were the same.

The devaluation of women's competence may be related to sexist beliefs about the reasons behind a man's versus a woman's success: People tend to believe that a woman's success is due to luck or hard work but a man's is due to his basic ability; hence, a man's resume, even though identical to a woman's, is rated higher. In a 1982 study, Yarkin, Town, and Wallston gave people precisely the same written description of the career of a successful banking officer, presenting this person as a man to half of the participants and as a woman to the remainder, and then asked the participants in the research to explain the banker's success. Without fail, people attributed the woman's success to good luck or hard work and perseverance (motivation), whereas the man's success was attributed to his basic superior ability. Because luck and motivation are temporary states that may disappear at any time, whereas superior ability is stable, a person who has been successful for the latter reason is seen as a better qualified and more reliable employee.

This devaluation of women's competence, when coupled with the tendency to assume that women's success is due to luck, undoubtedly affects how women are treated at work in face-to-face interactions: Over and over again in many studies, women report that their comments and suggestions are ignored or are ridiculed; that men making the identical comments receive praise whereas they do not, and that they are excluded from meetings, networks, lunches, and other activities that are part of the "old boy" network and of the road to career advancement (Feagin & Feagin, 1978; Harris & Associates, 1985; Henley, 1977; Krieger, 1990; Lott, 1987, 1989; Wolman & Frank, 1975). Likewise, in a recent Harris poll, men agreed with women's reports. *Men* reported that they have observed such discrimination against women (Harris & Associates, 1985).

Sexual Harassment at Work

A final example (of the many we could provide) of discrimination against women is the widespread sexual harassment of women in the workplace—as well as in high schools, colleges, and universities. Sexual harassment refers to (a) unwelcome sexual advances, (b) requests for sexual favors, and (c) any verbal or physical behavior of a sexual nature. It is illegal and has been defined as a form of discrimination against women by the Equal Employment Opportunity Commission (EEOC) and the U.S. government (Title VII of the Civil Rights Act of 1964). This means that it is illegal for coworkers, colleagues, supervisors, teachers, managers, employers, bosses, and professors to make unwanted sexual advances and sexual comments of any sort to women. Despite the law, however, large percentages of women report this kind of discrimination at work.

For example, in a large study of federal employees, Tangri, Burt, and Johnson (1982) found that 42% of women reported being sexually harassed in the past 2 years. Another independent study of federal workers published at about the same time—and conducted by the federal government—found similar results (U.S. Merit System Protection Board, 1981). Large studies of women working in the private sector (Gutek, 1985, 1992) likewise found that 53% of women reported at least one incident of sexual harassment at work and that the majority said and did nothing about it. The harassment included sexual comments and jokes as well as touching. Similarly, Paludi (1990) found frequent sexual harassment of women college students and faculty in U.S. colleges and universities. Likewise, results of a large, objective poll by *Newsweek* (October 1992) found that 21% of women reported being sexually harassed at work, and 42% reported that they knew other women who had been harassed. Issues regarding sexual harassment are addressed in Chapters 8 and 9.

WOMEN'S EXPERIENCES

These objective, scientific studies—many conducted by the federal government, which has nothing to gain by finding discrimination—indicate that widespread discrimination against women continues in America. The findings of these studies match what women have told us about their experiences. In an unpublished 1995 survey, we asked a random group of 120 women who were waiting in an airport (for flights to arrive or depart) to tell us the worst thing that has ever happened to or been done to them *because they are women*; we asked them to write down the worst experience with sexist discrimination that they have faced. Below are a few of their responses, reproduced verbatim.

> *Woman No. 2: Age 64, married, White.* When I was 24 in 1955, I went to work, and within a week, my boss said if I made another mistake, he would take down my pants and spank me, and [he] leered. I quit . . . I've not worked since then.
>
> *Woman No. 90: Age 20, single, White.* I have an experience every day: Someone [at work] comments about my breasts.
>
> *Woman No. 57: Age 21, single, Indian (from India).* [The worst thing?] Being flirted with by male coworkers or my bosses in almost every job that I've had.
>
> *Woman No. 55: Age 53, married, Native American.* [The worst thing was when] I was told I could not be a supervisor at General Dynamics in the machine shop [because I'm a woman]. I [eventually] made it and was rated No. 1 for 8 years. I was the first woman to do this. The male supervisors had heartburn, but they learned to deal with me.
>
> *Woman No. 64: Age 21, single, White.* I think the hardest thing for me is that I have to work twice as hard as a man [at my job] to prove myself, and even then it's not enough. I feel like the only way to succeed, especially at my work, is to wear a shorter skirt and tighter blouse. That alone makes

me furious because I know I can do a hell of a better job than most of my male counterparts.

Woman No. 93: Age 18, single, White. I work with all guys at work and they [said] that I have to do sexual favors for the bosses in order to get raises.

Woman No. 67: Age 26, single, Asian. [My] boss said to me that I don't need high education because I am a girl—girls should marry and have family.

Woman No. 107: Age 25, single, Black. I was denied a promotion because I am a woman.

Woman No. 86: Age 21, single, White. I am a cocktail waitress 5 days a week. . . . I get [sexual] comments all the time, but I pretty much ignore them . . . [but] sometimes I feel I put up with a little too much. I have to sort of expect it because it goes with the job, but sometimes I think, who are these guys and where are their morals and respect for women to say the things they do?

Woman No. 71: Age 21, single, White. Sexual harassment in the workplace. The guys I work with grab me and look up my skirt. When I told my manager what was going on, he just thought I was overreacting and making a big deal out of nothing. Nothing was ever done about the matter.

Woman No. 58: Age 45, married, homemaker, White. I was approached from behind and grabbed by . . . my supervisor. This happened when I was in high school years [ago], and I can still see his face and how horrible he was.

Woman No. 20: Age 57, single, White. As a young woman in the [19]50s, I took an aptitude test. I scored high on engineering interests and out-of-doors jobs. The test giver laughed when two job descriptions came up—forest ranger and engineer for a petroleum company. I didn't think it was funny at all then—and now. [Later, when] I was 38 years old, [I] got a job with the Forest Service on a firefighting crew, [but] I was too old for the job (for me)—I would have performed well in my 20s . . . but it was too late. . . . Now that I'm old, I have finally realized what young women don't have the opportunity to learn—until later: When I thought that people liked me because of myself, my personality, it was [instead] because of my perceived sexual availability. . . . Now that I've lost my looks, I know this to be true. I'm the same person but I'm treated like toxic waste. I'm invisible.

The women in this small survey indicated that sexual harassment occurs not only at work and school but in other settings as well:

Woman No. 50: Age 41, married, homemaker, White. I was about to be married and went shopping (by myself) for a couch. The salesman took me to the back room to supposedly show me something he thought I would like. [There] he said he wanted to kiss the bride. . . . He tried to get intimate with me, and I finally ran out of the store. I was so shocked and humiliated. I also felt guilty, thinking I provoked him. I am so angry [to this day] for not acting at the time to do something to this guy.

Woman No. 60: Age 56, married, Latina and White. I was hospitalized and on medication for pain—my psychologist and supposed friend (males) fondled my breasts while I was semi-awake. I had just had a hysterectomy! It was nauseating and I'll never forget it! (That was 28 years ago).

Woman No. 104: Age 19, single, college student, Black. [Recently] me and my best friend were in the mall shopping when two guys approached us trying to get our phone numbers and talking about how cute we were. I told one guy that I wasn't interested, and my friend told the other that she already had a man, which she did. Well, this angered them so bad that they started to call us names like "bitches" and every word they could think of.

The discrimination that women face consists, however, of more than discrimination in salaries and opportunities at work, and of far more than sexual harassment. Rather, in response to our question about the worst thing to happen to them because they are women, many women (of different ages and ethnic groups) wrote about being beaten up, sexually molested, or raped:

Woman No. 48: Age 23, single, Native American. I was forced to have sex with a man I was dating. Not a pleasant memory, and certainly the worst.

Woman No. 108: Age 22, single, White. A certain customer in my family's business continually harassed me when he came in. Besides the sexual advances . . . he went so far as to touch me in a demeaning way, at which time I struck him. . . . [also] an ex-boyfriend had tried to rape me. . . . I fought him off, told his family what had happened, but never pressed charges.

Woman No. 61: Age 22, single, Latina. I was robbed and sexually assaulted at gunpoint, September 15, 1995. I don't want to go into details.

Woman No. 54: Age 48, married, White. When I was 9 years old, my stepfather made me touch his penis. When I was 14, I was date-raped and became pregnant with my first child [as a result].

Woman No. 102: Age 19, single, college student, Black. The most recent thing that comes to mind happened on campus [after] eating brunch with three of my guy friends, [one of them] picked up his foot and kicked me in the butt.

Woman No. 33: Age 23, single, Asian. A (stranger) man showed me his genital area.

Woman No. 85: Age 24, single, college student, White. A boyfriend . . . hit me because I wore lipstick to a party.

Woman No. 63: Age 31, divorced, White. Ongoing physical abuse by my ex-husband (I have been divorced 9 years) . . . [also] rape—I don't care to elaborate, [and] sexual harassment on the job (very blatant and physical) by a coworker. When reported, my male supervisors did not respond. I quit my job and to the best of my knowledge, the perpetrator and managers involved are still employed.

Woman No. 84: Age 40, divorced, White. I was a victim of date rape. I am also very chesty (big on top) [and] I have so many [rude, sexual] remarks said to me . . . I have felt that I have to dress like a tomboy so I won't cause men to treat me like an object.

In addition to such blatant and physical acts, many women also listed subtle acts of discrimination, acts so slight that they have never been the object of scientific study. Indeed, *the most common answers* written in response to our question were about

- being treated as if they are too stupid
- being treated with a lack of respect
- being ignored, ridiculed, and not given credit for their work
- being ripped-off by people in service jobs (car mechanics, in particular)
- being discriminated against by bank tellers and waiters
- being called names like "bitch," "cunt," and "ho" (whore)

This subtle, pernicious, subversive, "sneaky" (as Woman No. 97 called it) discrimination was reported as ongoing in their lives and as acts that are hard to identify (let alone complain about) because they are like constant, low-level background noise. Yet, these garden-variety, subtle acts of everyday discrimination seemed to bother the women just as much as any physical or brutal discrimination because they are unfair—and it is the unfairness that angered the women:

Woman No. 88: Age 20, married, homemaker, Latina. I couldn't go out with friends because I was a girl, but my brother was allowed to. . . . I've also been told ugly sexual things in the street. [In addition] I was told by my uncles and men neighbors that all I was good for was cleaning, housewife, and gossip because I was a female!

Woman No. 96: Age 19, single, White. My boyfriend constantly makes sexist remarks about how I can't do things because I am a woman; he calls me sexist names [and] feels that . . . he can throw me around and touch me anywhere *he* pleases. . . . [Also] my parents have no rules for my brother because he is a guy, but I have ridiculous curfews just because I am a woman—they even admit that is the reason!

Woman No. 49: Age 34, married, Asian. Dealing with service-related workers—they are the worst, especially dealing with problems with my car—I have to ask my husband to call, they just treat you like you're stupid!

Woman No. 24: Age 42, divorced, Black. My brother has very sexist feelings about women. He doesn't extend them to me, but I am very offended by it because he does not respect his girlfriend—he is abusive to her. . . . It gets me into angry verbal confrontations with him!

Woman No. 97: Age 24, single, college student, White. I was told to keep my "place" concerning my boyfriend and that my going to school was making him feel inferior so I should stop. . . . I was raped, that would have to be the most sexist [thing] I've encountered. The rest [other types of discrimination] are much more sneaky and underlying, such as comments and innuendo and not being respected or taken seriously.

Woman No. 30: Age 18, single, White, college student. My senior year in high school, our economics teacher would give his lectures and ask questions. It seemed that every time a girl answered, we were wrong, but when a guy would answer (with the same thing the girl said), they were right!

Woman No. 105: Age 35, married, Asian. [The worst thing is] going to a meeting [at work] with all men in the room—you are ridiculed and mocked for asking "stupid" questions!

Some scientific evidence supports these women's complaints about subtle but pervasive discrimination in their daily lives. In a series of studies, for example, Henley (1977) found that women are in fact ignored when they speak and/or are interrupted, cut off, and talked over in a way that men are not. In two other studies, Lott (1987, 1989) found similar results. Likewise, several studies have proven that women and men are treated differently by people in service jobs (e.g., mechanics, waiters, salesclerks). For example, men in department stores are waited on before women, even if women arrive at the counter at the same time or long before the men; women are ignored by salesclerks and forced to wait (Stead & Zinkhan, 1986; Zinkhan & Stoiadan, 1984). But, beyond these studies, there are no studies of this softer type of discrimination because most research (understandably) focuses on brutal/physical acts of discrimination, such as battering, rape, and sexual harassment.

We believe, however, that it is time for the subtle discriminatory acts of everyday life to receive scientific attention as well. This is because the women in the survey reported above, as well as the women that we know personally as friends, students, colleagues, and family members, report over and over again that this subtle level is the level at which most discrimination occurs in their daily lives. Many women (thankfully) have not been sexually harassed by their boss, or beaten up or raped. Instead, what bothers many women is the daily, ongoing petty acts of discrimination—being ignored, treated as if they are stupid, excluded, ridiculed, called names, and treated in an unfair way by their families, lovers, employers, and coworkers alike.

PURPOSE OF THIS RESEARCH

Thus the purpose of the studies detailed here was to answer these basic questions that, to date, have been ignored by scientists:

- *How common is not only blatant but also subtle discrimination in women's lives?* How frequently are women called sexist names like "bitch," "cunt," or "whore"? How often must women endure listening to men tell degrading jokes about women? How often do women feel that they are being treated with a lack of respect? How often do women feel that they are being treated unfairly (because they are women) by their families, lovers, husbands, or neighbors? How frequently are women discriminated against by waiters, bank tellers, salesclerks, or mechanics and by professionals such as doctors and counselors? How many women walk around angry about some type of sexist discrimination they have faced?
- *What effect does sexist discrimination (subtle and blatant) have on women's physical and mental health?* Does it contribute to the common physical illnesses and to depression, anxiety, and other psychiatric symptoms and problems that are common in women, and are far more frequent among women than among men?

Some important studies have examined the impact of rape, battering, sexual harassment, and other forms of violence against women, finding that such violence *does* lead to psychiatric and physical symptoms and disorders among women (e.g., Goodman, Koss, & Russo, 1993; Koss, Koss, & Woodruff, 1991; Russo, 1995): Violence against women (brutal/physical sex discrimination) makes women sick and makes them crazy, literally and undeniably according to the scientific evidence. **But, thus far, no one has examined the physical or mental health impact on women of nonviolent sexist discrimination.** There are no studies of the role of discrimination in salaries, promotion, hiring, and other aspects of work on women's physical and mental health, and there are no studies of the psychological impact of the more subtle types of discrimination discussed here. Hence, we also set out to answer this question:

> ▨ *How common is work-related discrimination in women's lives, and what role does it play in women's mental health?* Does it lead to depression, anxiety, and the other psychiatric symptoms and problems that are common among women? Or does workplace discrimination only impair women's ability to support themselves and their children?

Providing scientific answers to these questions is important because the answers will highlight the frequency and the consequences of both work-related and subtle discrimination against women *for the very first time.* The answers will reveal the prevalence and the psychosocial and health costs and consequences of sexist discrimination.

In order to study the frequency and the health impact of work-related and subtle types of sex discrimination in women's lives, we needed a survey (questionnaire) instrument, a scale that could *measure* these experiences, but no such measure existed. Hence, in 1995, we created one that we call the *Schedule of Sexist Events* (SSE) and distributed it to 1,279 women (along with measures of symptoms) to answer the questions above. What we found is reported in this book in detail. We want to note immediately, however, that no scale, no matter how carefully and sensitively it was designed, can capture anyone's experiences. The feeling, the flavor, and the pain of the experiences are all lost between the cracks of the numbers of the *Schedule of Sexist Events,* as surely as they are with our comparable scale, the *Schedule of Racist Events,* which measures racism in the lives of African Americans (see Landrine & Klonoff, 1996a, 1996b). Yet, all such scales (including those measuring battering, sexual abuse, or treatment of the poor), by *quantifying* experiences, make it possible to scientifically (statistically) assess the impact of discrimination on people's physical and mental health, and such research is crucial to create social change.

Thus Part I of this book focuses on the frequency and the physical and mental health impact (correlates and consequences) of discrimination against women, endeavoring to answer the many questions posed above.

In Chapter 1, we describe the rationale for and content of the 20-item SSE that we created to measure the frequency of work-related and subtle sex discrimination in women's lives. Then, we detail the results of our first survey (Study 1), using the SSE, and report on the prevalence of various types of sexist discrimination in the lives of the 631 women who participated in that survey. We refer to these 631 women as Sample 1. We also examine the reliability, validity, and structure of the SSE.

In Chapter 2, we examine the data from the women in Sample 1 for any differences in experiencing discrimination based on a woman's age, ethnicity, and other status characteristics and report those findings in detail.

In Chapter 3, we examine the role of discrimination in the physical and psychiatric symptoms of the women in Sample 1.

In Chapter 4, we describe the results of our second survey (Study 2), using the SSE, and report on the prevalence of the various types of sexist discrimination in the lives of a new group of 652 women who participated in that survey; we refer to these 652 women as Sample 2. We also compare the findings from the two samples to assess similarity in experiences and ask: Did the women in the two samples report the same experiences? Do all women essentially experience the same types of sexist discrimination? Then we combine the samples to provide an overview of the nature and frequency of discrimination in the lives of all 1,279 women.

In Chapter 5, we examine the physical and mental health impact of sexist discrimination on the women in Sample 2. We also examine the role of ethnicity and of feminism in the impact of discrimination on women.

Next, in Chapter 6, we report on which specific type of sexist discrimination (e.g., at work, in personal relationships) plays the greatest role in women's symptoms, again by examining the women in Sample 2. Then, we present a theoretical model of how sexist discrimination causes symptoms in women and provide a brief summary of the chapters thus far.

With the prevalence and health impact of sexist discrimination in women's lives established, we then turn to Part II of the book, in which the focus is on steps women might take to deal with that discrimination.

In Chapter 7, Phyllis Bronstein, a clinical psychologist and feminist therapist from the University of Vermont, discusses ways that women (and their therapists) can deal with the stress of sexist discrimination in their lives, along with steps that women can take to cope with and decrease that discrimination. Dr. Bronstein also presents important insights, advice, and suggestions of many therapists (these provided verbatim from interviews) on how to understand and handle sexist discrimination and on how to decrease the harm that therapists have always known it causes to women's mental health.

In Chapter 8, Bernice Lott and Lisa M. Rocchio, psychologists and scholars from the University of Rhode Island, briefly discuss their study of how women usually cope with sexist discrimination and demonstrate that most women *do nothing about it*. They then devote the majority of their chapter to things women *can* do about it. They describe simple ways that women can network and organize to provide each other with social support and decrease the harmful effects and the frequency of sexist discrimination (sexual harassment in particular); they focus on a program that they have already developed and *that works*. Hence, Chapters 7 and 8 provide valuable information on immediate social and therapeutic remedies for sexist discrimination.

Then we turn to Part III of the book, where the focus is the law and discrimination against women. In Chapter 9, Lynne Wurzburg, J.D., and Robert H. Klonoff, J.D., attorneys from the well-known law firm Jones, Day, Reavis, & Pogue in Washington, D.C., discuss the legal definition of discrimination; the laws protecting women; and the major sex discrimination cases that have occurred. Hence, this chapter provides valuable information on the *legal* meaning of sex discrimination that might provide a resource for women considering legal action.

Finally, at the end of the book, we provide a brief Conclusions section that summarizes the meaning of all of the chapters for America's women on the eve of the 21st century.

Throughout this book, we focus primarily on nonviolent types of sexist discrimination—on work-related and subtle types of discrimination. We do not do so because we believe that such events are more important than brutal/physical discrimination (rape, battering) in women's lives. Rather, we do so because the impact of work-related and subtle discrimination on women has been neglected by scientists, and yet, we suspect that these acts are not only more common in most women's lives but also may be just as harmful to women as the more brutal, discriminatory events. Our suspicions aside, however, our approach to these studies was purely an objective, scientific one: We gave anonymous surveys to 1,279 women. These women completed those surveys voluntarily and without pressure, payment, promises, or even comments from us—for we were absent while they completed them. We then analyzed their self-reports of their own personal experiences, and we let those experiences speak for themselves.

ONE

Measuring Sexist Discrimination

The Schedule of Sexist Events

CONCEPTUALIZING DISCRIMINATION AGAINST WOMEN

The scientific evidence and the experiences of women that were reported in the Introduction all reveal that discrimination against women takes a wide variety of forms. Such discrimination includes (but is not limited to) being sexually harassed; being called sexist names such as "bitch"; being treated unfairly by family members and spouses/partners; being treated unfairly by teachers and professors; being discriminated against by people in service jobs (e.g., mechanics); and being discriminated against at

AUTHORS' NOTE: A brief version of Chapter 1 was published as E. A. Klonoff and H. Landrine, "The Schedule of Sexist Events: A Measure of Lifetime and Recent Sexist Discrimination in Women's Lives," *Psychology of Women Quarterly, 19,* 439-472, published by Cambridge University Press, 1995. This material is reprinted with the permission of Cambridge University Press.

work (e.g., in salaries, promotions). These various types of discrimination against women can all be conceptualized as specific **sexist events,** as **discriminatory acts or events that happen to women because they are women.** Throughout this book, we will refer to the variety of types of discriminatory acts against women as sexist events. There are several scientific reasons for and advantages to so doing.

Stress Research

One major, popular, and important area of contemporary research in the sciences is the study of stress as a cause of physical and mental symptoms, problems, and disorders. By *stress,* scientists mean specific events that can happen to anyone, causing wear and tear on the body and psyche. Some common major and minor stressful events that have been studied are shown in Table 1.1. As shown in the table, losing your job, moving, having a family member get sick, having fights and conflicts with loved ones, having problems at work, failing an exam, and the death of a loved one are examples of major stressful life events. These particular events are from a well-known stress scale, the PERI-Life Events Scale (PERI-LES; Dohrenwend, Krasnoff, Askenasy, & Dohrenwend, 1978). These events are inherently stressful in that they take a toll on the body and psyche and require time, energy, and adjustment. Many scientific studies have demonstrated that major stressful life events such as these cause a variety of physical and psychiatric symptoms, ranging from aches, pains, and colds to serious depression in women and men alike (Lazarus, 1966; Lazarus, DeLongis, Folkman, & Gruen, 1985).

Other stressful events shown in Table 1.1 are minor stressful events or *hassles.* These are annoying little events (e.g., losing one's car keys, getting stuck in a traffic jam) that similarly take a toll on the body and psyche. The minor stressful events shown in Table 1.1 are from a well-known and commonly used stress measure called the Hassles-Frequency scale (Hassles-Freq; Kanner, Coyne, Schaeffer, & Lazarus, 1981). Studies using that scale have shown that frequent hassles, like frequent major stressful life events, contribute to physical and psychiatric symptoms for women and men alike (Kanner et al., 1981). In the case of both major and minor stressful events, scientists measure the frequency of these events in people's lives and then define high stress as frequent, and low stress as infrequent, occurrence of these events.

TABLE 1.1 The Role of Major and Minor Stressors in Physical and Mental Health

Stressful Events	→	Immediate Effects (Changes in)	→	Long-Term Outcomes
Major events		**Cardiovascular system:**		Hypertension
Moved		Heart rate		Ulcer
Lost job		Blood pressure		Arthritis
Death in family		**Health habits/behavior:**		Cancer
Failed a course		Diet		Minor illnesses
Changed job		Exercise		Major disease
Got married		Rest		Heart disease
Retired		Smoking		Menstrual symptoms
Went on welfare		Alcohol use		Depression
Went off welfare		Drug use		Anxiety disorder
Trouble at work		**Immunological system:**		Obesity
Birth of child		Suppression of lympho-		Substance use disorder
Minor events		cytes, T, B, T_H, T_S, T_C		Other physical symptoms
Misplacing or losing things		cells		
Troublesome neighbors		**Depressed mood:**		
Social obligations		Suppression of lympho-		
Inconsiderate smokers		cytes, T, B, T_H, T_S, T_C		
Financial problems		cells		
		Anxiety		

How Stress Causes Symptoms

As shown in Table 1.1, major and minor stressful life events contribute to symptoms in a variety of ways. For example, when people are under high stress, they usually fail to sleep a full 8 hours; fail to eat full meals, instead grabbing a quick bite of junk food or skipping meals; and stay up late at night (Woods, Lentz, & Mitchell, 1993). Thus stressful events affect health by decreasing health-sustaining behaviors such as proper diet and rest; poor diet and lack of rest, in turn, play a major role in serious physical illnesses, including hypertension and cancer. Likewise, people who are under stress increase health-damaging behaviors such as smoking and drinking alcohol (Woods et al., 1993), and these, in turn, play a role in serious psychological and physical symptoms including hypertension, cancer, and depression. Causing changes in health habits and health behavior is only one of the ways (an indirect way) that stress causes illness, however.

In addition, stress directly affects the body by altering blood pressure and heart rate, thereby taxing the cardiovascular system (Taylor, 1995).

Likewise and most important, **stress directly affects the body by decreasing, suppressing, and compromising immunological functions** (Irwin et al, 1987; O'Leary, 1990). Because the immunological system is our first line of defense against disease, people under stress are more likely than those who are not to succumb to disease (see Taylor, 1995, pp. 535-541, and O'Leary, 1990, for reviews and summaries). Specifically, by literally decreasing and suppressing the lymphocytes that fight and destroy bacteria, viruses, and toxins, and by suppressing the circulating B, T, T_H, T_S, and T_C cells (the "killer" T cells) that kill invading microorganisms, stress leaves people open to attack by disease and so indirectly causes disease (Herbert & Cohen, 1993b; Irwin et al., 1986a, 1987; Naliboff et al., 1991). Diseases facilitated and indirectly caused in this manner by major stressful life events include:

- all infectious diseases among children whose families are under stress (Irwin et al., 1987; O'Leary, 1990)
- the common cold and other similar viral infections (O'Leary, 1990)
- herpes, chicken pox, mononucleosis, and Epstein-Barr virus in particular (Kiecolt-Glaser & Glaser, 1987; Kiecolt-Glaser et al., 1984a, 1985)

Likewise, studies have shown that even minor stressful life events (i.e., hassles) suppress immune functions and create disease (Levy et al., 1989). Indeed, even the stress of attending graduate school has been demonstrated consistently to cause immunosuppression and hence illness (Kiecolt-Glaser et al., 1984a, 1986; Taylor, 1995). Similarly, relationship stress, especially conflict with a partner and divorce and separation, suppresses immunological functions and opens people to disease (Kiecolt-Glaser et al., 1987, 1988a, 1988b, 1993). Finally, studies have also shown that depression is one of the major mechanisms through which stress compromises immune function: Stressful life events affect the psyche by creating depression, and both mild and severe depression cause immunosuppression (Herbert & Cohen, 1993a; Irwin et al., 1986a, 1986b, 1987; Kiecolt-Glaser et al., 1985), which then renders people vulnerable to invading viruses and bacteria. Indeed, such research suggests that depression is a physical and a psychological state in which mood *and* immunological functions *and* production of certain neuropeptides in the brain are all depressed (decreased). Thus the common observations that students tend to get sick just before or after final exams, that people tend to get sick over holidays (when they see their families), and that we all get sick when we have the most to do and can't afford to be ill (i.e., when we have the greatest stress) are all consistent with the scientific evidence on the stress-illness relationship.

Hence, when scientists state that stress causes disease or that a symptom is stress-related (due to stress), they do not mean that the symptom is "in your head." Rather, scientists mean that the physical or psychiatric symptom is a "real" one in a body and psyche that have been pushed to their limits and compromised, that simply cannot take any more: Stress is not merely correlated with physical and psychiatric symptoms and disorders. Rather, stress *causes* physical and psychiatric symptoms through the well-known and well-researched mechanisms described above.

Sexist Discrimination as Stress

The various types of discriminatory acts that women experience can be thought of as a special category of stressful events (sexist events) that are similar in many ways to the generic (can happen to anyone, male or female) major and minor stressful life events that have been the focus of stress research in psychology, preventive medicine, and public health for the past 20 years. We can conceptualize the various domains/types of sexist discrimination as sexist events and **view sexist events as gender-specific, negative life events, that is, as gender-specific stressors.** Sexist events can be viewed as gender-specific stressors because they are negative life events (stressors) that happen to women *because* they are women. There are several advantages to and benefits of conceptualizing discrimination against women as sexist events (as gender-specific stressors), described below.

Benefits of the Stressful-Events Approach to Sexist Discrimination

By conceptualizing sexist discrimination as sexist events that are analogous to generic stressful life events, theoretical models and lines of investigation from stress research (e.g., Lazarus, 1966; Lazarus et al., 1985; Lazarus & Launier, 1978) can be applied to the study of discrimination against women. Hence, for example, sexist events can be conceptualized as occurring frequently or infrequently and so might be measured in that manner, just as generic stressful life events are. Also, like generic stressful life events, sexist events can be conceptualized as acute (recent) and chronic (lifetime), and the impact of recent versus lifetime sexist discrimination can be examined. Similarly, a factor analysis of the various types of sexist events would be appropriate and informative; this would yield information on the various arenas in which sexist discrimination occurs and on the subtypes (factors)[1] of sexist discrimination, similar to the factors of generic stressful life events (e.g., work stress, relationship stress; see Dohrenwend et al., 1978). As is the case for the factors of generic life events, different factors of sexist events also should be differentially related to women's physical and mental health. For example, sexist discrimination on the part of loved ones and family members might be more strongly related to symptoms among women than sexist discrimination on the part of strangers, just as relationship stress is more strongly related to women's symptoms than is work-related stress.

Likewise, how women cope with sexist events can be studied; coping style and skills probably mediate the negative impact of sexist events, just as they mediate the impact of generic stressful life events (e.g., Billings & Moos, 1981): Sexist events, like generic stressful life events, probably have less of a negative impact on women who have good coping skills for handling stress. In addition, as is the case for generic stressful life events, so too, the negative impact of sexist events is likely to be mediated by social support (e.g., Cohen & Wills, 1985) and by some personality factors as such as "hardiness" (Kobasa, 1979): Sexist events no doubt have less of a negative impact on women who have strong, social support networks, and hardy, "tough" women may be less harmed by sexist events than other women.

Each of the above possibilities is worth investigating and simply entails applying and generalizing theories and research from the study of generic stressful events to the study of sexist events—with the hypothesis

---

1. Factor analysis is a data-reduction statistical technique that reduces data to its smallest constituents by grouping it into small, related groups called factors. For example, (1) having constant arguments with one's husband, (2) feeling overwhelmed by parental responsibilities that he fails to share, (3) having problems in one's sexual relationship with him, and (4) not getting along with his parents are all similar, highly related problems. Factor analysis would group these as Relationship Problems, thereby reducing four pieces of data (variables) to a single, more comprehensive variable. Likewise, (1) having a boss who is hostile, (2) a boss who makes unnecessary demands, (3) coworkers who are cold and competitive, and (4) a job one hates are also highly related, similar problems; factor analysis would group these as Work Problems. Hence, factor analysis would reduce all eight variables to two variables or factors (relationship versus work problems), making them easier to study and to discuss—the sole purpose of data reduction statistical techniques. Thus, instead of trying to discuss people's scores on these eight items, factor analysis allows one to discuss their scores on the two factors comprising those items. See the appendix for a full explanation of factor analysis.

that similar findings will be discovered. However, not all findings should be the same because sexist events and generic stressful life events are similar but not equivalent. Specifically, we theorize that sexist events differ from generic life events in these two important ways:

1. **We theorize that sexist events have an even greater negative impact on women's physical and mental health than generic stressful life events.** This is because sexist events are inherently demeaning, degrading, personal attacks upon and negative responses to something essential about the self that cannot be changed—being a woman. For example, sexist events such as being called a bitch or a cunt (like being called a nigger) are far more personal, offensive, and demeaning than generic life events such as losing your car keys or moving; hence, sexist events should harm women more than generic life events. In addition, **women have less control over sexist events** (just as Blacks have little or no control over racist events) than they do over generic life events, and this also might cause sexist events to be more harmful to women. For example, women cannot control sexist events, such as being sexually harassed on the street by construction workers or treated like an idiot by a car mechanic but women can control generic stressful life events, such as getting married, moving, or changing jobs—the latter are a woman's decision. Thus sexist discrimination is theorized to be even more damaging to women's physical and mental health than generic stressful events.

2. **We theorize that feminist consciousness is a unique personality factor that mediates the negative impact of sexist events.** By providing a cognitive framework for understanding sexism, feminist consciousness should decrease the perception of sexist events as one's own fault, increase active coping, and decrease the negative impact of these events.

In summary then, by conceptualizing discrimination against women as a gender-specific type of stressful event, theoretical models and types of research conducted in the study of generic stressful events can all be applied to the study of discrimination against women. Sexist discrimination can be brought into the mainstream of scientific research on the impact of stress on people's physical and mental health. By taking the stressful events approach, the study of discrimination against women can be rendered scientifically acceptable or mainstream, insofar as it is consistent with and coherent within the framework of contemporary scientific research. These are just a few of the advantages of conceptualizing the various types of discrimination against women as sexist (stressful) events.

The final and most important advantage of taking the stressful events approach to the analysis of sexist discrimination, however, is the strong body of existing scientific evidence demonstrating that stress causes illness. Countless, careful, laboratory scientific studies with humans and with animals (some cited above) have all demonstrated that stressful events (from constant noise to marital conflicts) cause psychiatric symptoms (such as depression and anxiety) and suppression of immunological functions, thereby rendering people vulnerable to and more likely to develop physical symptoms and diseases as well. Sexist events, *as simply another type of stressful event,* logically and necessarily have the same effect and play the same role in health: If relationship problems, constant noise, or attending graduate school are each sufficient stress to cause depression and suppression of immune functions (leading to disease), then being called sexist names, ignored, discriminated against at work, sexually harassed, assaulted, and treated as less of a person because one is a woman surely causes depression and suppresses immune functions as well. If stress causes symptoms through specific, well known mechanisms, the type of stress involved does not negate that causal relationship.

Hence, in this book, we do not endeavor to prove that sexist stressful events *cause* (or do not cause) symptoms among women (for example, by examining women's circulating T cells), because it has already been well-established that stressful events can and do cause symptoms. Rather, here we simply investigate how well sexist events predict women's symptoms. **If sexist events predict women's symptoms as well as or even better than the generic stressful events known to predict—because they cause—those very symptoms, then the role of sexist events in women's symptoms is necessarily and similarly a causal one.** We will return to this point at the end of the book.

With the role of stress in symptoms outlined and the advantages of taking a stressful events approach to the study of discrimination against women highlighted, we can turn to procedures for measuring sexist discrimination.

The Schedule of Sexist Events

We constructed the Schedule of Sexist Events with this generic-stressful life events model in mind, modeling our scale after the PERI-LES (Dohrenwend et al., 1978) and Hassles-Freq (Kanner et al., 1981) scales, the two major measures of major and minor stressful life events, respectively.

Hence, the items were intended to assess the frequency of specific sexist events in a woman's life recently (the past year) as well as in her entire lifetime. In constructing the items, we attempted to capture an array of types/domains of discrimination against women. The scale is shown in Figure 1.1. We then distributed this scale to a sample of women as described below.

Study 1 Method

Participants

In our study, 631 women completed a questionnaire. Their ages ranged from 18 to 73 years (mean = 32.14, σ = 11.74 years, median = 29 years). They included 403 Whites and 228 women of color (117 Latinas, 38 African Americans, 25 Asian Americans, and 46 members of other ethnic groups). Of the total, 292 were single, 238 were married, and 101 were divorced, separated, or widowed. The majority (340) had taken some college classes, whereas 129 had a high school education or less, and 119 had college or graduate degrees. Their incomes ranged from zero to $400,000 per year (mean = $34,058, σ = $34,370).[2] We will refer to these 631 women henceforth as Sample 1.

Procedure

Women were approached in classrooms and sororities on a large college campus and asked to complete an anonymous survey; 294 college students completed it. In addition, women were approached in nine small office buildings and asked to complete the questionnaire. Five visits also were made to the local airport, where women waiting for flights were asked to complete the survey. Through the latter two procedures, a total of 337 adult women from the community completed the questionnaire.

---

2.   The mean is the average for a group. The standard deviation (σ) is the average or typical (or standard) amount by which the scores differ (deviate) from the mean (hence: standard deviation); it gives an indication of the dispersion (spread) of the scores and hence a global view of the sample. Thus, the mean (32.14 years) and σ (11.74 years) for age for this sample indicate that the average age was 32 and that most of the women were between the ages of 19 (mean minus standard deviation) and 44 (mean plus standard deviation); the standard distance between most women's ages and the mean age was 11.74 years. See the appendix for a further discussion of σ.

Please think carefully about your life as you answer the questions below. For each question, read the question and then answer it twice: Answer once for what your ENTIRE LIFE (from when you were a child to now) has been like, and then once for what the PAST YEAR has been like. Circle the number that best describes events in YOUR ENTIRE LIFE, and in the PAST YEAR, using these rules:

Circle *1* = If the event has *NEVER* happened to you
Circle *2* = If the event happened *ONCE IN A WHILE (less than 10% of the time)*
Circle *3* = If the event happened *SOMETIMES (10-25% of the time)*
Circle *4* = If the event happened *A LOT* (26-49% of the time)
Circle *5* = If the event happened *MOST OF THE TIME (50-70% of the time)*
Circle *6* = If the event happened *ALMOST ALL OF THE TIME (more than 70% of the time)*

1. How many times have you been treated unfairly by *teachers or professors* because you are a woman?
    How many times IN YOUR ENTIRE LIFE?   1   2   3   4   5   6
    How many times IN THE PAST YEAR?   1   2   3   4   5   6

2. How many times have you been treated unfairly by your *employer, boss, or supervisors* because you are a woman?
    How many times IN YOUR ENTIRE LIFE?   1   2   3   4   5   6
    How many times IN THE PAST YEAR?   1   2   3   4   5   6

3. How many times have you been treated unfairly by *your coworkers, fellow students, or colleagues* because you are a woman?
    How many times IN YOUR ENTIRE LIFE?   1   2   3   4   5   6
    How many times IN THE PAST YEAR?   1   2   3   4   5   6

4. How many times have you been treated unfairly by *people in service jobs* (by *store clerks, waiters, bartenders, waitresses, bank tellers, mechanics, and others*) because you are a woman?
    How many times IN YOUR ENTIRE LIFE?   1   2   3   4   5   6
    How many times IN THE PAST YEAR?   1   2   3   4   5   6

5. How many times have you been treated unfairly by *strangers* because you are a woman?
    How many times IN YOUR ENTIRE LIFE?   1   2   3   4   5   6
    How many times IN THE PAST YEAR?   1   2   3   4   5   6

6. How many times have you been treated unfairly by *people in helping jobs* (by *doctors, nurses, psychiatrists, case workers, dentists, school counselors, therapists, pediatricians, school principals, gynecologists, and others*) because you are a woman?
    How many times IN YOUR ENTIRE LIFE?   1   2   3   4   5   6
    How many times IN THE PAST YEAR?   1   2   3   4   5   6

7. How many times have you been treated unfairly by *neighbors* because you are a woman?
    How many times IN YOUR ENTIRE LIFE?   1   2   3   4   5   6
    How many times IN THE PAST YEAR?   1   2   3   4   5   6

8. How many times have you been treated unfairly by *your boyfriend, husband, or other important man in your life* because you are a woman?
    How many times IN YOUR ENTIRE LIFE?   1   2   3   4   5   6
    How many times IN THE PAST YEAR?   1   2   3   4   5   6

9. How many times were you *denied a raise, a promotion, tenure, a good assignment, a job, or other such thing at work that you deserved* because you are a woman?
    How many times IN YOUR ENTIRE LIFE?   1   2   3   4   5   6
    How many times IN THE PAST YEAR?   1   2   3   4   5   6

Figure 1.1. Schedule of Sexist Events (SSE)

10. How many times have you been *treated unfairly by your family* because you are a woman?

How many times IN YOUR ENTIRE LIFE?	1	2	3	4	5	6
How many times IN THE PAST YEAR?	1	2	3	4	5	6

11. How many times have people *made inappropriate or unwanted sexual advances to you* because you are a woman?

How many times IN YOUR ENTIRE LIFE?	1	2	3	4	5	6
How many times IN THE PAST YEAR?	1	2	3	4	5	6

12. How many times have people *failed to show you the respect that you deserve* because you are a woman?

How many times IN YOUR ENTIRE LIFE?	1	2	3	4	5	6
How many times IN THE PAST YEAR?	1	2	3	4	5	6

13. How many times have you *wanted to tell someone off for being sexist?*

How many times IN YOUR ENTIRE LIFE?	1	2	3	4	5	6
How many times IN THE PAST YEAR?	1	2	3	4	5	6

14. How many times have you been *really angry about something sexist that was done to you?*

How many times IN YOUR ENTIRE LIFE?	1	2	3	4	5	6
How many times IN THE PAST YEAR?	1	2	3	4	5	6

15. How many times were you *forced to take drastic steps* (such as *filing a grievance, filing a lawsuit, quitting your job, moving away, and other actions*) to deal with some sexist thing that was done to you?

How many times IN YOUR ENTIRE LIFE?	1	2	3	4	5	6
How many times IN THE PAST YEAR?	1	2	3	4	5	6

16. How many times have you *been called a sexist name like bitch, cunt, chick, or other names?*

How many times IN YOUR ENTIRE LIFE?	1	2	3	4	5	6
How many times IN THE PAST YEAR?	1	2	3	4	5	6

17. How many times have you *gotten into an argument or a fight about something sexist that was done or said to you or done to somebody else?*

How many times IN YOUR ENTIRE LIFE?	1	2	3	4	5	6
How many times IN THE PAST YEAR?	1	2	3	4	5	6

18. How many times have you been *made fun of, picked on, pushed, shoved, hit, or threatened with harm* because you are a woman?

How many times IN YOUR ENTIRE LIFE?	1	2	3	4	5	6
How many times IN THE PAST YEAR?	1	2	3	4	5	6

19. How many times have you *heard people making sexist jokes or degrading sexual jokes?*

How many times IN YOUR ENTIRE LIFE?	1	2	3	4	5	6
How many times IN THE PAST YEAR?	1	2	3	4	5	6

20. How *different* would your life be now if you *HAD NOT BEEN* treated in a sexist and unfair way

THROUGHOUT YOUR ENTIRE LIFE?

the same	a little different	different in a few ways	different in a lot of ways	different in most ways	totally different
1	2	3	4	5	6

IN THE PAST YEAR?

1	2	3	4	5	6

Figure 1.1. Continued

Materials

The major instrument in the questionnaire was the Schedule of Sexist Events (SSE), shown in Figure 1.1. The SSE is a self-report inventory consisting of 20 items to be rated on scales that range from 1 = *the event never happened* to 6 = *the event happens almost all of the time.* The 20 questions assess the frequency with which a woman has experienced sexist events of various types in a diversity of settings, ranging from discrimination at work to battering. Each item in the SSE is completed twice, once for the frequency of these sexist events in a woman's entire life (Lifetime Sexist Events scale) and once for the frequency of these events in the past year (Recent Sexist Events scale). These two kinds of data are examined separately and can be treated as two separate subscales.

In addition to the SSE, all women received a page requesting demographic information (age, ethnic group, education, income, etc.). Finally, the Beck Depression Inventory (BDI; Beck, Ward, Mendelson, Mock, & Erbaugh, 1961); the PERI-LES (Dohrenwend et al., 1978); the Hopkins Symptom Checklist (HSCL-58; Derogatis, Lipman, Rickles, Uhlenhuth, & Covi, 1974); the Spielberger State-Trait Anxiety Inventory (STAI; Spielberger, Gorsuch, & Lushene, 1970); the Hassles-Freq Scale (Kanner et al., 1981), and the Premenstrual Tension Syndrome Scale (PMTS; Condon, 1993) also were distributed. These measures of symptoms were used in the analyses reported in Chapters 3 and 5 and are described in detail in Chapter 3.

Study 1 Results

Frequency of Lifetime Sexist
Events/Discrimination

Of the 631 women in the sample, only 6 (1%) reported never experiencing a sexist event/discrimination of any type in their entire lives; the majority (99%) of the sample reported experiencing sexist events at least once in their lives, with some events reported more frequently by the sample than others. Table 1.2 displays data on the percentage of women who indicated experiencing each type of sexist event in their lifetimes: The columns indicate how frequently each sexist event occurred, and cells show the percentage of women reporting that frequency. The last column on the right (column 7) shows the percentage of women *who have ever,* in their entire lives, experienced the sexist event in question (irrespective of frequency); the full content of each item is shown in Figure 1.1.

TABLE 1.2 Percentage of the Sample Reporting Specific Sexist Events in Their Lifetimes

	Lifetime Frequency of the Event: Percentage of Time It Happened to Her						
Questionnaire Item	1 Never Happened	2 Up to 10% of the Time	3 10-25% of the Time	4 26-49% of the Time	5 50-70% of the Time	6 >70% of the Time	Ever Happened (100% minus column 1)
1. Sexism by teachers	46.9	35.4	12.0	4.1	1.0	0.6	53.10
2. Sexism by employers	39.9	30.5	18.7	6.4	3.1	1.5	60.10
3. Sexism by colleagues	41.9	34.4	16.4	5.4	1.5	0.5	58.10
4. Sexism by people in service jobs	23.0	36.8	24.0	11.5	2.9	1.8	77.00
5. Sexism by strangers	26.8	40.6	21.5	7.5	2.6	1.0	73.20
6. Sexism by people in helping jobs	40.9	34.4	15.8	5.5	1.8	1.5	59.10
7. Sexism by neighbors	66.4	23.8	7.0	1.6	0.3	0.8	33.60
8. Sexism by boyfriend, mate	25.1	30.7	21.2	14.1	5.0	3.9	74.90
9. Sexism at work	59.6	25.7	8.8	3.4	2.1	0.3	40.40
10. Sexism by family	54.5	21.9	10.9	6.0	3.6	3.1	45.50
11. Sexually harassed	18.0	30.0	26.3	16.2	5.0	4.4	82.00
12. Got no respect	17.3	44.1	21.2	12.1	3.4	2.0	82.70
13. Wanted to tell someone off	14.8	35.1	22.0	15.6	6.5	6.0	85.20
14. Angry about sexism	24.3	40.8	19.4	8.0	3.6	3.9	75.70
15. Took drastic steps	80.9	15.2	2.4	0.3	0.7	0.5	19.10
16. Called sexist names	17.8	39.5	22.1	12.9	4.6	3.1	82.20
17. Argued over sexism	34.1	37.4	17.6	7.0	2.6	1.3	65.90
18. Was picked on, harmed	43.6	32.6	13.5	5.7	3.1	1.5	56.40
19. Heard sexist jokes	5.9	22.8	27.1	25.1	10.1	9.0	94.10
	The Same as Now	A Little Different	Different in a Few Ways	A Lot Different	Different in Most Ways	Totally Different	Would be different (100% − column 1)
20. How different your life would be without lifetime sexism	30.3	28.2	23.8	12.3	3.0	2.5	69.70

NOTE: For the complete wording of the items, see Figure 1.1.

33

As shown in Table 1.2, the most common sexist event was being forced to listen to sexist jokes, something that 94.1% of the sample reported experiencing. Other common sexist events (i.e., those experienced by the majority of the sample) were being called sexist names (82.2%); being treated with a lack of respect (82.7%); wanting to tell someone off for being sexist (85.25%); feeling very angry about something sexist that has happened (75.7%); and being discriminated against by strangers (73.2%) and by people in service jobs (77%) because one is a woman. A frighteningly large percentage of the sample, 56.4%, reported being picked on, hit, shoved, or threatened with harm because they were women; 40.4% reported being denied a raise or promotion because they were women, and 19.1% reported filing a lawsuit or labor grievance, quitting their jobs, or taking some other drastic step in response to sexist discrimination.

Frequency of Recent Sexist Events/Discrimination

Table 1.3 displays similar data for sexist events experienced in the past year. Only 19 of the 631 women (3%) reported never experiencing any sexist event in the previous year; 97% of the sample reported experiencing some type of sexist discrimination in the previous year, with some types being more common for the sample than others. As shown in Table 1.3, common recent sexist events (experienced at least once by the women in the previous year—column 7, rightmost) were being forced to listen to sexist jokes (83.8%); wanting to tell someone off for being sexist (72.1%), and being treated unfairly by people in service jobs because one is a woman (61.9%). Substantial numbers of women reported that (in the previous year) they were discriminated against by their boss/employer (32.1%); denied a promotion or raise because they were women (18.3%); picked on, hit, pushed, or threatened with harm because they were women (29.4%); and filed a lawsuit or quit their jobs (8.7%) in response to sexist discrimination.

These findings highlight the magnitude and the seriousness of workplace and other discrimination against women. They also underscore the need for scientific research on the role of such discrimination in poverty among women and in women's physical and mental health.

Ethnic Differences in the Frequency
of Lifetime and Recent Sexist Events

As shown in Figure 1.2, White women ($n = 403$) and minority women ($n = 228$) reported highly similar experiences with sexist events in their

TABLE 1.3 Percentage of the Sample Reporting Sexist Events in the Past Year

	Recent Frequency of the Event: Percentage of Time It Happened to Her						
Questionnaire Item	1 Never Happened	2 Up to 10% of the time	3 10-25% of the Time	4 26-49% of the Time	5 50-70% of the Time	6 >70% of the Time	Ever Happened (100% minus column 1)
1. Sexism by teachers	75.2	18.6	3.7	1.5	0.5	0.5	24.80
2. Sexism by employers	67.9	19.2	6.2	3.3	2.3	1.0	32.10
3. Sexism by colleagues	63.5	23.9	8.7	2.3	1.3	0.2	36.50
4. Sexism by people in service jobs	38.1	39.4	14.7	5.6	1.8	0.5	61.90
5. Sexism by strangers	41.4	42.3	11.8	2.5	1.3	0.7	58.60
6. Sexism by people in helping jobs	59.6	29.1	7.3	2.3	1.2	0.5	40.40
7. Sexism by neighbors	80.3	14.4	3.8	1.0	0.5	0	19.70
8. Sexism by boyfriend, mate	49.8	29.2	11.1	4.9	2.5	2.5	50.20
9. Sexism at work	81.7	12.2	3.0	1.8	1.0	0.3	18.30
10. Sexism by family	70.9	18.0	4.2	2.9	1.5	2.5	29.10
11. Sexually harassed	44.6	28.1	16.6	5.5	2.8	2.4	55.40
12. Got no respect	38.2	39.5	12.8	5.6	3.0	1.0	61.80
13. Wanted to tell someone off	27.9	36.4	16.1	10.3	4.6	4.8	72.10
14. Angry about sexism	47.9	31.5	10.8	4.4	2.3	3.1	52.10
15. Took drastic steps	91.3	5.4	1.0	0.8	0.8	0.7	8.70
16. Called sexist names	46.2	33.0	10.9	5.4	3.0	1.5	53.80
17. Argued over sexism	56.3	27.7	8.1	4.6	1.8	1.5	43.70
18. Was picked on, harmed	70.6	21.2	3.9	2.3	1.0	1.0	29.40
19. Heard sexist jokes	16.2	36.7	19.7	14.4	6.7	6.2	83.80
	The Same as Now	A Little Different	Different in a Few Ways	A Lot Different	Different in Most Ways	Totally Different	Would be different (100% – column 1)
20. How different your life would be without recent sexism	47.9	28.2	13.6	7.2	1.6	1.5	52.10

NOTE: For the complete wording of the items, see Figure 1.1.

35

lifetimes. For example, 94.7% of White women and 93.1% of minority women reported being forced to listen to sexist jokes in their lifetimes. Although there were many similarities, some differences also are clear in Figure 1.2.

Similarly, Figure 1.3 compares the experiences of White and minority women with recent (past year) sexist discrimination, with marked similarities and differences clear again. For example, 36.6% of minority women, compared with 25.4% of White women, reported being picked on, hit, shoved, or threatened with harm in the previous year because they were women. As will be clear in statistical analyses reported in Chapter 2, some of these ethnic differences are statistically significant,[3] with minority women reporting more frequent sexist discrimination than White women in specific domains. Other important status differences (e.g., by age, marital status, social class) in experiencing lifetime and recent sexist events are also detailed in Chapter 2.

These descriptive data are provided in detail because they indicate that sexist discrimination is an experience common to all women and was rampant in the United States in 1995. These data are consistent with the literature and the personal reports detailed in the Introduction.

We turn now to an analysis of the structure, reliability, and validity of the SSE. Before the SSE can be used to study the role of sexist events in symptoms among women, the scale must be demonstrated to be reliable and valid. The reader is referred to the appendix, "Understanding the Statistics Used in This Book," for a more detailed explanation of the statistics that follow and of their necessity.

Factor Structure of the SSE-Lifetime and SSE-Recent

Factor Analysis of Lifetime Sexist Events

The ratings given by Sample 1 to the items for Lifetime Frequency were separated from those for Past Year Frequency and analyzed as their own scale, SSE-Lifetime. These data were entered into a principle components analysis (PCA) with an orthogonal rotation, and factors were retained based on an eigenvalue equal to or greater than 1.00. These results are displayed in Table 1.4 (with item numbers and their factor loadings), along

---

3. The phrase *statistically significant* (or simply "significant") means (a) not by chance, not random, and (b) in all probability also true for all women in the country—not just for our sample. See the appendix for details.

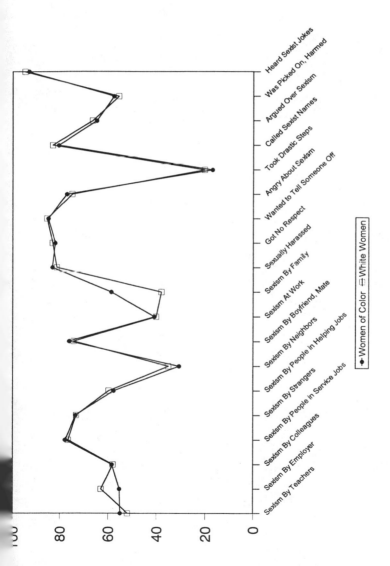

Figure 1.2. Percentage of Sample Reporting Lifetime Sexist Events, White Women Versus Minority Women

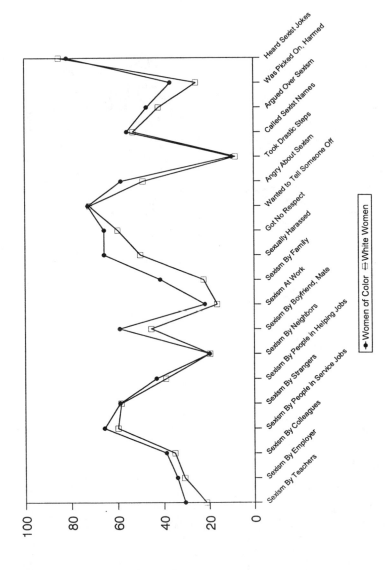

Figure 1.3. Percentage of Sample Reporting Recent (Past Year) Sexist Events, White Versus Minority Women

TABLE 1.4 Principal Components Analysis of the SSE-Lifetime
(Four Factors, 58.8% of Variance)

Factor	Questionnaire Item	Loading
Factor 1. Sexist Degradation and Its Consequences (40.1% of variance)		
	16. Called sexist names	.77
	17. Argued over sexism	.73
	19. Heard sexist jokes	.71
	13. Wanted to tell someone off	.71
	14. Angry about sexism	.67
	11. Sexually harassed	.67
	12. Got no respect	.62
	18. Was picked on, harmed	.58

Mean score = 20.40, σ = 7.55, eight items, Cronbach's α = .896

Factor 2. Sexist Discrimination in Distant Relationships (7.8% of variance)

	4. Sexism by people in service jobs	.69
	6. Sexism by people in helping jobs	.68
	7. Sexism by neighbors	.64
	5. Sexism by strangers	.64
	1. Sexism by teachers	.63
	3. Sexism by colleagues	.49

Mean score = 11.75, σ = 4.40, six items, Cronbach's α = .816

Factor 3. Sexism in Close Relationships (5.9% of variance)

	10. Sexism by family	.73
	8. Sexism by boyfriend, mate	.68
	20. How different would your life be now	.66

Mean score = 9.31, σ = 3.86, three items, Cronbach's α = .67

Factor 4. Sexist Discrimination in the Workplace (5.0% of variance)

	15. Took drastic steps	.76
	9. Sexism at work	.72
	2. Sexism by employers	.64

Mean score = 4.97, σ = 2.23, three items, Cronbach's α = .675

Total SSE-Lifetime: Mean score = 43.91, σ = 14.51, twenty items, Cronbach's α = .92

NOTE: For the complete wording of the items, see Figure 1.1.

with internal-consistency reliability data for each factor and for the SSE-Lifetime subscale as a whole.

As shown, the 20 items of the SSE-Lifetime emerged as four factors, accounting for 58.8% of the variance. We named these factors Sexist

Degradation and Its Consequences (40.1% of the variance), Sexist Discrimination in Distant Relationships (7.8%), Sexism in Close Relationships (5.9%), and Sexist Discrimination in the Workplace (5.0%).

Factor analyses of the SSE-Lifetime were then repeated to assure that the above factor structure would hold for all women, irrespective of their backgrounds. Similar PCAs (i.e., with an orthogonal rotation and eigenvalue > 1.00 to retain factors) were conducted separately for the 294 college students and for the 337 community women. These (shown in Table 1.5) indicated that the factor structure of the SSE-Lifetime held across these two groups of women and was essentially the same for both. Thus the SSE-Lifetime factors can be employed in research with college students as well as with community samples.

Likewise, to assure that the factor structure of the SSE-Lifetime applies to women irrespective of ethnicity, similar PCAs were conducted separately for the 228 women of color and the 403 White women. These are shown in Table 1.6 and indicated that the factor structure of the SSE-Lifetime held well across ethnicity. The difference between the factors by ethnicity was that four factors emerged for White women and only three for women of color; this is because, for women of color, all items on sexism in relationships (close or distant) loaded together. The items that loaded in the factors were similar enough, however, to suggest that the general factor structure of the SSE-Lifetime can be used for all ethnic groups. Reliability data for women of color, college students, community women, and White women (not shown here) also were similar to those displayed in Table 1.4 for the entire sample.

Thus Lifetime Sexist Events can be conceptualized as falling into four general types or arenas, corresponding to the four factors; the 20 items can be discussed and understood in terms of four factors. The relationships between these types/arenas of sexist discrimination and women's behavior, health, and mental health can be examined.

Factor Analysis of Recent Sexist Events

The ratings given by Sample 1 to the items for Recent (past year) Frequency were separated from those for Lifetime and analyzed as their own scale, SSE-Recent. These data (for the sample as a whole) were entered into a similar PCA. These results are displayed in Table 1.7, along with internal consistency reliability data for each factor and for the SSE-Recent as a whole.

TABLE 1.5 Factor Analyses for Student Versus Community Participants: SSE-Lifetime

	College Women (N = 294), four factors, 58.9%			Community Women (N = 337), four factors, 58.1%	
Factor	Questionnaire Item	Loading	Factor	Questionnaire Item	Loading
Factor 1. Sexist Degradation and Its Consequences (39.5% of variance, college women; 38.1% of variance, community women)			**Factor 1.**		
	16. Called sexist names	.78		16. Called sexist names	.76
	13. Wanted to tell someone off	.77		11. Sexually harassed	.69
	17. Argued over sexism	.75		17. Argued over sexism	.69
	19. Heard sexist jokes	.72		14. Angry about sexism	.65
	14. Angry about sexism	.68		18. Was picked on, harmed	.64
	12. Got no respect	.59		19. Heard sexist jokes	.64
	11. Sexually harassed	.57		12. Got no respect	.60
	18. Was picked on, harmed	.50		13. Wanted to tell someone off	.58
Factor 2. Sexist Discrimination in Distant Relationships (8.3% of variance, college women; 8.2% of variance, community women)			**Factor 2.**		
	7. Sexism by neighbors	.71		4. Sexism by people in service jobs	.73
	6. Sexism by people in helping jobs	.69		1. Sexism by teachers	.70
	4. Sexism by people in service jobs	.65		6. Sexism by people in helping jobs	.69
	5. Sexism by strangers	.63		5. Sexism by strangers	.65
	1. Sexism by teachers	.53		7. Sexism by neighbors	.60
				3. Sexism by colleagues	.56
Factor 3. Sexist Discrimination in the Workplace (5.9% of variance, college women; 6.4% of variance, community women)			**Factor 3.**		
	15. Took drastic steps	.77		15. Took drastic steps	.73
	9. Sexism at work	.71		9. Sexism at work	.71
	2. Sexism by employer	.64		2. Sexism by employer	.62
Factor 4. Sexism in Close Relationships (5.2% of variance, college women; 5.5% of variance, community women)			**Factor 4.**		
	20. How different life would be	.70		10. Sexism by family	.83
	10. Sexism by family	.69		8. Sexism by boyfriend, mate	.61
	8. Sexism by boyfriend, mate	.66		20. How different life would be	.49

NOTE: For the complete wording of the items, see Figure 1.1.

41

TABLE 1.6 Factor Analyses for Women of Different Ethnic Groups: SSE Lifetime

	White Women (N = 403), four factors, 57.2%			Women of Color (N = 228), three factors, 57.7%	
Factor	Questionnaire Item	Loading	Factor	Questionnaire Item	Loading
Factor 1. Sexist Degradation and Its Consequences (37.1% of variance)			**Factor 1.** Sexist Degradation and Its Consequences (44% of variance)		
	16. Called sexist names	.72		16. Called sexist names	.79
	11. Sexually harassed	.71		17. Argued over sexism	.78
	14. Angry about sexism	.70		13. Wanted to tell someone off	.74
	13. Wanted to tell someone off	.69		19. Heard sexist jokes	.74
	19. Heard sexist jokes	.69		18. Was picked on, harmed	.72
	17. Argued over sexism	.67		14. Angry about sexism	.66
	12. Got no respect	.66		11. Sexually harassed	.63
				12. Got no respect	.62
Factor 2. Sexist Discrimination in Distant Relationships (8.1% of variance)			**Factor 2.** Sexist Discrimination in Distant and Close Relationships (7.9% of variance)		
	4. Sexism by people in service jobs	.66		6. Sexism by people in helping jobs	.78
	7. Sexism by neighbors	.65		4. Sexism by people in service jobs	.76
	6. Sexism by people in helping jobs	.63		5. Sexism by strangers	.69
	1. Sexism by teachers	.62		8. Sexism by boyfriend, mate	.65
	5. Sexism by strangers	.61		1. Sexism by teachers	.56
	3. Sexism by colleagues	.49		7. Sexism by neighbors	.52
				20. How different life would be	.50
Factor 3. Sexism in Close Relationships (6.4% of variance)			**Factor 3.** Sexist Discrimination in the Workplace (5.8% of variance)		
	10. Sexism by family	.72		15. Took drastic steps	.79
	8. Sexism by boyfriend, mate	.65		9. Sexism at work	.69
	20. How different life would be	.62		2. Sexism by employer	.63
	18. Was picked on, harmed	.54			
Factor 4. Sexist Discrimination in the Workplace (5.6% of variance)					
	9. Sexism at work	.74			
	2. Sexism by employer	.67			
	15. Took drastic steps	.67			

NOTE: For the complete wording of the items, see Figure 1.1.

TABLE 1.7 Principal Components Analysis of the SSE-Recent: Four
Factors, 54.4% of Variance

Factor	Questionnaire Item	Loading
Factor 1. Sexist Degradation and Its Consequences (36.3% of variance)		
	13. Wanted to tell someone off	.72
	19. Heard sexist jokes	.71
	16. Called sexist names	.69
	14. Angry about sexism	.68
	11. Sexually harassed	.68
	17. Argued over sexism	.65
	12. Got no respect	.58
	18. Was picked on, harmed	.47
Mean score = 16.16, σ = 6.91, eight items, Cronbach's α = .88		
Factor 2. Sexist Discrimination in Distant Relationships (7.3% of variance)		
	4. Sexism by people in service jobs	.74
	6. Sexism by people in helping jobs	.67
	5. Sexism by strangers	.64
	7. Sexism by neighbors	.54
	1. Sexism by teachers	.51
Mean score = 7.96, σ = 2.95, five items, Cronbach's α = .74		
Factor 3. Sexist Discrimination in the Workplace (5.7% of variance)		
	9. Sexism at work	.72
	2. Sexism by employer	.67
	15. Took drastic steps	.62
	3. Sexism by colleagues	.51
Mean score = 5.57, σ = 2.47, four items, Cronbach's α = .70		
Factor 4. Sexism in Close Relationships (5.0% of variance)		
	8. Sexism by boyfriend, mate	.69
	10. Sexism by family	.59
	20. How different life would be	.53
Mean score = 5.33, σ = 2.57, three items, Cronbach's α = .61		
Total SSE Year Mean score = 35.03, σ = 12.44, 20 items, Cronbach's α = .90		

NOTE: For the complete wording of the items, see Figure 1.1.

As shown, the items emerged again as four factors, in this case
accounting for 54.4% of the variance. These factors were nearly identical
to those that emerged for the SSE-Lifetime and so were similarly named
Sexist Degradation and Its Consequences (36.3% of the variance), Sexist
Discrimination in Distant Relationships (7.3%), Sexist Discrimination in

the Workplace (5.7%), and Sexism in Close Relationships (5.0%). PCAs were not repeated for community versus college women, or for White versus minority women for the SSE-Recent because the data for SSE-Lifetime strongly suggested that the factor structure of the items holds well across these groups.

Thus Recent Sexist Events also can be conceptualized as falling into four general types, corresponding to the four factors. The relationships between these types of recent sexist events and women's behavior can be examined and compared with the role of lifetime sexist discrimination.

Factor scores were computed for each woman for each factor of the SSE-Lifetime and SSE-Recent. These were the sum of the ratings the women had given to each item in the factor in question. Correlations among the factors were then examined by using these total factor scores, as shown in Table 1.8. Despite the rotation for orthogonal factors, scores on the factors of the SSE-Lifetime and of the SSE-Recent were highly correlated. Each factor was necessarily highly correlated with the total score on the SSE-Lifetime (sum of all lifetime ratings) and on the SSE-Recent (sum of all past year ratings).

Reliability of the SSE[4]

Internal Consistency Reliability. As indicated in the factor analyses, the SSE-Lifetime and SSE-Recent scales, as well as their factors, exhibited high internal consistency reliability. The items of the SSE-Lifetime and of the SSE-Recent had total scale Cronbach's α of .92 and .90, respectively, indicating highly reliable scales. Internal consistency for the SSE-Lifetime factors (1 to 4) were .89, .82, .67, and .68, respectively. For the factors (1 to 4) of the SSE-Recent, Cronbach's α were .88, .74, .70, and .61, respectively.

Split-Half and Test-Retest Reliability. Split-half reliability for the SSE-Lifetime and SSE-Recent scales were $r = .87$ and $r = .83$, respectively ($p = .0005$ for both). Internal consistency and split-half were judged to be the best way to assess the reliability of the scales. Test-retest reliability was judged to be a less than adequate manner of assessing the reliability of the

---

4. Reliability is the extent to which a test or scale measures whatever it measures in a consistent, stable, reliable manner. There are several types of reliability; see appendix for a discussion of each.

TABLE 1.8 Correlations Among Factors of the SSE-Lifetime and SSE-Recent

	Factor 2	Factor 3	Factor 4	Total
SSE-Lifetime factors				
Factor 1	.64	.61	.50	.92
Factor 2		.57	.57	.84
Factor 3			.47	.77
Factor 4				.69
SSE-Recent (past year) factors				
Factor 1	.54	.54	.59	.93
Factor 2		.56	.46	.75
Factor 3			.43	.73
Factor 4				.74

NOTE: All correlations were significant at $p < .0005$ by 2-tailed t test.
Factor 1. Sexist Degradation and Its Consequences
Factor 2. Sexist Discrimination in Distant Relationships
Factor 3. Sexism in Close Relationships
Factor 4. Sexist Discrimination in the Workplace

two scales because a single sexist event occurring on any day in a woman's life would change her SSE-Lifetime and SSE-Recent scores, the latter score in particular. Nonetheless, a preliminary analysis of the test-retest reliability of the scales was conducted by distributing the scale to a small group of college women in a sorority ($n - 50$) once, and then again 2 weeks later. In light of the above concern, the ensuing test-retest reliability of $r = .70$ for SSE-Lifetime and $r = .63$ for SSE-Recent ($p = .005$ for both) was encouraging. These data suggest that the SSE-Lifetime and SSE-Recent scales are highly reliable.

Validity of the SSE[5]

Given our theory that sexist events are gender-specific stressors in women's lives and are analogous to other types of stressful events, the validity of the SSE can be established in two ways. The first is to examine the relationship between scores on the SSE and other measures of stressful

---

5. Validity is the extent to which a test or scale measures what it claims to measure and is the most important quality of all scales and tests—more important than reliability. There are many ways to demonstrate validity, but few of these are easy, and controversies regarding the "proof" of validity remain. How, for example, would one establish the validity of an intelligence test—prove that it actually measures intelligence rather than something else?

events. If the SSE correlates with other measures of stressful events *at least as well as those measures correlate with each other,* then its (convergent) validity as a measure of (gender-specific) stressful events has been established. Thus we examined the extent to which scores on the SSE correlated with scores on the PERI-LES (Dohrenwend et al., 1978) and the Hassles-Freq (Kanner et al., 1981) scales. These two scales are highly reliable and valid measures of generic stressful events and have well-established relationships to behavioral indicators of stress. These data are shown in Tables 1.9 and 1.10.

As indicated in Table 1.9, the correlation between the PERI-LES and the Hassles-Freq scale was $r = .32$ for our sample. Also shown in Table 1.9 is that the total SSE-Recent score correlated with the PERI-LES $r = .27$, and the total SSE-Lifetime score correlated with the PERI-LES $r = .27$. Likewise, the total SSE-Recent score correlated with the Hassles-Freq scale $r = .24$, and the total SSE-Lifetime score also correlated with the Hassles-Freq scale $r = .24$. An r- to z-score transformation (Hays, 1981) revealed that none of these correlations differed significantly from the others. Thus, while all of the correlations are low, the SSE correlated with two well-known measures of stressful events as well as those measures did with each other. These data suggest that the SSE is a valid measure of stressful events. Likewise, Table 1.10 displays the correlations among the factors of the SSE-Lifetime and Recent, the PERI-LES, and Hassles-Freq scales. As shown, most of the factors correlated well with the measures of generic stress.

The more powerful way of establishing the validity of the SSE is to demonstrate that scores on it are strongly related to stress-related physical and psychiatric symptoms (concurrent validity). We address this topic in Chapter 3.

DISCUSSION OF STUDY 1

One source of concern about this study is that **we have no evidence indicating that the sexist events reported by the sample were actually experienced**; what we could have here are perceptions rather than factual reporting or response-style differences and biases among the women. There are three reasons to reject this hypothesis:

> 1. These self-reports are consistent with non-self-report data from other studies.

TABLE 1.9 Relationship Between SSE-Lifetime, SSE-Recent, and Two Measures of Stressful Events

	SSE-Recent	PERI-LES	Hassles-Freq
SSE-Lifetime	$.75^a$	$.27^b$	$.24^c$
SSE-Recent		$.27^d$	$.24^e$
PERI-LES			$.32^f$

NOTE: PERI-LES is the PERI-Life Events Scale (Dohrenwend et al., 1978). Hassles-Freq is the Hassles-Frequency scale (Kanner et al., 1981). All correlations shown are significant at $p = .00005$.
a. $n = 613$.
b. $n = 538$.
c. $n = 538$.
d. $n = 534$.
e. $n = 534$.
f. $n = 551$.

2. The pattern of self-reports we obtained was neither random nor extreme.

3. All other scales that measure the frequency of stressful events use similar self-reports and treat them as accurate, factual descriptions of events in people's lives.

Where other data are concerned, several studies (detailed in the Introduction) indicate that women are paid less than men, even when occupying the same job, with the same title and education, and these data *are not self-reports.* The prevalent report of discrimination at work found for this sample is consistent with such data, suggesting that women's self-reports are accurate. Likewise, the well-documented bias against women in medical treatment described earlier is consistent with women's reports here of being discriminated against by such professionals.

In addition, the pattern of reports of specific sexist events also suggests accurate reporting. For example, women were *likely* to report being forced to listen to sexist jokes (83.8% of the sample reported this) in the previous year but were *unlikely* to report filing a lawsuit or labor grievance (only 8.7% reported this) in the previous year. Furthermore, most women reported that the various sexist events occur about 10% to 50% of the time in their lives and in the past year; very few reported that any of these events occur more frequently, say 51% to 100% of the time. If these data solely reflect a bias toward reporting events, one would expect frequent reports of all events, or a random pattern, rather than the frequent reporting of only a few highly probable events and the infrequent reporting of lower probability events. In addition, if these findings merely reflect the desire to report unpleasant experiences, then women who reported high

TABLE 1.10 Relationships Among SSE Factors and Two Measures of Stressful Events

	Factor 1 Sexist Degradation and Its Consequences	Factor 2 Sexist Discrimination in Distant Relationships	Factor 3 Sexism in Close Relationships	Factor 4 Sexist Discrimination in the Workplace	Total
SSE-Lifetime factors					
Hassles-Freq	.21	.19	.22	.22	.24
PERI-LES	.26	.23	.21	.17	.27
SSE-Recent Factors					
Hassles-Freq	.19	.20	.17	.23	.29
PERI-LES	.28	.15	.19	.18	.27

NOTE: PERI-LES is the PERI-Life Events Scale (Dohrenwend et al., 1978). Hassles-Freq is the Hassles-Frequency Scale (Kanner et al., 1981). All correlations shown are significant at $p = .00005$; $N = 551$ for each r.

sexist events should have reported high generic stressful events as well. The correlation between SSE scores and scores on the PERI-LES would be high if all we had here was a case of reporting bias. But the correlations were all low. Women reported frequent sexist events but not frequent generic stressful life events. This, too, suggests efforts to report actual experiences accurately.

Finally, we note that the SSE was modeled after the PERI-LES, the Hassles-Freq, and other scales that assess stressful events. The self-reports entailed in the SSE do not differ from those entailed in these other scales, and reports on those scales have been treated as accurate, factual reports of events in people's lives. **There appears to be no reason to assume that reports of sexist events are any more or less accurate than reports of generic stressful events.** Thus we treat these self-reports as similarly factual descriptions of the experiences of the sample and assume that women endeavor to be as accurate as they can when reporting sexist or generic stressful events.

Hence the data here confirm and are consistent with the evidence reviewed in the Introduction, indicating that women face ongoing discrimination against them: 97% to 99% of women in this sample reported being discriminated against in some form or another *because* they were women, with 40% reporting salary and other types of discrimination in the workplace.

We can now turn to an examination of status differences among the women of Sample 1 in experiences with sexist discrimination/events.

TWO

Social Status Differences in Experiencing Sexist Discrimination

As noted previously, the 631 women in Sample 1 were diverse in terms of age, education, ethnic group, income, and the like. In this chapter, we report on the extent to which these status differences were associated with different scores on the SSE-Lifetime and SSE-Recent Scales. Such data will reveal whether a woman's social class, age, ethnicity, or other status characteristics play a role in her chances of being discriminated against.

RESULTS

Source of Participants

To examine whether the source of the participants (college students vs. women from the community) played a role, a multivariate analysis of variance (MANOVA)[1] with follow-up analyses of variance (ANOVAs) was

1. Multivariate analysis of variance and analysis of variance (ANOVA) are statistics used to determine if two groups studied differ from each other in statistically significant ways. Both analyze the variance, *the differences*, among groups, and hence their names. Both compare the differences within a group (within-group variance) to the differences between groups (between-groups variance) to determine if groups truly differ or not. There must be more differences *between* two groups of people than *within* either group for the groups to be said to truly differ *from each other.* For example, for Black women and White women to differ in their attitudes about abortion, the differences between the two groups of women must exceed the

conducted on the total SSE-Lifetime and SSE-Recent scores; these data are shown in Table 2.1. As indicated, the college students had higher scores (reported experiencing sexist events more frequently) than the community women, in the past year as well as in their lifetimes. These differences are probably largely an artifact of age, however. As indicated later here, there were significant age differences in scores on the scale, with younger women reporting more discrimination than older ones, as other studies have found (e.g., Klein, 1984). The college student women were significantly younger than the community women (χ^2 = 105.423, df = 1, p = .000005); the correlation (phi) between age (22 and younger vs. 23 and older) and source (student vs. community) was .41 (p = .0005). Because source of participants may not be a psychologically meaningful variable, because the factor structure of the scales held irrespective of source (see Chapter 1), and because differences in scores based on the source of the participants are likely to be at least in part an artifact of these age differences, no further analyses of the data by source of participants are presented. We caution researchers that scores for college students might be higher than for community samples and that generalizations from one to another should be limited.

Income/Social Class

The annual income of the women ranged from zero to $400,000. The mean income was $34,058 ($\sigma$ = $34,370), and the median was $27,000. To assess possible social class/income differences in reporting sexist events, participants were divided into three groups representing the zero to 33rd percentile ($19,000 or less, n = 166), the 34th to 66th percentile ($19,200-$39,000, n = 134), and the upper third of the sample ($40,000 and above, n = 138). A MANOVA was conducted with these three groups and two dependent variables, total SSE-Lifetime and total SSE-Recent scores. This MANOVA was not significant (T^2 = .011, $F(4, 932)$ = 1.27, p = .29) and none of the follow-up ANOVAs were significant, indicating that there were no income differences in frequency of sexist discrimination. To assure that

---

differences between both groups. If White women (within-group) differ so much from each other in their attitudes that they differ more among themselves than they do from Black women, then the two groups do not differ from each other. MANOVA and ANOVA are simply the ratio of the within- to the between-groups variance; the larger this ratio (called F), the more the groups differ. Analysis of variance examines group differences on a single variable, measure, or experience, whereas multivariate analysis of variance examines group differences on many (multi) variables (variates) simultaneously. See appendix for further description.

TABLE 2.1 Differences (ANOVAs) in Total Sexist Events Reported by
Participant Source[a]

| | College Women | Community Women |
	(N = 294)	(N = 337)
Sexist Events-Lifetime	47.13	41.14
Sexist Events-Recent	38.24	32.26

a. MANOVA: Hotelling's $T^2 = .063$, Exact $F(2, 61038) = 19.26$, $p < .0005$.
b. $df = 1, 611$.
*$p < .0005$.

no income differences existed, t tests were conducted comparing extreme income groups: We compared the 15% of the sample with the lowest incomes ($8,000 per year or less, $n = 98$) with the 15% of the sample with the highest incomes (greater than $60,000 per year, $n = 71$) on total SSE-Lifetime and total SSE-Recent scores. Neither of these t tests was significant (SSE-Lifetime, $t = .33$, $df = 167$, $p = .74$; SSE-Recent, $t = .59$, $df = 165$, $p = .56$). Thus we conclude that there are no income differences on the SSE and that sexist discrimination, therefore, does not vary with a woman's social class.

Education

Education was examined as another possible indicator of a woman's social class; education differences also could represent response-style differences and thereby alter reporting. The education levels of the participants ranged from a high school diploma or less ($n = 113$) to some college courses taken ($n = 309$), to an undergraduate or graduate degree ($n = 109$). Possible education differences were assessed through a MANOVA, using these three groups and two dependent variables, total SSE-Lifetime score and total SSE-Recent score. The MANOVA was significant for SSE-Lifetime only, $T^2 = .026$, $F(4, 1136) = 3.63$, $p = .006$. The post-hoc Tukey comparisons (at $\alpha = .05$) revealed that women with some college education (mean score = 45.38) scored higher than those with a high school diploma (mean score = 41.18), with no differences between these two groups and the group of women with a college or graduate degree (mean score = 44.15) on the total SSE-Lifetime score. Because only two of the education groups differed on only one of the scores, we conclude that education is not related to frequency of sexist discrimination. As will be seen in the cluster analysis later, education and income (in the context of age, ethnicity, and marital status) did not predict (had nonsignificant main effects on) the frequency of sexist events experienced.

Thus a woman's level of education does not alter her experiences with sexist discrimination, and her income similarly does not play a role. When adding the lack of education differences to the lack of income differences and considering these to be measures of social class, we conclude that **women are discriminated against irrespective of their social class.** Finally, given that education might be associated with differences in responses to written questionnaires, and that no education differences appeared, we suggest that women's reports of sexist discrimination are not an artifact of response styles and thereby represent their experiences.

Age

A few researchers (Klein, 1984) have found that younger women tend to report more sexist discrimination than older ones. This has been interpreted as a birth cohort effect, that is, as meaning that women born in different generations or eras (before and after the women's movement) differ in their perceptions of the acceptability of gender discrimination as a result of the women's movement, so that younger women report more discrimination than their older cohorts. Age differences have not been interpreted as differences in *experiencing* discrimination but rather as differences in reporting it (Klein, 1984). Because we know of no empirical evidence for the cohort interpretation, however, it is not clear what the age differences found in previous interview studies mean. Analyses of age differences are shown in Tables 2.2 and 2.3.

As shown in Table 2.2, women 22 years old and younger reported more frequent sexist discrimination for their entire lives than women ages 30 to 39, but not more than women 23 to 29 or than women 40 and older. Likewise, women ages 22 and younger reported experiencing sexist discrimination more frequently in the past year than did women ages 23 to 29, 30 to 39, and 40 to 55 years old; yet women 23 to 29 did not differ from those 40 to 55. Thus, for Lifetime Sexist Events, the pattern of scores by age was not consistent with the birth-cohort hypothesis, which predicts that scores should be higher for women born after the women's movement (e.g., 1960). To better assess the birth cohort question, we investigated age

TABLE 2.2 Differences (ANOVAs) in Total Sexist Events Reported by Participant Age[a]

Total Sexist Events Score	Group 1 22 and < (N = 170)	Group 2 23-29 (N = 143)	Group 3 30-39 (N = 140)	Group 4 40-55 (N = 127)	SS	F[b]
Lifetime	47.16	43.47	41.08	44.35	2,921.79	4.79*
Recent	40.76	35.35	31.54	31.79	8,588.67	20.35**

NOTE: Post-hoc Tukey tests ($\alpha = .05$) SSE Lifetime: 1 > 3; Post-hoc Tukey tests ($\alpha = .05$) SSE Recent: 1 > 2 > 3; 1 > 4; 2 ≯ 4, 3 ≯ 4.
a. MANOVA: Hotelling's $T^2 = .1446$, $F(6, 1146) = 13.81$, $p < .0005$.
b. $df = 3,575$.
*$p < .003$; **$p < .0005$.

differences on the factors of the SSE-Lifetime and SSE-Recent, using total factor scores; these data are shown in Table 2.3.

As shown in Table 2.3 (top of table), younger women's (18- to 22-year-olds) higher scores on total SSE-Lifetime were the result of more frequent reports of Sexist Degradation (Factor 1), something they reported more frequently than all other age groups. Likewise, women 18 to 22 also reported more frequent Sexist Discrimination in Distant Relationships (Factor 2) when compared with the 30- to 39-year-olds, but not when compared with the other two age groups; young women did not, for example, report discrimination in distant relationships more frequently than women 40 to 55. In addition, on Factor 4, the oldest group of women (40 to 55) reported significantly more frequent discrimination at work than all of the younger groups. No age differences in sexist treatment in close relationships in one's entire lifetime appeared. Hence, these results did not support the birth cohort hypothesis. Likewise, data on the SSE-Recent factors are shown at the bottom of Table 2.3, where it is clear that the age groups differed on all of the SSE-Recent factors. Again, however, the pattern of age differences did not support the birth cohort hypothesis. Thus, these data similarly suggest that there are complex differences in how women of different ages are treated in specific domains.

Ethnicity

Data on ethnic differences in reporting sexist discrimination are presented in Tables 2.4 and 2.5. As shown in Table 2.4 (top), women of color reported significantly more frequent sexist discrimination than did

TABLE 2.3 Age Differences (MANOVAs) on Factors of SSE-Lifetime and SSE-Recent, Using Total Factor Scores

	Group 1: 22 and <	Group 2: 23-29	Group 3: 30-39	Group 4: 40-55	SS	F^a	Tukey Tests on Factor at $\alpha = .05$
				ANOVAs			
SSE-Lifetime factors[b]							
1. Sexist Degradation and Its Consequences	22.77	20.29	18.48	19.91	1,476.88	9.19***	1 > 2, 3, 4
2. Sexist Discrimination in Distant Relationships	12.29	11.72	10.86	12.28	193.15	3.39*	1 > 3; 4 > 3; 1, 2, 3 > 4
3. Sexism in Close Relationships	7.05	6.69	6.47	6.96	30.47	1.16	
4. Sexist Discrimination in the Workplace	4.86	4.75	4.88	5.63	63.46	4.27**	4 > 1, 2, 3
SSE-Recent factors[c]							
1. Sexist Degradation and Its Consequences	19.77	16.19	14.16	13.75	3,410.40	27.74***	1 > 2 > 3 = 4
2. Sexist Discrimination in Distant Relationships	8.84	7.90	7.29	7.64	200.09	7.98***	1 > 2 = 3 = 4
3. Sexist Discrimination in the Workplace	6.12	5.65	4.85	5.53	121.76	7.04***	1 = 2 = 4 > 3
4. Sexism in Close Relationships	5.83	5.40	4.90	4.70	112.86	6.53***	1 > 3, 4

a. $df = 3,568$ for SSE-Lifetime factors; $df = 3,559$ for SSE-Recent factors.
b. MANOVA: Hotelling's $T^2 = .1133$, $F(12, 1691) = 5.32$, $p = .0005$.
c. MANOVA: Hotelling's $T^2 = .1742$, $F(12, 1664) = 8.05$, $p = .0005$.
*$p = .02$; **$p = .005$; ***$p = .0005$.

TABLE 2.4 Ethnic Differences in Reporting Sexist Events:
Lifetime and Recent

	ANOVAs			
	White Women (N = 403)	Women of Color (N = 228)	SS	F
Differences on Total SSE Scores[a]				
Lifetime	47.20	50.80	1,608.14	6.18[b]*
Recent	33.51	37.32	1,799.72	11.45[b]**
				,
Differences on Factors of SSE-Lifetime and SSE-Recent				
SSE-Lifetime factors[c]				
1. Sexist Degradation and Its Consequences	24.67	25.60	124.36	1.46[d]
2. Sexist Discrimination in Distant Relationships	11.22	11.63	25.08	1.28[d]
3. Sexism in Close Relationships	8.89	9.99	173.61	12.05[d]**
4. Sexist Discrimination in the Workplace	4.95	4.85	1.50	0.29[d]
				,
SSE-Recent factors[e]				
1. Sexist Degradation and Its Consequences	17.13	19.26	645.46	11.14[f]**
2. Sexist Discrimination in Distant Relationships	5.41	5.63	6.43	1.02[f]
3. Sexist Discrimination in the Workplace	7.67	8.26	50.65	5.09[f]
4. Sexism in Close Relationships	3.47	4.21	76.61	20.45[f]**

a. MANOVA: Hotelling's T^2 = .021, Exact $F(2, 538)$ = 5.71, p = .004.
b. df = 1,539.
c. MANOVA: Hotelling's T^2 = .034, Exact $F(4, 619)$ = 5.28, p = .0001.
d. df = 1,622.
e. MANOVA: Hotelling's T^2 = .037, Exact $F(4, 613)$ = 5.70, p =.0001.
f. df = 1,616.
*p = .01; **p =.001.

White women, in their lifetimes, as well as in the past year. At the bottom of Table 2.4, ethnic differences on the factors (using the factor structure for the entire sample and total factor scores) of the SSE-Lifetime and SSE-Recent are shown in order to better understand these differences. As indicated, women of color scored higher than White women on the total SSE-Lifetime score because they reported significantly more frequent sexism in their close, personal relationships with men and family (Factor 3).

TABLE 2.5 Specific Ethnic Differences in Reporting Sexist Events: Total Factor Scores, Lifetime and Recent

	White Women (n = 403)	Black Women (n = 38)	Latinas (n = 117)	Asian Women (n = 25)	ANOVAs		Tukey Tests on Factor at α = .05
					SS	F^a	
SSE-Lifetime factors[b]							
1. Sexist Degradation and Its Consequences	20.03	19.21	20.24	21.9	1,114.77	0.75	
2. Sexist Discrimination in Distant Relationships	11.59	11.44	11.66	12.68	29.41	0.54	
3. Sexism in Close Relationships	6.41	6.81	7.49	8.13	156.39	6.30**	Latinas > Whites Asians > Whites
4. Sexist Discrimination in the Workplace	4.98	4.81	4.94	5.04	1.22	0.08	
SSE-Recent factors[c]							
1. Sexist Degradation and Its Consequences	15.45	15.22	16.82	18.39	340.04	2.78*	Asians >Whites
2. Sexist Discrimination in Distant Relationships	7.73	8.69	8.00	7.80	34.39	1.48	
3. Sexist Discrimination in the Workplace	5.43	5.42	5.78	5.88	14.53	0.85	
4. Sexism in Close Relationships	4.82	5.47	6.09	6.52	188.69	11.85**	Asians > Whites Latinas > Whites

a. $df = 3,563$ for SSE-Lifetime factors; $df = 3,553$ for SSE-Recent factors.
b. MANOVA: Hotelling's $T^2 = .052$, $F(12, 1686) = 2.44$, $p = .004$.
c. MANOVA: Hotelling's $T^2 = .088$, $F(12, 1646) = 4.04$, $p = .0005$.
*$p = .04$; **$p = .0005$.

Likewise, women of color scored higher than White women on the total SSE-Recent score because they reported more frequent Sexist Degradation (i.e., being called sexist names, being picked on, pushed, shoved) and more Sexism in Close Relationships than did White women. There were no ethnic differences in the frequency of sexist discrimination at work or in distant relationships.

To interpret these findings in a culturally sensitive manner, we conducted these analyses again on the four separate ethnic groups (White women and Asian, African, and Latino American women) to assess which groups differed on the factors; those results are shown in Table 2.5.

As shown in Table 2.5 (top, Lifetime scores), not all minority women differed from White women in reporting sexism in their personal relationships (Factor 3) over their lifetimes. Rather, Latinas and Asian Americans reported more frequent sexist treatment in their personal relationships (experiences with men and family members) than did White women; no other ethnic differences on the Lifetime factors appeared.

Ethnic differences on the factors of SSE-Recent are shown at the bottom of Table 2.5; two differences emerged. Asian American women reported more frequent Sexist Degradation (Factor 1; i.e., name-calling) than did White women, and both Asian American women and Latinas reported more frequent sexism in close relationships (Factor 4) than did White women.

These data suggest that ethnicity plays a role in sexist discrimination against women and that women of color experience more frequent sexist discrimination in certain domains than do White women. We note that the greater discrimination reported by minority women was limited to being called sexist names and to their personal relationships with family members and loved ones who **are likely to be of the same ethnic group as the women**; hence, these reports cannot be said to be an artifact of misinterpreting racist discrimination for sexist discrimination.

Marital status

Finally, marital status differences in reporting sexist discrimination are shown in Table 2.6. As shown (top of table), single (never married) women reported experiencing sexist discrimination significantly more often than married women for their lifetimes and for the past year. To

TABLE 2.6 Marital Status Differences in Reporting Sexist Events

	ANOVAs			
	Single Women	Married Women	SS	F
Differences on Total SSE Scores				
Lifetime	46.57	40.24	5,094.78	25.69[b]*
Recent	38.73	31.20	7,201.86	47.70[b]*
Differences on Factors of **SSE-Lifetime and SSE-Recent**				
SSE-Lifetime factors[c]				
1. Sexist Degradation and Its Consequences	21.91	18.19	1,740.35	33.49[d]*
2. Sexist Discrimination in Distant Relationships	12.42	10.82	322.91	17.53[d]*
3. Sexism in Close Relationships	7.13	6.09	137.39	15.91[d]*
4. Sexist Discrimination in the Workplace	5.02	4.87	2.84	0.55[d]
SSE-Recent factors[e]				
1. Sexist Degradation and Its Consequences	18.20	13.83	2,360.33	53.36[f]*
2. Sexist Discriminatiion in Distant Relationships	8.57	7.15	248.06	30.35[f]*
3. Sexist Discrimination in the Workplace	5.99	5.12	94.85	15.69[f]*
4. Sexism in Close Relationships	5.78	4.71	139.94	23.00[f]*

a. MANOVA: Hotelling's $T^2 = .093$, Exact $F(2, 511) = 23.84$, $p = .0005$.
b. $df = 1,512$.
c. MANOVA: Hotelling's $T^2 = .087$, Exact $F(4, 505) - 10.94$, $p = .0005$.
d. $df = 1,508$.
e. MANOVA: Hotelling's $T^2 = .113$, Exact $F(4, 496) = 14.05$, $p = .0005$
f. $df = 1,499$.
*$p = .0005$.

understand the source of these differences, single women and married women were compared on the factors of the SSE-Lifetime and SSE-Recent (bottom of Table 2.6). As indicated, for their lifetimes, single women reported more frequent sexist discrimination than married women for every domain except work. For the past year, single women reported more frequent sexist discrimination than did married women in every domain. Although some of the differences between the means were small (e.g., Lifetime and Recent Factor 3) and perhaps of no practical significance, differences on some factors (Lifetime and Recent Factor 1) were large.

Overall Analysis of Status Differences

Cluster Analysis of Cases[2]

Although several status variables were related to experiencing sexist events when analyzed alone, such relationships may not hold when analyzing all of those variables simultaneously; in the context of other status variables, an effect might drop out. To assess this overall relationship between the status variables and frequent versus infrequent experiences of sexist events, a cluster analysis with all of the status variables included (age, education, income, ethnicity, and marital status) and with total SSE-Lifetime and SSE-Recent scores was performed. For this analysis, age was entered as a continuous variable (actual ages), and all other variables were coded as follows: marital status was coded as -1 = married, 1 = single; ethnicity was coded as -1 = White, 1 = Black, 2 = Latina, and 3 = Asian American; education was coded as -1 = high school diploma or less, 0 = some college, and 1 = college degree or higher; and income was coded as 1 = \$19,000 or less, 2 = \$19,200-39,000, and 3 = > \$40,000 per year. These cluster analyses are shown in Table 2.7. At the top of the table is the result when we requested two groups (clusters), and at the bottom is the result when we requested three significantly different groups.

As shown at the top of Table 2.7, women who reported frequent sexist events versus those who reported infrequent sexist events differed on all status variables except education and income. Those experiencing frequent sexist events were significantly younger, likely to be unmarried, and likely to be minorities. The prototypical woman (cluster center) who experienced sexist events frequently was a 26-year-old, unmarried, minority woman.

---

2. Cluster analysis of cases is the same as MANOVA except that the groups being compared (to see if they differ) are constructed by the computer program instead of selected ahead of time by the researcher. For example, we could have divided the women into those with high Recent Sexist Events and those with low Recent Sexist Events (researcher-defined groups) using any SSE-Recent score we liked, and then conducted a MANOVA comparing these groups on income, age, ethnicity, education, and so on. Instead, we asked the computer to construct groups (called clusters) who differed in a statistically significant way on as many of these variables as possible, and then waited to see whether status characteristics would be something on which the clusters differed significantly. While identical to a MANOVA, cluster analysis is also more objective: In MANOVA, we could divide the women into groups using any Sexist Events score we liked as the dividing line for high versus low groups, and hence have the potential to force certain results to appear. In cluster analysis, we have no control over how the groups are defined—such that SSE scores did not have to be included as a variable on which the clusters differed.

TABLE 2.7 Cluster Analysis of Cases

	Two Clusters			
	Frequent Events	Infrequent Events	MS	F (df = 1,339)
SSE-Lifetime	60.26	36.92	38,976.92	445.98***
SSE Recent	49.82	29.49	29,565.49	386.89***
Age	25.86	31.77	2,498.11	23.58***
Marital status	0.49 (single)	−0.05 (married)	21.20	22.76***
Ethnicity	0.13 (minority)	−0.27 (white)	11.41	5.98*
Education	−0.06 (high school graduate)	−0.04 (high school graduate)	0.03	0.76
Income	1.87 (medium)	1.97 (medium)	0.78	1.06

	Three Clusters				
	Frequent	Moderately Frequent	Infrequent	MS	F (df = 2,338)
SSE-Lifetime	71.39	50.90	33.36	24,269.36	408.82***
SSE-Recent	63.56	40.36	26.74	20,033.09	439.56***
Age	23.17	27.06	33.61	2,420.44	24.37***
Marital status	0.53 (single)	0.46 (single)	−0.25 (married)	22.29	25.77***
Ethnicity	0.40 (minority)	−0.03 (any ethnicity)	−0.35 (white)	9.12	4.76**
Education	−0.13 (high school graduate)	−0.02 (more high school than college)	−0.05 (more high school than college)	0.16	0.37
Income	1.83 (medium)	1.89 (medium)	2.00 (medium)	0.69	0.98

*p = .01; **p = .009; ***p = .0005.

The prototypical woman (cluster center) who experienced sexist events infrequently was a 32-year-old, married, White woman.

The bottom of Table 2.7 shows a similar analysis in which we requested three groups (clusters) who differ significantly on total SSE-Lifetime, SSE-Recent, and the status variables. As shown, again neither education nor social class was related to these clusters; instead, the sexist events clusters differed by age, ethnicity, and marital status. The prototypical woman (cluster center) who reported experiencing highly frequent sexist events was a 23-year-old, unmarried, minority woman. The prototypical woman who reported experiencing moderately frequent sexist events was a 27-year-old, unmarried woman of any ethnicity. The prototypical woman who reported experiencing sexist events infrequently was a 34-year-old, married, White woman. These results strongly suggest that age, ethnicity, and marital status are related to experiencing sexist discrimination, whereas education and social class are not relevant. In the context of the other status variables, the effect for education (found in the previous MANOVA) dropped out and so can be dismissed.

An additional analysis (logit-loglinear model fitting) not shown here revealed that the effect for marital status held only for White women. Being single was associated with a high frequency of sexist events for White women only; for women of color, a high frequency of sexist events appeared irrespective of marital status. This analysis alters the meaning of the marital status effects found earlier here, when that variable was examined individually in a MANOVA. The marital status effect seen in previous (MANOVA) analyses must be qualified.

Discussion

Women on welfare and wealthy women reported similar experiences with sexist discrimination, and women with doctorate degrees reported experiences similar to those of young women in high school. This absence of education and social class differences is perhaps consistent with what feminists might expect: The privilege associated with higher social class or education does not exempt women from their status as women in a patriarchal society. Women who differ in social class, education, and culture may indeed differ in their customs, socialization experiences, behavioral patterns, and even their inner lives, but they nonetheless have one thing in common: the way they are treated in the world for being women (Lott, 1990).

Simultaneously, we did find large age differences. Because these were not consistent with the birth cohort hypothesis, they suggest that there may be complex age differences in how women are treated. It may be the case that younger women (18 to 22) do experience more frequent sexist degradation (e.g., name-calling) than older ones. Where Sexist Discrimination in Distant Relationships (with physicians, store clerks, mechanics) is concerned, it is quite possible that very young (18 to 22) and older (>40) women both experience more frequent discrimination than the other age groups. Likewise, it is conceivable that women 40 to 55 years old experience more frequent sexist treatment at work than their younger counterparts. At present, there is no theoretical framework for interpreting these differences because older (ages 40 to 55) groups of women are rarely included in studies in feminist psychology and because age differences within samples typically are not reported by researchers. However, these data suggest that young and older women differ significantly in how they are treated as women in the world, and thereby **may differ significantly in their experience of gender.** This, in turn, raises questions on the appropriateness of generalizing from the 18- to 22-year-old women who constitute many of feminist psychology's samples, for their experiences of discrimination (and so of gender) may not match those of their older counterparts. Replicating classic, feminist psychological studies with older groups of women to assess the extent to which the results hold may clarify the nature of age differences; the need to include older women in future studies is clear.

The same may be the case for the marital status effects found here, in which single White women experienced more frequent gender discrimination than married White women. Our data suggest that (White) single women and married women differ significantly in how they are treated as women in the world and consequently also may experience gender differently. These marital status differences may reflect differences in how (White) women behave, as well as differences in the extent to which they are perceived as knowing their "place." For example, some studies (e.g., Gigy, 1980) suggest that unmarried women tend to have higher occupational status than their married counterparts and tend to be characterized by their unique "self-assertiveness, determination, or independence" (Lott, 1994, p. 335). Thus, unmarried (White) women may behave in an assertive, independent manner that elicits punishment (gender discrimination), and/ or they may occupy high status (occupational) positions that similarly elicit punishment (discrimination) to teach them their "place" in both cases.[3] In any event, like the age differences we found, these marital status differences (for White women) similarly lack an interpretive, theoretical framework. They imply, however, that generalizing from largely unmarried, college student samples to other women may be inappropriate and that reporting and controlling for marital status in future research may be beneficial.

In addition to these two interesting status differences was the finding that women of color experience more frequent sexist discrimination than White women in certain arenas. The irony here is that (despite recent efforts) women of color are by and large ignored by feminist psychology, feminist social science, and women's studies and were similarly neglected by the women's movement. Whether their experience of more frequent gender discrimination in the 1990s is in part a result of such previous neglect (e.g., the failure of the women's movement to address minority women's lives) is a reasonable question. In any case, the women who experience gender discrimination *least* often (White women) have received much of feminism's attention, whereas those who experience sexist discrimination *most* often (women of color) are the very women feminist social science ignores. No better evidence for the need to bring cultural diversity to feminist research could be presented; in the context of these data, continuing to neglect women of color in our work is simply indefensible.

Why women of color experience more frequent gender discrimination in specific domains (Sexist Degradation; Sexism in Close Relationships) then becomes the question. Where close relationships are concerned, we suggest that the differences reflect cultural differences in the prevalence of highly traditional gender roles. This interpretation, as well as the ethnic differences data, is consistent with others (e.g., Landrine, 1995). For example, these findings are consistent with data indicating that many Latino (Falicov, 1982) and Asian American (Root, 1995) families emphasize highly traditional gender roles, in which women are expected to be subservient and are treated as inferior. The reason that Asian American

---

3. These differences in how women are treated based on their marital status are unlikely to be an artifact of sexual orientation because only 30% of adult, never-married women report being lesbians (Gigy, 1980).

women reported more frequent Sexist Degradation than all other ethnic groups cannot be ascertained at present.[4]

We can now turn to Chapter 3, in which we present data on the physical and mental health correlates and consequences of sexist discrimination for this sample.

---

4.   Although the ethnic differences shown here are differences among Latinas, Asians, and Whites, some differences for African Americans also emerged. For example, on Recent Events Factor 2 (Sexism in Distant Relationships), post-hocs revealed that African American women scored higher than White women. However, because the overall F was not significant, we did not report that finding. The complex ethnic differences in these data go beyond those reported here and require further study.

THREE

Physical and Psychiatric Correlates of Sexist Discrimination

As mentioned in Chapter 1, numerous studies have found that women are more likely than men to exhibit a variety of psychiatric symptoms—depression and anxiety foremost among those (Landrine, 1992; McGrath, Strickland, Keita, & Russo, 1990; Rickel, Gerrad, & Iscoe, 1984). Depression is the most common diagnosis received by women who seek mental health services, whether they are White, Black, or Latino (Russo, Amaro, & Winter, 1987; Russo & Sobel, 1981). For example, findings from the Epidemiological Catchment Area (ECA) Program of the National Institute of Mental Health, based on community surveys, revealed higher rates of depressive disorders, anxiety disorders, and somatization disorders (i.e., stress-related symptoms) for women than for men (Myers et al., 1984; Robins et al., 1984; see Russo & Green, 1993, for a more complete discussion of these and other gender differences in psychiatric disorders).

AUTHORS' NOTE: A brief version of Chapter 3 was published as H. Landrine, E. A. Klonoff, J. Gibbs, V. Manning, and M. Lund, "Physical and Psychiatric Correlates of Gender Discrimination: An Application of the Schedule of Sexist Events," *Psychology of Women Quarterly, 19,* 473-492, published by Cambridge University Press, 1995. This material is reprinted with the permission of Cambridge University Press.

Explaining These Patterns

Attempts to explain women's higher rate of depressive, somatization, and anxiety disorders have focused on biological, psychological, social, and cultural variables (Nolen-Hoeksema, 1990; Russo & Green, 1993), suggesting that no one theory fully accounts for women's higher risk (McGrath et al., 1990; Weissman & Merikangas, 1986). Evidence does suggest, however, that women's higher exposure (than men) to generic stressful life events is a significant contributing factor (Aneshensel, Frerichs, & Clark, 1981; Belle, 1990; Cleary & Mechanic, 1983; Kessler & McLeod, 1984; McGrath et al., 1990; Newmann, 1986, 1987; Russo & Green, 1993). As noted in Chapter 1, stressful events have been demonstrated to play a significant role in depression and anxiety among women and men alike (Lazarus, 1966; Lazarus & Launier, 1978; Thoits, 1984). In addition, stress also contributes to acute physical symptoms and to physical illnesses (these more common among women than men (see Klonoff & Landrine, 1992; Marcus & Siegel, 1982; Verbrugge, 1980, 1985, 1986, 1989) by

▓ decreasing health-sustaining behaviors (e.g., number of meals eaten, number of hours of sleep)

▓ increasing health-damaging behaviors such as smoking and alcohol consumption (e.g., Woods et al., 1993)

▓ compromising immune functions, as discussed in Chapter 1

Thus the fact that women experience higher levels of generic stressful life events than men do explains in part why women have higher rates of depressive, anxiety, and somatization disorders than men (Kessler, Price, & Wortman, 1985) and of acute physical illnesses as well.

Although generic (can happen to anyone) stressors and hassles undoubtedly play a role in women's higher rate of depressive, anxiety, and somatic symptoms, women's higher rate of generic stressful life events is not sufficient to explain their extraordinary rates of these symptoms and disorders, and so additional variables are required. Foremost among these additional variables are the stressors that women experience but that men do not (i.e., gender-specific stressors, see Russo, 1995). Although these gender-specific stressors are not assessed by generic stress scales, they nonetheless not only contribute to women's anxiety and depressive symptoms but indeed may account for women's higher rate of such symptoms (Russo, 1995).

Two general types of gender-specific stressful life events have been investigated and clearly demonstrated to erode women's physical and mental health. The first are **role-related stressors,** including multiple role strain, role overload, and role conflict (Aneshensel, 1986; Baruch & Barnett, 1986; Pugliesi, 1988; Reifman, Biernat, & Lang, 1991; Repetti, Matthews, & Waldron, 1989; Verbrugge, 1986; Waldron & Jacobs, 1989). These terms refer to the stress inherent in being a parent, worker employed outside of the home, and spouse/partner simultaneously. Such multiple roles can be overwhelming, requiring more time than anyone has, and the behavioral demands in one of these roles can and often do contradict those in another; problems with multiple roles occur for women rather than for men. The second type of gender-specific stressors are **brutal and physical gender-specific stressors** (Russo, 1995), including battering, rape, sexual harassment, and other forms of violence against women (Goodman et al., 1993; Koss et al., 1991).

Studies suggest that including these two types of gender-specific stressors along with the more generic ones increases our ability to predict and explain stress-related symptoms (anxiety, depression, somatization) among women, as well as women's higher rate of these symptoms. Such work has been fruitful and strongly suggests that a general stress-coping model is a beneficial approach to understanding women's rate of specific disorders *if and only if* the gender-specific stressors, contexts, and realities of women's lives are included and addressed (Russo, 1995). Attempts to understand stress-related symptoms among women that ignore the reality of ongoing sexism are as limited and inadequate as an effort to understand stress-related symptoms among Blacks while ignoring the meaning of race and the prevalence of racism.

In this chapter, we focus not on the role-related or the brutal/physical forms of sexism but instead on the pernicious, subtle sexist events measured by our scale, because their role in women's symptoms has never been examined. Hence, in this chapter, we set out to discover the extent to which sexist events, relative to generic life events and hassles, predicted the symptoms of the women in Sample 1. Previous studies already have shown that scores on scales measuring stressful life events predict symptoms among women well, even when controlling for social support (Wohlgemuth & Betz, 1991), and other studies have shown that daily hassles predict women's symptoms even better than do major life events (Monroe, 1982). The question to be answered here is: Do sexist events predict women's symptoms even better than generic events?

SYMPTOMS OF FOCUS

Depression, Anxiety, Somatization

Clearly, symptoms related to depression and anxiety are the most relevant to investigate, not only because their relationship to stress is well-known, but also because these are the psychiatric symptoms that women exhibit significantly more frequently than men, as noted above. Thus these symptoms were measured with several different scales: Scores on the Spielberger State-Trait Anxiety Inventory (STAI; Spielberger et al., 1970) and on the Beck Depression Inventory (BDI; Beck et al., 1961) were examined as measures of anxiety and of depression, respectively.

In addition, scores on the Hopkins Symptom Checklist (HSCL-58; Derogatis et al., 1974) were examined. This well-known scale yields six important symptom-related scores. In addition to a total symptom score (HSCL Total), scores on the five subscales (Anxiety, Depression, Obsessive-Compulsive, Interpersonal Sensitivity, and Somatization) can be computed to examine different types of symptoms. The HSCL Anxiety subscale is somewhat similar to the STAI. The HSCL Depression subscale is somewhat similar to the BDI but focuses more on lack of motivation, withdrawal, and hopelessness than on sadness. These can be compared with scores on the STAI and BDI to yield a clear picture of the relationship between stress, depression, and anxiety among these women. In addition, the Obsessive-Compulsive subscale of the HSCL is relevant, capturing symptoms of unremitting, irresistible but ego-alien (unwanted, unfamiliar) thoughts, feelings, and actions. The HSCL Interpersonal Sensitivity subscale is quite important to examine because it assesses feelings of personal inadequacy and inferiority, low self-esteem, and self-deprecation. Finally, the HSCL Somatization subscale is highly relevant to this investigation because it assesses the stress-related physical symptoms (e.g., headaches, gastrointestinal and cardiovascular symptoms, pain) that women (as detailed above) report more frequently than men.

Premenstrual Symptoms

In addition to the above symptoms, we were interested in premenstrual symptoms because some form of so-called premenstrual syndrome (PMS) is reported by 70% to 90% of women and thus accounts for many of women's complaints of depression and anxiety as well as for frequent physician visits (Reid & Yen, 1981). PMS is a highly controversial (e.g., Ruble, 1977), ostensible syndrome characterized by reports of psychiatric (depression, anxiety, confusion) and physical (bodily pain, headaches, temperature changes) symptoms 4 to 7 days prior to menses. Not only do at least 70% of women report these symptoms, but 30% of those report that the symptoms are incapacitating (Reid & Yen, 1981). Although evidence for a biological etiology of these symptoms is sketchy at best (Reid & Yen, 1981), evidence for a social-psychological (stress-related) etiology is strong. An enormous number of cross-sectional (comparing current groups) and longitudinal (analyses of one group of people over time) studies have demonstrated that stress is a good predictor of reporting these symptoms, with stress in relationships among the best of predictors (e.g., Beck, Gevirtz, & Mortola, 1990; Coughlin, 1990; Futternman, Jones, Miccio-Fonseca, & Quigley, 1992; Heilbrun & Frank, 1989; Gannon, Luchetta, Pardie, & Rhodes, 1989; Woods, 1984; Woods, Dery, & Most, 1982; Woods, Most, & Longnecker, 1985). We assessed these symptoms with the Premenstrual Tension Syndrome Scale (PMTS; Condon, 1993).

METHOD

The 631 women of Sample 1 completed several scales in addition to the SSE. Specifically,

- 551 of the women also received the PERI-Life Events Scale (PERI-LES; Dohrenwend et al., 1978) and the Hassles Frequency Scale (Hassles-Freq; Kanner et al., 1981), which measure major and minor generic stressors
- 99 of these 551 women received the BDI
- A separate 89 received the STAI
- Another 99 received the PMTS
- Another 125 received the HSCL-58

Thus, most of the sample received three scales measuring major, minor, and sexist stressful events. Then, small groups also received one of several different symptom measures. This procedure assured that each woman's questionnaire was about the same length and was not so long as to be intolerable, yet it assured that many different symptom measures could be used. Which woman received which symptom questionnaire was random. The questions to be answered are:

- Do sexist events predict women's symptoms?
- If so, how well?
- Do they predict women's symptoms better than generic major and minor stressful events do?

To answer these questions, we ran 10 stepwise, multiple regression analyses (see Appendix for an explanation), one for each of the 10 symptom measures. In all 10 regressions, we used four predictors: scores on SSE-Lifetime, scores on SSE-Recent, scores on the PERI-LES, and scores on the Hassles-Freq.[1] Thus two measures of sexist stress and two of generic stress were used to predict women's symptoms on 10 symptom measures, and the question was: What will be selected by the computer program as the best predictor of those symptoms? The results are shown in Table 3.1.

RESULTS

Sexist Stress Versus Generic Stress and Women's Symptoms

As shown in Table 3.1,

- The single best predictor of women's total psychiatric and physical symptoms, as measured by the (HSCL) Total Score, was SSE-Lifetime. SSE-Lifetime was the best and the only predictor selected, accounting for 16.65% of the variance in women's symptoms.
- Likewise, the single best predictor of women's somatic (physical) symptoms, as measured by the HSCL Somatization Scale, was SSE-Lifetime;

1. Using both SSE-Lifetime and SSE-Recent scores in the same regression could raise concern, because these scores might be regarded as linearly dependent (i.e., SSE-Lifetime scores could be argued, theoretically, to encompass SSE-Recent scores). We note that while lifetime *experiences* with discrimination necessarily include and encompass recent experiences, this linear relationship is not the case for lifetime and recent *scores* on the scale. Rather, SSE-Lifetime and SSE-Recent scores correlated a maximum of $r = .75$, with 56% overlap—far from a perfect relationship (see Chapter 1). Nonetheless, to address this potential concern, we also have analyzed these data by running two sets of regressions, one using SSE-Recent scores and generic stressors and another using SSE-Lifetime scores and generic stressors (see Landrine et al., 1995), so that the two types of SSE scores were not in the same regression. We found the same results reported here, namely, SSE-scales were better predictors than generic stress scales for 7 of the 10 symptom measures—and for the same 7 of 10 reported in this chapter.

In that alternative analyses (presented in Landrine et al., 1995), we also used hierarchical regressions to examine the extent to which SSE scores contributed to the variance in women's symptoms above and beyond that accounted for by generic stressors, which were entered in the first step. Results were similar to and consistent with those reported here. The current analysis, in conjunction with those reported elsewhere, is acceptable.

TABLE 3.1 Stepwise Regressions Predicting Women's Symptoms from SSE-Lifetime, SSE-Recent, PERI-LES, and Hassles-Freq scores

Symptom Measure	Predictor Selected	R	R^2	Sum of Squares	F (df)		p
Hopkins Total Symptoms Score	Step 1: SSE-Lifetime	.408	.1665	4,984.05	17.78	(1,89)	.0001
Hopkins Somatization subscale	Step 1: SSE-Lifetime	.327	.1069	276.27	12.69	(1, 106)	.0006
Hopkins Obsessive-Compulsive subscale	Step 1: SSE-Recent	.319	.1024	187.19	11.86	(1,104)	.0008
Hopkins Interpersonal Sensitivity subscale	Step 1: SSE-Recent	.349	.1219	212.19	14.71	(1,106)	.0002
	Step 2: PERI-LES	.405	.1639	285.58	10.29	(2,105)	.0001
Hopkins Depression subscale	Step 1: SSE-Recent	.356	.1265	422.97	13.91	(1,96)	.0003
Hopkins Anxiety subscale	Step 1: SSE-Lifetime	.363	.1314	100.27	15.89	(1,105)	.0001
Beck Depression Inventory	Step 1: Hassles-Freq	.345	.1193	321.92	10.56	(1,78)	.0017
	Step 2: PERI-LES	.407	.1659	447.77	7.66	(2,77)	.0009
Spielberger Trait Anxiety Scale	Step 1: Hassles-Freq	.364	.1322	1,623.99	12.95	(1,85)	.0005
Spielberger State Anxiety Scale	Step 1: PERI-LES	.275	.0755	1,015.81	6.78	(1,83)	.0109
PMTS Menstrual Symptoms Scale	Step 1: SSE-Lifetime	.374	.1402	672.82	13.38	(1,82)	.0004
	Step 2: Hassles-Freq	.426	.1817	871.61	8.99	(2,81)	.003

NOTE: PERI-LES = PERI-Life Events Scale (Dohrenwend et al., 1978) and Hassles-Freq = the Hassles Frequency Scale (Kanner et al., 1981).

it was not only the best but also the only predictor selected, accounting for 10.69% of the variance.

▓ The single best predictor of women's obsessive-compulsive symptoms, measured by that subscale of the HSCL, was SSE-Recent, which was the only predictor selected, accounting for 10.24% of the variance.

▓ The best predictor of women's interpersonal sensitivity symptoms (e.g., feelings of inferiority and inadequacy, low self-esteem), as measured by that subscale of the HSCL, was SSE-Recent, which alone accounted for 12.19% of the variance. Scores on the PERI-LES were selected as the second best predictor of these symptoms, accounting for an additional 4.2% of the variance. Thus, together, SSE-Recent and PERI-LES scores accounted for 16.39% of the variance.

▓ The single best predictor of women's symptoms of depression, measured by that subscale of the HSCL, was SSE-Recent. SSE-Recent was the only predictor selected, accounting for 12.65% of the variance.

▓ The single best predictor of women's symptoms of anxiety, measured by that subscale of the HSCL, was SSE-Lifetime, which was the only predictor selected, accounting for 13.14% of the variance.

▓ The single best predictor of women's symptoms of depression, when measured by the BDI, was Hassles-Freq, which alone accounted for 11.93% of variance. Scores on the PERI-LES were selected as the second best predictor of Beck scores, accounting for an additional 4.66% of the variance. Thus, the two generic stress measures together accounted for 16.59% of the variance, and neither SSE-Recent nor SSE-Lifetime was selected as a predictor.

▓ Likewise, when anxiety was measured by the Spielberger scales, SSE-Lifetime and SSE-Recent were not predictors of women's symptoms of anxiety. Instead, the best and only predictor of trait (stable) anxiety symptoms among women was the Hassles-Freq, which accounted for 13.22% of the variance. The best and only predictor of state (temporary) anxiety symptoms was the PERI-LES, which was the only predictor selected, accounting for 7.55% of the variance.

▓ Finally, the best predictor of women's (physical and psychiatric) menstrual symptoms (PMTS scale) was SSE-Lifetime, which accounted for 14.02% of the variance. The Hassles-Freq was selected as the second best predictor, accounting for an additional 4.15% of the variance, such that, together, SSE-Lifetime and Hassles-Freq scores accounted for 18.17% of the variance.

DISCUSSION

Experiences with sexist discrimination (SSE-Lifetime and/or SSE-Recent scores) were the single best predictor of women's total physical and psychiatric symptoms, somatic symptoms, obsessive-compulsive symptoms, interpersonal sensitivity symptoms, and menstrual symptoms, and they were the best predictor of women's depressive symptoms and anxiety symptoms as well, depending on how the latter two symptoms were measured. Scores on the SSE scales were better predictors of women's symptoms than were scores on generic stress scales for the majority (7 of the 10) of the types and measures of symptoms. Sexist stress thus appears to be a more powerful variable contributing to women's symptoms than generic stress. These findings are important because previous studies found that daily hassles and major life events were good predictors of physical and psychiatric symptoms among women, particularly daily hassles. Our data indicate that experiences with sexist discrimination also play a powerful role, a role by and large more powerful than that of generic stress. This suggests the need for new models of women's symptoms that highlight the role of generic, sexist, and other types of gender-specific stressors (role-related and brutal/physical) and explore causal links among the various stressors and symptoms. We present such a model later in this book.

One concern about these findings is that in 3 of the 10 measures, SSE scores were not the best predictor of symptoms, and yet, they were the best predictor of those symptoms when a different measure of the symptoms was used. Scores on the SSE were not predictors of symptoms of anxiety when measured by the two STAI scales, but they were the best predictors when anxiety was measured by the HSCL Anxiety scale. Likewise, scores on the SSE were not predictors of symptoms of depression when measured by the BDI, but they were the best predictors of depression when measured by the HSCL Depression scale. We believe that this inconsistency is largely an artifact of the size of samples. The number of women who completed the HSCL Depression and Anxiety scales was far larger than the number who completed the STAI anxiety and BDI scales; this difference may account for the failure of SSE scores to be predictors of the latter measures. This interpretation is supported by the data presented in Chapter 5. In the study reported in that chapter, a new sample of women completed the HSCL Depression scale, and the Center for Epidemiological Studies Depression scale (CES-D; Radloff, 1977) and BDI Depression scales, with greater numbers of women completing the latter. SSE scores contributed significantly to all three measures of depression, once larger samples were involved, *and their contribution was the same* irrespective of the measure of depression used. Hence, we conclude that experiences with sexist discrimination contribute to women's symptoms of anxiety and depression, in addition to contributing to the various other symptoms measured here.

The relationship between sexist discrimination and women's symptoms was a moderately strong one: Sexist stress alone accounted for 10.24% to 16.65% of the variance in women's symptoms when examining all women in the sample as a whole. Theoretically, however, the relationship between sexist discrimination and women's symptoms may be stronger for some groups of women than for others, and hence, the 10% to 17% of the variance accounted for here may underestimate the contribution of sexism to women's symptoms. For example, the relationship between sexist discrimination and symptoms may be stronger for minority women than for White women simply because minority women report a higher frequency of sexist events. Likewise, the relationship could be stronger for younger women than for their older counterparts, because older women may have greater legal, financial, and social resources for coping with discrimination. Similarly, the relationship between sexist discrimination and symptoms might be stronger for nonfeminist women than for feminist women; feminism may mediate the negative impact of sexism by providing women with an explanation and external attribution, thereby decreasing internal (self-blame) attributions. Hence, the strength of the discrimination-symptom relationship found here may be the minimum rather than the maximum relationship. We address these issues in later chapters.

In summary, sexist discrimination is a powerful predictor of psychiatric and physical symptoms among women and is, by and large, a better predictor of those symptoms than is generic stress. Although the precise relationship between sexist discrimination and symptoms may vary with women's social status and endorsement of feminism (both possibilities are analyzed later), these data nonetheless support this preliminary conclusion: **Common, garden-variety sexist discrimination plays an important role in women's symptoms and a greater role than generic stressful life events.** Given that generic stressful life events have been demonstrated to *cause* the symptoms in question, it is highly likely that sexist events similarly cause those same symptoms—and that this is how and why they were found here to be related to those symptoms.

We turn now to a replication of these studies with a new sample.

Replication and Extension of the Schedule of Sexist Events

In this chapter, we present a replication of the study reported in Chapter 1. The purposes of the replication were (1) to assess the extent to which a new sample of 652 women reported similar frequencies of the various sexist events; (2) to examine the degree to which similar reliability data were obtained; and (3) to examine the extent to which similar relationships between scores on the SSE and status variables were obtained. We then combine the scores of Sample 1 (the standardization sample, $N = 631$) with those of the current sample, to provide norms on the scale based on 1,268 women. Next, we present an extension of the scale in which we added an appraisal dimension to it for this new sample; this yielded an alternative version of the scale, the Schedule of Sexist Events-Revised.

STUDY 2

Participants

A new sample of 652 women completed an anonymous questionnaire. The sample consisted of 439 college students and 213 women from the community. They represented 405 White and 247 minority women (42

Blacks, 136 Latinas, 45 Asian/Pacific Islanders, and 24 members of other ethnic minority groups). The majority (380 or 58.6%) were single (unmarried), 30.4% (197) were married, and the remainder were separated, widowed, or divorced. Their ages ranged from 17 to 73 years (mean = 27.93, σ = 10.75 years). Their incomes ranged from zero (for some college students) to $100,000 per year (mean = $18,075, σ = $17,126, median = $18,000).

Procedure

The procedure used for this study was identical to that used in the first study: Women were approached in classrooms on a large college campus and asked to complete an anonymous survey; 439 college students completed it. In addition, women were approached in six small office buildings and asked to complete the questionnaire. Five visits also were made to the local airport, where women waiting for flights were asked to complete the survey. This resulted in participation by 213 adult women from the community.

Materials

The major instrument in the questionnaire was the Schedule of Sexist Events-Revised (SSE-R), shown in Figure 4.1. The SSE-R consists of the SSE with an appraisal dimension added. The various items in the SSE are completed three times for the SSE-R, once for the frequency (on a 6-point scale) of the sexist event in the past year (Recent Sexist Events scale), once for the frequency (on a 6-point scale) of the sexist event in a woman's entire lifetime (Lifetime Sexist Events scale), and then once to appraise the stressfulness of that event ("How stressful was this for you?," answered on a 6-point scale). This appraisal dimension is the only difference between the SSE and the SSE-R. All 652 women received the SSE-R and a page requesting demographic information.

RESULTS: REPLICATION OF THE SSE

Frequency of Lifetime Sexist Events for the New Sample

Only 3 of the 652 women (0.46%) reported never experiencing any type of sexist discrimination in their entire lifetime; 99.95% of the sample

---

Please think carefully about your life as you answer the questions below. For each item, read the question and then answer it three times: Answer once for what your ENTIRE LIFE (from when you were a child to now) has been like, then once for what the PAST YEAR has been like; finally, rate how stressful having this happen to you was on a scale from 1 = Not at all stressful to 6 = Extremely stressful. Circle the number that best describes events in YOUR ENTIRE LIFE, and in the PAST YEAR, using these rules:

Circle **1** = If the event has **NEVER** happened
Circle **2** = If the event happened **ONCE IN A WHILE (less than 10% of the time)**
Circle **3** = If the event happened **SOMETIMES (10-25 % of the time)**
Circle **4** = If the event happened **A LOT (26 - 49% of the time)**
Circle **5** = If the event happened **MOST OF THE TIME (50-70% of the time)**
Circle **6** = If the event happened **ALMOST ALL OF THE TIME (more than 70% of the time)**

1. How many times have you been treated unfairly by **teachers or professors** because you are a woman?

How many times IN YOUR ENTIRE LIFE?	1	2	3	4	5	6
How many times IN THE PAST YEAR?	1	2	3	4	5	6
	Not at all Stressful				Extremely Stressful	
How stressful was this for you?	1	2	3	4	5	6

NOTE: For the SSE-R, the appraisal dimension shown above is repeated for all items except the last item (Item 20).

Figure 4.1. Sample Item From the SSE-R

reported experiencing some type of sexist discrimination at some point in their lives. As shown in Table 4.1 (far right-hand column), common sexist events (experienced at least once by large percentages of women) were

- Hearing sexist jokes (93.6 % of the sample, or 610 women)
- Being called sexist names (86.4% or 563 women)
- Wanting to tell people off for being sexist (87.4%)
- Being sexually harassed (89.8%)
- Being discriminated against by people in service jobs (waiters, mechanics, store clerks, bank tellers, etc., 78.8%).

A frighteningly large percentage of the women (62.5% or about 407 women) reported being picked on, hit, shoved, or threatened with harm at least once in their lives (Item 18) because they were women. Some sexist events (e.g., hearing a sexist joke, 93.6% of the sample) obviously were more common experiences for the women than others (e.g., being discriminated against by neighbors, 38%) and probably were *significantly* more common. We did not test for significant differences in the frequency of specific Lifetime Sexist Events because our purpose here is replication (assessment of the similarity of findings with two samples); we extend our permission to others to conduct such analyses of the data shown in Table 4.1.

Frequency of Recent Sexist Events for the New Sample

Likewise, only 11 of the 652 women (1.7%) reported never experiencing any type of sexist discrimination in the previous year; 98.3% reported some type of sexist event in the previous year, with some events being common for the sample. As shown in Table 4.2 (column 7), common sexist events (experienced at least once by large percentages of women in the past year) were

- Hearing sexist jokes (86.1% of the sample or 561 women experienced this at least once *in the past year*)
- Being called sexist names (65.6% or about 427 women were called "bitch," "cunt," etc. in the past year)
- Wanting to tell people off for being sexist in the past year (78.2% or about 509 women)
- Being treated with a lack of respect because one is a woman (70.1% or about 457 women)

As shown in Table 4.2 (Item 18), 35.4% of the women (about 230 women) reported being picked on, hit, shoved, or threatened with harm in the previous year because they were women.

Again, it is clear that some sexist events (e.g., hearing a sexist joke, 86.1% of the sample) obviously were more common experiences for the women than others (e.g., filing a lawsuit or labor grievance or quitting one's job because of sexism at work, 14.6%), and probably were *significantly* more common. We did not test for significant differences in the frequency of specific Recent Sexist Events for reasons described above regarding Lifetime Events, and we invite others to do so. As in Chapter 1, we note that highly probable events (such as hearing a sexist joke) were reported

TABLE 4.1 Percentage of Sample 2 Reporting Specific Sexist Events in Their Lifetimes

Questionnaire Item	Lifetime Frequency of the Event: Percentage of Time It Happened to Her						Ever Happened (100% minus column 1)
	1 Never Happened	2 Up to 10% of the Time	3 10-25% of the Time	4 26-49% of the Time	5 50-70% of the Time	6 >70% of the Time	
1. Sexism by teachers	39.9	36.3	17.0	4.2	1.6	1.1	60.1
2. Sexism by employer	36.1	27.1	20.7	8.8	4.3	2.9	63.9
3. Sexism by colleagues	33.0	31.7	18.7	10.8	4.5	1.2	67.0
4. Sexism by people in service jobs	21.2	29.1	24.0	14.9	7.6	3.1	78.8
5. Sexism by strangers	23.2	39.2	21.8	9.3	5.0	1.5	76.8
6. Sexism by people in helping jobs	40.3	33.8	14.5	6.5	3.4	1.5	59.7
7. Sexism by neighbors	62.0	23.4	7.8	4.4	1.4	1.1	38.0
8. Sexism by boyfriend, mate	21.7	26.2	21.4	13.7	9.8	7.1	78.3
9. Sexism at work	57.9	21.5	10.4	5.8	3.0	1.4	42.11
10. Sexism by family	43.4	21.5	13.4	9.7	6.8	5.1	56.6
11. Sexually harrassed	10.2	26.0	20.6	21.6	13.4	8.2	89.8
12. Got no respect	15.3	28.9	23.6	16.8	10.2	5.2	84.7
13. Wanted to tell someone off	12.6	23.6	22.0	18.1	11.0	12.7	87.4
14. Angry about sexism	22.5	30.2	21.3	11.1	7.3	7.6	77.5
15. Took drastic steps	72.7	16.7	4.2	2.0	2.6	1.7	27.3
16. Called sexist names	13.6	28.6	19.9	17.5	10.7	9.7	86.4
17. Argued over sexism	25.7	31.1	21.0	12.1	6.3	3.9	74.3
18. Was picked on, harmed	37.5	28.7	15.3	11.1	4.5	2.9	62.5
19. Heard sexist jokes	6.4	16.7	20.3	23.4	17.5	15.7	93.6
	The Same as Now	A Little Different	Different in a Few Ways	A Lot Different	Different in Most Ways	Totally Different	Would Be Different (100% – column 1)
20. How different life would be	23.5	26.6	24.0	15.8	4.5	5.7	76.50

80

TABLE 4.2 Percentage of Sample 2 Reporting Sexist Events in the Past Year

Questionnaire Item	Recent Frequency of the Event: Percentage of Time It Happened to Her						
	1 Never Happened	*2 Up to 10% of the Time*	*3 10-25% of the Time*	*4 26-49% of the Time*	*5 50-70% of the Time*	*6 >70% of the Time*	*Ever Happened (100% minus column 1)*
1. Sexism by teachers	71.2	20.5	5.8	1.4	1.0	0.2	28.8
2. Sexism by employer	63.1	18.0	9.0	4.6	3.6	1.7	36.9
3. Sexism by colleagues	55.9	22.9	13.2	4.1	2.2	1.7	44.1
4. Sexism by people in service jobs	34.4	34.1	17.7	9.7	3.0	1.1	65.6
5. Sexism by strangers	39.1	38.3	13.3	4.9	3.4	0.9	60.9
6. Sexism by people in helping jobs	60.9	23.8	10.1	2.8	2.0	0.3	39.1
7. Sexism by neighbors	79.0	14.0	4.4	1.3	0.8	0.5	21.0
8. Sexism by boyfriend, mate	38.7	26.4	13.4	10.2	5.5	5.8	61.3
9. Sexism at work	77.5	13.4	5.0	1.9	0.8	1.4	22.5
10. Sexism by family	57.7	20.5	8.5	4.9	5.3	3.1	42.3
11. Sexually harassed	33.3	26.3	14.5	11.7	6.7	7.5	66.7
12. Got no respect	29.9	33.4	17.6	9.0	5.4	4.7	70.1
13. Wanted to tell someone off	21.8	30.7	17.0	11.2	8.3	11.1	78.2
14. Angry about sexism	40.4	28.2	12.2	8.0	5.3	5.9	59.6
15. Took drastic steps	85.4	8.7	2.7	1.6	0.6	1.1	14.6
16. Called sexist names	34.4	28.6	14.2	9.8	6.3	6.7	65.6
17. Argued over sexism	44.3	28.1	13.9	6.1	4.2	3.4	55.7
18. Was picked on, harmed	64.6	19.7	6.9	4.2	2.8	1.7	35.4
19. Heard sexist jokes	13.9	26.2	20.1	16.5	12.6	10.6	86.1
	The Same as Now	*A Little Different*	*Different in a Few Ways*	*A Lot Different*	*Different in Most Ways*	*Totally Different*	*Would be different (100% – column 1)*
20. How different life would be	39.7	21.1	21.9	9.9	3.9	3.6	60.30

by many women, whereas highly unlikely events (such as filing a lawsuit or grievance or quitting one's job) were reported by few women, with large percentages of women (e.g., 62%) reporting that certain sexist events (e.g., being treated unfairly by neighbors) never happened to them in their entire lifetimes (Table 4.1). **This pattern suggests efforts to accurately report events and is similar to patterns found in Sample 1,** as will be seen momentarily.

Comparing the Frequency of Sexist Events for Two Samples

In Figure 4.2, total percentages of each sample who reported that sexist events had ever occurred (irrespective of frequency) are presented graphically to highlight the similarities and differences between the samples. As shown in Figure 4.2, it appears that compared to Sample 1 (demarcated by circular points), larger percentages of Sample 2 (demarcated by square points) reported the occurrence (ever) of each sexist event in their lifetimes, as well as in the past year. Simultaneously, it is clear that the patterns across the samples are remarkably similar, with (for example) hearing sexist jokes the most common experience to ever occur for both samples, and with filing lawsuits/grievances being an uncommon experience for both samples. The data in Figure 4.2 are categorical data on the occurrence (*ever* versus *never* happened) of the various sexist events; these are the values shown in the far right-hand column of Tables 4.3 and 4.4. The similarities across samples (shown in Figure 4.2) strongly suggest efforts to accurately report one's experiences.

In Table 4.3, the frequency of the various Lifetime Sexist Events for Sample 1 and Sample 2 are displayed, with obvious similarities in the patterns across the samples. In Table 4.4, reports of the frequency of the various Recent Sexist Events for Sample 1 and Sample 2 likewise are displayed, with clear similarities in patterns again. The similarities across the samples (shown in Tables 4.3 and 4.4) likewise suggest that self-reports on the SSE are accurate reports of women's experiences: **It is extremely unlikely that fabricated, exaggerated, or random reports of sexism from two independent samples would yield such similar results in the reported specific frequencies** (on 6-point scales) **of specific sexist acts.** Because these data represent ratings of the frequencies of the sexist events on a continuous (1 to 6) scale, means and standard deviations can be derived and statistically compared.

(text continued on p. 88)

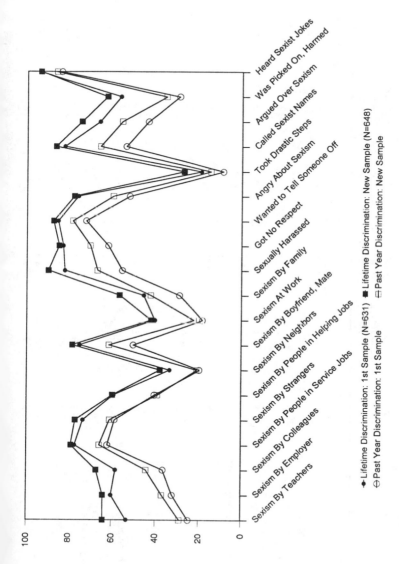

Figure 4.2. Percentage of Samples Reporting Occurrence of Sexist Discrimination

TABLE 4.3 Frequency of Lifetime Sexist Events for Sample 1 and Sample 2

Questionnaire Item	1 Never Happened	2 Up to 10% of the Time	3 10-25% of the Time	4 26-49% of the Time	5 50-70% of the Time	6 > 70% of the Time	Ever Happened (100% minus column 1)
1. Sexism by teachers							
Sample 1	46.9	35.4	12.0	4.1	1.0	0.6	53.1
Sample 2	39.9	36.3	17.0	4.2	1.6	1.1	63.9
2. Sexism by employer							
Sample 1	39.9	30.5	18.7	6.4	3.1	1.5	60.1
Sample 2	36.1	27.1	20.7	8.8	4.3	2.9	63.9
3. Sexism by colleagues							
Sample 1	41.9	34.4	16.4	5.4	1.5	0.5	58.1
Sample 2	33.0	31.7	18.7	10.8	4.5	1.2	67.0
4. Sexism by people in service jobs							
Sample 1	23.0	36.8	24.0	11.5	2.9	1.8	77.0
Sample 2	21.2	29.1	24.0	14.9	7.6	3.1	78.8
5. Sexism by strangers							
Sample 1	26.8	40.6	21.5	7.5	2.6	1.0	73.2
Sample 2	23.2	39.2	21.8	9.3	5.0	1.5	76.8
6. Sexism by people in helping jobs							
Sample 1	40.9	34.4	15.8	5.5	1.8	1.5	58.1
Sample 2	40.3	33.8	14.5	6.5	3.4	1.5	59.7
7. Sexism by neighbors							
Sample 1	66.4	23.8	7.0	1.6	0.3	0.8	33.6
Sample 2	62.0	23.4	7.8	4.4	1.4	1.1	38.0
8. Sexism by boyfriend, mate							
Sample 1	25.1	30.7	21.2	14.1	5.0	3.9	74.9
Sample 2	21.7	26.2	21.4	13.7	9.8	7.1	78.3
9. Sexism at work							
Sample 1	59.6	25.7	8.8	3.4	2.1	0.3	40.4
Sample 2	57.9	21.5	10.4	5.8	3.0	1.4	42.1

	The Same as Now	A Little Different	Different in a Few Ways	A Lot Different	Different in Most Ways	Totally Different	Would be different (100% − column 1)
Sample 1	54.5	21.9	10.9	6.0	3.6	3.1	45.5
Sample 2	43.4	21.5	13.4	9.7	6.8	5.1	56.6
11. Sexually harassed							
Sample 1	18.0	30.0	26.3	16.2	5.0	4.4	82.0
Sample 2	10.2	26.0	20.6	21.6	13.4	8.2	89.8
12. Got no respect							
Sample 1	17.3	44.1	21.2	12.1	3.4	2.0	82.7
Sample 2	15.3	28.9	23.6	16.8	10.2	5.2	84.7
13. Wanted to tell someone off							
Sample 1	14.8	35.1	22.0	15.6	6.5	6.0	85.2
Sample 2	12.6	23.6	22.0	18.1	11.0	12.7	87.4
14. Angry about sexism							
Sample 1	24.3	40.8	19.4	8.0	3.6	3.9	75.7
Sample 2	22.5	30.2	21.3	11.1	7.3	7.6	77.5
15. Took drastic action							
Sample 1	80.9	15.2	2.4	0.3	0.7	0.5	19.1
Sample 2	72.7	16.7	4.2	2.0	2.6	1.7	27.3
16. Called sexist names							
Sample 1	17.8	39.5	22.1	12.9	4.6	3.1	82.2
Sample 2	13.6	28.6	19.9	17.5	10.7	9.7	86.4
17. Argued over sexism							
Sample 1	34.1	37.4	17.6	7.0	2.6	1.3	65.9
Sample 2	25.7	31.1	21.0	12.1	6.3	3.9	74.3
18. Was picked on, harmed							
Sample 1	43.6	32.6	13.5	5.7	3.1	1.5	56.4
Sample 2	37.5	28.7	15.3	11.1	4.5	2.9	62.5
19. Heard sexist jokes							
Sample 1	5.9	22.8	27.1	25.1	10.1	9.0	94.1
Sample 2	6.4	16.7	20.3	23.4	17.5	15.7	93.6
20. How different life would be							
Sample 1	30.3	28.2	23.8	12.3	3.0	2.5	69.7
Sample 2	23.5	26.6	24.0	15.8	4.5	5.7	76.5

TABLE 4.4 Frequency of Recent Sexist Events for Sample 1 and Sample 2

Questionnaire Item	1 Never Happened	2 Up to 10% of the Time	3 10-25% of the Time	4 26-49% of the Time	5 50-70% of the Time	6 > 70% of the Time	Ever Happened (100% minus column 1)
1. Sexism by teachers							
Sample 1	75.2	18.6	3.7	1.5	0.5	0.5	24.8
Sample 2	71.2	20.5	5.8	1.4	1.0	0.2	28.8
2. Sexism by employer							
Sample 1	67.9	19.2	6.2	3.3	2.3	1.0	32.1
Sample 2	63.1	18.0	9.0	4.6	3.6	1.7	36.9
3. Sexism by colleagues							
Sample 1	63.5	23.9	8.7	2.3	1.3	0.2	36.5
Sample 2	55.9	22.9	13.2	4.1	2.2	1.7	44.1
4. Sexism by people in service jobs							
Sample 1	38.1	39.4	14.7	5.6	1.8	0.5	61.9
Sample 2	34.4	34.1	17.7	9.7	3.0	1.1	65.6
5. Sexism by strangers							
Sample 1	41.4	42.3	11.8	2.5	1.3	0.7	58.6
Sample 2	39.1	38.3	13.3	4.9	3.4	0.9	60.9
6. Sexism by people in helping jobs							
Sample 1	59.6	29.1	7.3	2.3	1.2	0.5	40.4
Sample 2	60.9	23.8	10.1	2.8	2.0	0.3	39.1
7. Sexism by neighbors							
Sample 1	80.3	14.4	3.8	1.0	0.5	0.0	19.7
Sample 2	79.0	14.0	4.4	1.3	0.8	0.5	21.0
8. Sexism by boyfriend, mate							
Sample 1	49.8	29.2	11.1	4.9	2.5	2.5	50.2
Sample 2	38.7	26.4	13.4	10.2	5.5	5.8	61.3
9. Sexism at work							
Sample 1	81.7	12.2	3.0	1.8	1.0	0.3	18.3
Sample 2	77.5	13.4	5.0	1.9	0.8	1.4	22.5

	The Same as Now	A Little Different	Different in a Few Ways	A Lot Different	Different in Most Ways	Totally Different	Would be different (100% − column 1)
Sample 1	70.9	18.0	4.2	2.9	1.5	2.5	29.1
Sample 2	57.7	20.5	8.5	4.9	5.3	3.1	42.3
11. Sexually harassed							
Sample 1	44.6	28.1	16.6	5.5	2.8	2.4	55.4
Sample 2	33.3	26.3	14.5	11.7	6.7	7.5	66.7
12. Got no respect							
Sample 1	38.2	39.5	12.8	5.6	3.0	1.0	61.8
Sample 2	29.9	33.4	17.6	9.0	5.4	4.7	70.1
13. Wanted to tell someone off							
Sample 1	27.9	36.4	16.1	10.3	4.6	4.8	72.1
Sample 2	21.8	30.7	17.0	11.2	8.3	11.1	78.2
14. Angry about sexism							
Sample 1	47.9	31.5	10.8	4.4	2.3	3.1	52.1
Sample 2	40.4	28.2	12.2	8.0	5.3	5.9	59.6
15. Took drastic action							
Sample 1	91.3	5.4	1.0	0.8	0.8	0.7	8.7
Sample 2	85.4	8.7	2.7	1.6	0.6	1.1	14.6
16. Called sexist names							
Sample 1	46.2	33.0	10.9	5.4	3.0	1.5	53.8
Sample 2	34.4	28.6	14.2	9.8	6.3	6.7	65.6
17. Argued over sexism							
Sample 1	56.3	27.7	8.1	4.6	1.8	1.5	43.7
Sample 2	44.3	28.1	13.9	6.1	4.2	3.4	55.7
18. Was picked on, harmed							
Sample 1	70.6	21.2	3.9	2.3	1.0	1.0	29.4
Sample 2	64.6	19.7	6.9	4.2	2.8	1.7	35.4
19. Heard sexist jokes							
Sample 1	16.2	36.7	19.7	14.4	6.7	6.2	83.8
Sample 2	13.9	26.2	20.1	16.5	12.6	10.6	86.1
20. How different life would be	The Same as Now	A Little Different	Different in a Few Ways	A Lot Different	Different in Most Ways	Totally Different	Would be different (100% − column 1)
Sample 1	47.9	28.2	13.6	7.2	1.6	1.5	52.1
Sample 2	39.7	21.1	21.9	9.9	3.9	3.6	60.3

TABLE 4.5 ANOVA of Mean Frequency of Various Lifetime Sexist Events for Two Samples

SSE Item	Sample 1 Mean (σ)	Sample 2 Mean (σ)	SS	F	p
1. Sexism by teachers	1.789 (.945)	1.942 (1.012)	6.759	7.035	.008
2. Sexism by employer	2.065 (1.15)	2.247 (1.287)	9.637	6.424	.011
3. Sexism by colleagues	1.905 (.975)	2.273 (1.232)	39.405	31.635	.00005
4. Sexism by people in service jobs	2.417 (1.15)	2.669 (1.31)	18.591	12.134	.001
5. Sexism by strangers	2.224 (1.069)	2.382 (1.161)	7.18	5.749	.017
6. Sexism by people in helping jobs	1.971 (1.067)	2.028 (1.166)	0.934	0.739	.390
7. Sexism by neighbors	1.472 (.808)	1.618 (.999)	6.218	7.468	.006
8. Sexism by boyfriend, mate	2.521 (1.313)	2.854 (1.508)	32.229	16.025	.00005
9. Sexism at work	1.628 (.947)	1.773 (1.168)	6.083	5.332	.021
10. Sexism by family	1.928 (1.311)	2.306 (1.515)	41.477	20.542	.00005
11. Sexually harassed	2.765 (1.309)	3.288 (1.445)	79.518	41.679	.00005
12. Got no respect	2.467 (1.124)	2.933 (1.381)	63.066	39.414	.00005
13. Wanted to tell someone off	2.819 (1.346)	3.331 (1.559)	76.179	35.707	.00005
14. Angry about sexism	2.388 (1.247)	2.740 (1.492)	36.087	18.946	.00005
15. Took drastic action	1.269 (.6754)	1.498 (1.041)	15.252	19.458	.00005
16. Called sexist names	2.557 (1.192)	3.118 (1.512)	91.77	40.027	.00005
17. Argued over sexism	2.120 (1.103)	2.546 (1.36)	52.696	34.054	.00005
18. Was picked on, harmed	1.982 (1.158)	2.24 (1.319)	19.362	12.491	.00005
19. Heard sexist jokes	3.388 (1.321)	3.768 (1.478)	42.042	21.291	.00005
20. How different life would be	2.361 (1.235)	2.684 (1.386)	30.393	17.552	.00005

Thus a MANOVA was conducted to compare these frequency ratings. Results revealed that the total (frequency ratings on all 20 items) SSE Lifetime and SSE Recent scores of Sample 2 were significantly higher than those of Sample 1, Hotelling's $T^2 = .0485$, Exact $F(2, 1262) = 32.16$, $p = .0005$. Means for Sample 2 and Sample 1 on the SSE-Lifetime were 50.19 and 43.69, respectively ($SS = 13336.62$, ANOVA $F(1, 1263) = 52.24$, $p = .0005$). On the SSE-Recent, they were 40.71 and 34.65, respectively ($SS = 111599.28$, ANOVA $F(1, 1263) = 59.86$, $p = .0005$). Follow-up ANOVAs on the Lifetime and Recent items are shown in Tables 4.5 and 4.6, respectively.

TABLE 4.6 ANOVA of Mean Frequency of Various Recent Sexist Events for Two Samples

SSE Item	Sample 1 Mean (σ)		Sample 2 Mean (σ)		SS	F	p
1. Sexism by teachers	1.338	(.706)	1.396	(.759)	.923	1.711	.191
2. Sexism by employer	1.544	(1.015)	1.732	(1.195)	9.654	7.809	.005
3. Sexism by colleagues	1.521	(.857)	1.796	(1.147)	20.775	20.048	.00005
4. Sexism by people in service jobs	1.954	(1.009)	2.184	(1.159)	14.451	12.174	.001
5. Sexism by strangers	1.795	(.888)	2.002	(1.10)	11.730	11.637	.001
6. Sexism by people in helping jobs	1.568	(.859)	1.632	(.957)	1.091	1.314	.252
7. Sexism by neighbors	1.264	(.618)	1.323	(.769)	.938	1.911	.167
8. Sexism by boyfriend, mate	1.878	(1.162)	2.375	(1.509)	67.602	36.907	.00005
9. Sexism at work	1.266	(.694)	1.379	(.895)	3.479	5.371	.021
10. Sexism by family	1.536	(1.082)	1.870	(1.323)	30.627	20.728	.00005
11. Sexually harassed	2.030	(1.24)	2.554	(1.566)	75.103	37.307	.00005
12. Got no respect	1.962	(1.058)	2.426	(1.393)	58.982	38.167	.00005
13. Wanted to tell someone off	2.401	(1.333)	2.896	(1.612)	67.124	30.454	.00005
14. Angry about sexism	1.899	(1.169)	2.284	(1.493)	40.542	22.337	.00005
15. Took drastic action	1.159	(.657)	1.268	(.7975)	3.234	6.011	.014
16. Called sexist names	1.889	(1.112)	2.470	(1.525)	92.165	51.089	.00005
17. Argued over sexism	1.711	(1.046)	2.091	(1.337)	39.544	27.185	.00005
18. Was picked on, harmed	1.409	(.822)	1.674	(1.138)	19.202	19.229	.00005
19. Heard sexist jokes	2.755	(1.382)	3.226	(1.556)	60.832	27.948	.00005
20. How different life would be	1.903	(1.131)	2.270	(1.347)	36.872	23.666	.00005

As shown, the mean frequency ratings given by Sample 2 were statistically significantly higher than those given by Sample 1 for nearly every Lifetime and Recent sexist events item. The differences between the means of the two samples on the items nonetheless were quite small. For example, for lifetime ratings of the frequency of hearing sexist jokes (Table 4.5), the means for the samples were 3.388 (Sample 1) and 3.768 (Sample 2) respectively, and this minor (0.38 point) difference was statistically significant at the $p = .00005$ level. Similarly, mean recent (past year) ratings of the frequency of wanting to tell people off about their sexist behavior were 2.401 and 2.896 for Samples 1 and 2, respectively, and this minor (0.495 point) mean difference similarly was statistically significant at the p = .00005. **No significant difference between the samples on any item exceeded 0.5 points.** Such small mean differences between the samples undoubtedly were statistically significant because of the enormous statistical power inherent in our sample sizes and are unlikely to be of any practical significance. Thus these statistically but not practically significant differences do not cast aspersions on the scale and lead us to conclude that, despite such apparent differences, the experiences of the two samples were remarkably similar, in terms of both the types of sexism that they experienced (Figure 4.2) and the specific frequency with which they experienced various types of sexist events (Tables 4.3 to 4. 6).

Furthermore, these small but significant mean differences between the samples on the SSE-Lifetime and SSE-Recent items also are likely to be an artifact of the status differences between the samples. Specifically, Sample 2 (mean age = 27.93, σ = 10.75) is significantly younger (by 4.21 years on the average) than Sample 1 (mean age = 32.14, σ = 11.74) t test for unequal variances, $t(df$ = 1231.46) = 6.62, p = .0005. Because both Sample 2 data and those from Sample 1 (Chapter 2) found that younger women score higher than their older counterparts on the SSE scales, these age differences between the samples are likely to account for the higher scores of Sample 2. Indeed, in Study 1 (Chapter 2), we found that women 22 years old and younger had the highest scores on the SSE; a significantly greater percentage of women in Sample 2 were 22 years old or younger (43.8%) compared with the percentage (28%) in Sample 1, $\chi^2(3)$ = 38.998, p = .000005. Likewise, a significantly greater percentage of the women in Sample 2 (58.6%), compared with those in Sample 1 (46.7%), were single, $\chi^2(2)$ = 23.95, p = .00001, and Study 1 (as well as the data presented later here for Sample 2) found that single women tended to score higher on the SSE than their married counterparts.

Thus the age and marital status differences between the samples probably account for the statistically (but perhaps not practically) significant higher scores of Sample 2.

Comparing the Reliability of
SSE Scales for Two Samples

Table 4.7 displays the SSE reliability data obtained from Sample 2 and compares those findings with those for Sample 1 (reported in Chap-

TABLE 4.7 Reliability of the Schedule of Sexist Events With Two Samples

	Internal Consistency Reliability (Cronbach's α)		Split-Half Reliability (r)[a]	
	Lifetime Sexist Events	Recent Sexist Events	Lifetime Sexist Events	Recent Sexist Events
Sample 1 (N = 631)	.92	.90	.87	.83
Sample 2 (N = 652)	.92	.90	.87	.84

a. All rs are significant at p < .0005.

ter 1). As shown, the reliability coefficients obtained were identical for the two samples. These data suggest that the SSE is a highly reliable scale.

Status Differences on the SSE
for the New Sample

A set of MANOVAs were conducted to assess the extent to which the ethnic, age, and marital status differences on the SSE found with Sample 1 would emerge for the current sample as well, and to examine the degree to which no education and social class differences on the SSE would be found with this sample and thereby match previous findings for Sample 1.

Income/Social Class. To assess possible income/social class differences on the SSE, participants were divided (as in Chapter 2) into three income groups representing the zero to 33rd income percentile for the sample ($7,999 or less, n = 160), the 34th to 66th percentile ($8,000-$19,999 , n = 150), and the upper third of the sample ($20,000 and higher, n = 184); 131 women did not report their incomes and were excluded from these analyses, which are based on 494 women. A MANOVA comparing these three income groups on total SSE-Lifetime and SSE-Recent scores (dependent variables) was significant, Hotelling's $T^2 = 0.06907$, $F(4, 978) = 8.444$, $p = .0005$. Follow-up ANOVAs revealed no income differences on the SSE-Lifetime score, $SS = 625.44$, $F(2, 491) = 1.10$, $p = .333$, but significant differences on the SSE-Recent score, $SS = 4825.25$, $F(2, 491) = 11.04$, $p = .0005$. Post-hoc Tukey comparisons at $\alpha = .05$ (shown in Table 4.8) revealed that the wealthiest group of women reported

TABLE 4.8 Analyses of Income Differences on SSE-Recent

Post-hoc Analyses	Group 1 0-$7,999 n = 160	Group 2 $8,000-19,999 n = 150	Group 3 $20,000 and > n = 184
Mean SSE-Recent score	44.24	42.18	36.99
SSE-Recent score σ	16.32	15.48	12.64
SSE-Recent score range	20.00-97.33	20.00-94.00	20.00-79.00
95% Confidence Interval of mean	41.69-46.78	39.68-44.68	35.16-38.83

Tukey HSD at α = .05: Group 3 < 60 Groups 1 and 2

Income × Ethnicity χ^2	White Women n = 325	Women of Color n = 176
0-$7,999	91 (56.2%)[a]	71 (43.8%)
$8,000-$19,999	97 (63.4%)	56 (36.6%)
$20,000 and >	137 (73.7%)	49 (26.3%)

$\chi^2 (2) = 11.82, p = .003$

Income × Age χ^2	22 years and <	23 to 29 years	30 to 39 years	40 to 55 years
0-$7,999	121 (75.2%)[a]	24 (14.9%)	10 (6.2%)	6 (3.7%)
$8,000-$19,999	76 (50.0%)	47 (30.9%)	22 (14.5%)	7 (4.6%)
$20,000 and >	12 (6.8%)	44 (24.9%)	64 (36.2%)	57 (32.2%)

$\chi^2 (6) = 207.83, p = .000005$

Income × Marital Status χ^2	Single	Married	All Others
0-$7,999	140 (86.4%)	14 (8.6%)	8 (4.9%)
$8,000-$19,999	108 (70.6%)	27 (17.6%)	18 (11.8%)
$20,000 and >	37 (19.9%)	111 (59.7%)	38 (20.4%)

$\chi^2 (4) = 177.11, p = .000005$

a. All percentages shown are row percents; they sum to 100% across rows only.

significantly less frequent sexist events in the previous year than did the other two income groups.

Such social class differences were not found for Sample 1 and so further analyses (shown in Table 4.8) to ascertain their meaning were conducted. These analyses suggested that the income differences may be an artifact of ethnicity, insofar as 73.7% of the wealthiest group were White women, and the White women (results presented below) scored lower on SSE-Recent than did the women of color in Sample 2. Likewise, the income differences could be an artifact of age, insofar as the majority of the women in the highest income group were older (30 to 55), and the older women in this sample scored lower than their younger counterparts on the SSE-Recent (results presented below). Similarly, the income differences could be an artifact of marital status because the highest-income group tended to be married or separated, widowed, or divorced, whereas the lowest-income group was single, and these other marital status groups scored lower on SSE-Recent than did single women. Given these three strong relationships between income and other status variables, we conclude that the sole income difference on SSE-Recent that emerged here is an artifact of these other status variables (age, ethnicity, and marital status).

Education. As in Study 1, women were divided into three education groups: those with a high school diploma ($n = 99$), those with some college education ($n = 386$), and those with undergraduate and graduate degrees ($n = 162$); the five women who did not report their education levels were excluded from these analyses. A MANOVA with follow-up ANOVAs revealed no education differences in scores on the SSE-Lifetime, $F(2, 635) = 1.38$, $p = .251$, or SSE-Recent, $F(2, 635) = 1.88$, $p = .154$, in a manner matching findings for Sample 1. As in Study 1 (Chapter 2), the lack of education differences suggests no education-based response-style effects.

Age. Significant age differences in scores on the SSE were found for Sample 1, thus the age groups analyzed in that study were the focus of this analysis. Women were divided into four age groups representing women 22 years old and younger ($n = 283$), ages 23 to 29 years ($n = 141$), ages 30 to 39 years ($n = 118$), and ages 40 to 55 years ($n = 104$); the six women who were older than age 55 were excluded from these analyses. A MANOVA with these four age groups and with SSE-Lifetime and SSE-Recent total scores as dependent variables was significant, Hotelling's $T^2 = 0.1686$, $F(6, 1262) = 17.73$, $p = .0005$. Follow-up ANOVAs revealed no differences between the age groups on SSE-Lifetime, $SS = 1424.39$, $F(3, 633) = 1.64$, $p = .18$, but significant differences on SSE-Recent, $SS = 7653.41$, $F(3, 633) = 11.64$, $p = .0005$. Post-hoc comparisons (shown in Table 4.9) revealed that younger women reported significantly more frequent sexist events in

TABLE 4.9 Age Differences on the SSE Recent Total Score

	Group 1 22 years and >	Group 2 23 to 29 years	Group 3 30 to 39 years	Group 4 40 to 55 years
Mean SSE-Recent score	44.20	40.74	35.97	36.70
SSE-Recent score σ	15.52	15.50	11.91	14.78
SSE-Recent score range	20.00-97.33	20.00-93.00	20.00-82.00	20.00-99.00
95% Confidence Interval				
of mean	42.37-46.03	38.14-43.34	33.78-38.16	33.79-39.61

Post-hoc Tukey HSD at α = .05: Group 1 > Groups 3 and 4

the past year than did the two oldest groups of women. These findings are similar to those found for Sample 1.

Ethnicity. Results found for Sample 1 revealed that women of color reported significantly more frequent sexist events than did White women. A MANOVA comparing the White ($n = 405$) and minority ($n = 247$) women in Sample 2 on the total SSE-Lifetime and SSE-Recent scores was significant, Hotelling's $T^2 = 0.0249$, $F(2, 640) = 7.983$, $p = .0005$. The follow-up ANOVAs revealed no ethnic differences on SSE Lifetime, $SS = 339.96$, $F(1, 641) = 1.17$, $p = .28$, but significant difference on SSE-Recent, $SS = 2398.20$, $F(1, 641) = 10.63$, $p = .001$, with women of color (mean SSE-Recent = 43.19) again reporting significantly more frequent sexist events than White women (mean SSE-Recent = 39.20). Further analyses of these data (by specific ethnic groups) were not conducted in order to decrease the number of consecutive significance tests. Thus women of color in Sample 2 as a whole scored higher than White women on the SSE-Recent in a manner similar to findings with Sample 1.

Marital Status. Finally, analyses of marital status effects for Sample 1 revealed that single (never married) women scored higher on the SSE-Lifetime and SSE-Recent than married women, with no analysis of divorced, separated, and widowed women conducted. Thus here we divided women into three marital status groups: single ($n = 380$), married ($n = 197$), and separated, widowed, or divorced ($n = 75$); we then conducted a MANOVA comparing their scores on the SSE-Lifetime and SSE-Recent. This MANOVA was significant, Hotelling's $T^2 = 0.135$, $F(4, 1268) = 21.44$,

TABLE 4.10 Marital Status Differences on the SSE-Recent and
SSE-Lifetime Total Scores

	Group 1	Group 2	Group 3
	Single Women n = 376	Married Women n = 194	All Others n = 69
Mean SSE-Recent score	43.44	36.33	38.41
SSE-Recent score σ	15.37	13.24	16.04
SSE-Recent score range	20.00-97.33	20.00-82.00	20.00-99.00
95% Confidence Interval of mean	41.88-44.99	34.45-38.20	34.56-42.26

Post-hoc Tukey HSD at α = .05: Group 1 > Groups 2 and 3

Mean SSE-Lifetime score	50.38	48.34	54.69
SSE-Lifetime score σ	16.15	17.38	20.08
SSE-Lifetime score range	20.00-101.00	22.00-98.00	20.00-114.00
95% Confidence Interval of mean	48.74-52.02	45.88-50.79	49.87-59.51

Post-hoc Tukey HSD at α = .05: Group 3 > Group 2

p = .0005. The follow-up ANOVAs revealed marital status differences again on both the SSE-Lifetime, SS = 2076.20, $F(2, 636)$ = 3.59, p = .028, and SSE-Recent, SS = 6892.31, $F(2, 636)$ = 15.67, p = .0005. Post-hoc comparisons (shown in Table 4.10) revealed that single women reported more frequent sexist discrimination in the past year than did all other groups of women, whereas separated/widowed/divorced women reported more frequent sexist events in their entire lives than did married women.

On the whole then, the frequency of sexist events reported, specific patterns of sexist events reported, reliability of the scale, and status differences on the scale were similar for the two independent samples of women.

Norms on the SSE for 1,279 Women

Given the above similarities, scores of Sample 1 (n = 631) and Sample 2 (n = 652) were combined to arrive at norms for the SSE-Lifetime and SSE-Recent total scores, based on all 1,279 women.

SSE Lifetime Scores. The possible range of SSE-Lifetime scores is 20 to 120, and the obtained range was 20 to 118. The mean (standard error),

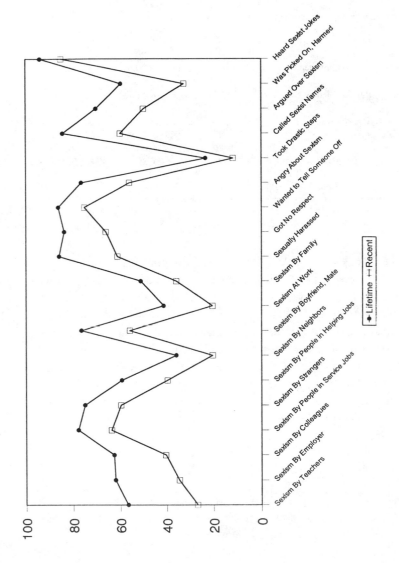

Figure 4.3. Percentage of Combined Samples (*N* = 1,279) Reporting Occurrence of Sexist Events

median, and mode were 47.22 (0.457), 44.00, and 37.00, respectively. Standard deviation, variance, kurtosis, and skewness were 16.27, 264.61, 0.674, and 0.857, respectively. Average SSE-Lifetime scores can be defined as those within ±1 σ of the mean, or scores of 30.95 to 63.49, representing 900 women or 70.98% of the sample. Low SSE-Lifetime scores can be defined as those > −1 σ below the mean, or scores of 30.00 and below, representing 175 women or 13.80% of the sample. High SSE-Lifetime scores can be defined as those > +1 σ above the mean, or scores of 64.00 and above, representing 193 women or 15.22% of the sample. On the average, then, 70% of a random sample of women can be expected to score within ±1 σ of the mean reported here, with the remaining 30% scoring around them at the low (15%) and high (15%) ends.

SSE-Recent Scores. The possible range of SSE-Recent scores is 20 to 120, and the obtained range was 20 to 103; these scores logically should (indeed, must) be lower than Lifetime scores for any subject or sample. The mean (standard error), median, and mode were 37.97 (0.399), 34.00, and 27.00, respectively. Standard deviation, variance, kurtosis, and skewness were 14.17, 200.83, 1.59, and 1.26, respectively. Average SSE-Recent scores can be defined as those within ±1 σ of the mean, or scores of 23.00 to 52.63, representing 976 women or 77.52% of the sample. Low SSE-Recent scores can be defined as those > −1 σ below the mean, or scores below 23.00, representing 91 women or 7.23% of the sample. High SSE-Recent scores can be defined as those > +1 σ above the mean, or scores of 53.00 and higher, representing 192 women or 15.25% of the sample. On the average, about 78% of a random sample of women can be expected to score within ±1 σ of the mean reported here, with the remaining 22% of the sample scoring around them at the low (7%) and high (15%) ends.

Although we recommend use of continuous SSE scores in research, the above cut-off points can be used to define groups in specific types of statistical analyses, to define high and low cases for legal, clinical, and other decisions, and to evaluate the representativeness of new samples.

Finally, with the two samples combined, we computed the percentage of the 1,279 women who reported *ever* experiencing sexist discrimination in their lives and in the past year, irrespective of the frequency of those experiences (categorical data from column 7 from both samples). These data are shown in Figure 4.3 and can be used as norms.

EXTENSION OF THE SSE:
ADDING AN APPRAISAL DIMENSION

As described thus far, the SSE measures the frequency with which women have experienced various types of sexist events. Thus the SSE is an **events measure** of stress: It focuses on the frequency with which people experience specific events that are known or presumed to be stressful and/or harmful, and it assumes that the presence or absence (as well as the frequency) of these events therefore should be related to symptoms. The SSE was modeled after and is similar to other events measures of stress, such as the Hassles Frequency Scale (Hassles; Kanner et al., 1981) and the PERI-Life Events Scale (PERI-LES; Dohrenwend et al., 1978). Like these scales, the SSE rests on the assumption that **certain kinds of events or experiences are necessarily and inherently stressful.** Although this events approach is the most common way to measure stress, there is an alternative strategy.

The alternative approach to measuring stress focuses on the appraisal (evaluation) of life situations or events as stressful and uses scales such as the Perceived Stress Scale (PSS-14; Cohen et al., 1983) and the Hassles Intensity Scale (Kanner et al., 1981). The logic behind **appraisal measures** of stress is that people differ in the extent to which they appraise (evaluate) and experience precisely the same event as stressful: One person may be unnerved by an event, whereas, another might dismiss that same event as inconsequential. Theoretically, the event would have a greater negative mental and physical health impact on the individual who appraised the event as stressful and have little impact on the individual who appraised the event as inconsequential. Thus appraisal dimensions are added to some generic stress scales. For example, the Hassles Scale has two dimensions: On the *Frequency* dimension, people rate the frequency of experiencing various hassles, and on the *Intensity* dimension, they rate the extent to which they appraised each hassle as stressful (intense). The Intensity dimension tends to be more strongly related to symptoms than the Frequency dimension (Kanner et al., 1981). Hence, appraisal approaches to measuring stress are useful and important (for discussion, see Cohen, 1986; Lazarus et al., 1985; Lazarus & Folkman, 1986). Studies have found that the more negative (high, extreme) the appraisal of a generic stressor, the greater its role in symptoms.

Thus we added an appraisal dimension to the SSE, as shown in Figure 4.1 (the SSE-R). Below, we report basic data on women's appraisals of sexist events. Then, in Chapter 5, we provide an analysis of the role of the appraisal versus the frequency of sexist events in psychiatric symptoms among the new sample of women.

Appraisal Dimension

As noted earlier, in addition to rating the frequency of each sexist event in the past year and in their lifetimes, women in Sample 2 also appraised 19 of the 20 sexist events (appraisal ratings were not collected on the last item, "How different would your life be now?"). The stressfulness of each sexist event was appraised on scales that ranged from 1 = *not at all stressful* to 6 = *extremely stressful.* Like SSE-Lifetime and SSE-Recent, these appraisal ratings can be treated as a separate scale (SSE-Appraisal), and the role of such appraisals in women's physical and mental health can be assessed. These appraisals are shown in Table 4.11.

As shown, the various types of sexist events were a source of stress for the women, with some events appraised as stressful by large percentages of the sample (*column 7*). Events that were appraised as a source of stress for many women (at least 70% of the sample, *column 7*) were being treated unfairly by a boyfriend, husband, lover (71.6%); being sexually harassed (83.2%); being treated with a lack of respect (77.2%); wanting to tell people off about their sexist behavior (78%); being called sexist names (75%); and hearing sexist jokes (74.5%). Likewise, these particular sexist events were rated as very stressful (ratings of 5 and 6, *columns 5 and 6*) by substantial numbers of women: Sexism on the part of boyfriends was so rated by 27% (176 women); being called sexist names was very stressful for 16.8% (109 women); experiencing pent-up anger about sexism was very stressful for 22.2% (145 women); and being treated with a lack of respect was very stressful for 21.6% (141 women). Thus, **the events found stressful by many women appeared to be those from the Sexist Degradation and Its Consequences, and Sexism in Close Relationships factors.**

The mean appraisal ratings (*column 8*) and the very stressful ratings (*columns 5 and 6*) for some events clearly were higher than for others and perhaps significantly so, **with the highest appraisal ratings appearing to be on items from the Sexist Degradation and Its Consequences, and**

TABLE 4.11 Appraisal of Sexist Events by Sample 2

	Percentage of Sample Reporting Stressfulness of Each Sexist Event						Sexism as	
Questionnaire Item	1 Not at all stressful	2	3	4	5	6 Extremely Stressful	Source of Stress (100% − column 1)	Mean Rating
1. Sexism by teachers	49.2	18.2	15.4	8.5	5.6	3.1	50.80	2.12
2. Sexism by employer	40.0	17.1	17.3	9.4	8.1	8.1	60.00	2.53
3. Sexism by colleagues	41.8	21.8	18.3	7.0	5.6	5.6	58.20	2.29
4. Sexism by people in service jobs	31.1	27.7	17.7	12.2	6.9	4.4	68.90	2.49
5. Sexism by strangers	39.0	27.4	18.6	8.6	4.4	2.0	61.00	2.18
6. Sexism by people in helping jobs	48.6	21.4	12.1	8.9	6.1	2.9	51.40	2.11
7. Sexism by neighbors	69.2	15.7	7.6	3.2	2.3	1.9	30.80	1.59
8. Sexism by boyfriend, mate	28.4	16.6	15.9	12.1	10.8	16.2	71.50	3.09
9. Sexism at work	60.2	13.4	10.6	6.0	3.2	6.6	39.80	1.99
10. Sexism by family	46.9	15.4	12.1	9.1	7.1	9.4	53.10	2.43
11. Sexually harassed	16.8	21.8	19.6	17.1	10.0	14.6	83.20	3.26
12. Got no respect	22.8	23.3	19.8	12.5	11.3	10.3	77.20	2.97
13. Wanted to tell someone off	22.0	23.6	18.0	11.6	12.5	12.3	78.00	3.06
14. Angry about sexism	26.5	21.2	17.5	12.6	10.5	11.7	73.50	2.94
15. Took drastic steps	72.0	5.2	5.0	4.9	4.2	8.7	28.00	1.90
16. Called sexist names	25.0	22.6	17.3	10.1	9.5	15.4	75.00	3.03
17. Argued over sexism	32.1	20.8	18.2	13.1	9.1	6.8	67.90	2.67
18. Was picked on, harmed	42.5	15.9	11.3	11.3	6.3	12.6	57.50	2.61
19. Heard sexist jokes	25.5	27.2	19.9	10.7	9.3	7.5	74.50	2.74

Sexism in Close Relationships factors. We did not analyze for such significant differences and extend our permission to others to conduct the many analyses of the data in Table 4.11 which are needed to illuminate the kinds of sexist events that women appraise/experience as stressful.

Finally, the split-half reliability of the 19-item SSE-Appraisal scale was $r = .886$ ($p = .0005$), and the internal consistency reliability was $.927$; these values are similar to those obtained for the SSE-Recent and SSE-Lifetime scales for both samples. The correlation between the SSE-Lifetime and SSE-Appraisal was $r = .80$ ($n = 634$, $p = .0005$) and between the SSE-Recent and SSE-Appraisal, the correlation was $r = .69$ ($p = .0005$).

DISCUSSION OF STUDY 2

Sample 2 was significantly younger than Sample 1 and also consisted of a significantly greater percentage of unmarried women. In addition, Sample 2 (mean annual income $18,075, $\sigma = \$17,126$) was significantly poorer than Sample 1 (mean annual income = $34,058, $\sigma = \$34,370$), earning (on the average) about $15,983 less per year than Sample 1 (t test for unequal variances = 8.96, $df = 651.74$, $p = .0005$). Despite these significant differences in age, marital status, and income, however, the scores of the two samples on the SSE-Lifetime and SSE-Recent were remarkably similar in terms of the specific events that were common versus uncommon experiences for the women (Figure 4.2; Tables 4.3 and 4.4). Similarly, differences on the SSE by age, ethnicity, and marital status (Tables 4.9 and 4.10) found with Sample 2 replicate those found with Sample 1 (on the whole and for the most part) and were remarkably similar to findings of Study 1. Likewise, the internal consistency and split-half reliability data obtained for the two samples were identical (Table 4.7). Thus, the findings of this replication suggest that the SSE is a reliable instrument that can be used with women who vary in age, income, education, and ethnicity; the implication is that similar patterns of results will be obtained across samples. The alternative version of the SSE presented in Figure 4.1 (SSE-R) contains a third dimension, SSE-Appraisal, which is reliable and can be used in future research. Indeed, in the next chapter, we examine the role of the frequency versus appraisal of sexist events in psychiatric symptoms among the 652 women (Sample 2) who participated in Study 2.

Finally, as with Sample 1, we again found in Sample 2 that sexist discrimination was rampant, with 99% of women reporting being discriminated against in some form or another and with 22.5% to 42.1% reporting being discriminated against at work in salaries and promotions. Because the similarities in the findings for the two samples suggest *accurate reporting,* these reports of prevalent sexist discrimination have major social, political, and psychological implications.

FIVE

Appraisal Versus Frequency of Sexist Discrimination in Women's Symptoms

In Chapter 3, we found that the best predictor of symptoms among women (on the whole) was scores on the SSE, which were better predictors than scores on the two generic stress inventories. Because sexist events were better predictors than generic stressful events in the prior study, we did not include a measure of generic stressful events in this study. Instead, in this study, we sought only to test hypotheses about which aspect of sexist events (lifetime frequency, past-year frequency, or appraisal) best predict women's symptoms. Thus, in this chapter, we test and discuss three hypotheses about the frequency versus appraisal of sexist discrimination in the symptoms of the women of Sample 2.

METHOD

All 652 women received the SSE-R and a page requesting demographic information. A random subset of 470 of the women also received the Hopkins Symptom Checklist (HSCL; Derogatis et al., 1974) as a measure of a variety of psychiatric and physical symptoms. In addition, another (separate) random subset of the sample (n = 145) received the Beck

Depression Inventory (BDI; Beck et al., 1961) and the Center for Epidemiological Studies Depression scale (CES-D; Radloff, 1977) as alternative measures of depression instead of receiving the HSCL. Likewise, a random 145 women received the Premenstrual Tension Syndrome Scale (PMTS; Condon, 1993) along with either the HSCL or with the BDI and CES-D. This procedure assured that each woman's questionnaire was about the same length and yet many different symptom measures could be used. The PMTS, it should be noted, can yield two scores: total physical and psychiatric symptoms exhibited in the 4 to 7 days before menses and total symptoms exhibited during menses. Unlike our use of this scale in Chapter 3, in this chapter, we use both of these PMTS scores.

HYPOTHESIS 1:
APPRAISAL VERSUS
FREQUENCY OF SEXIST EVENTS

We hypothesized that the frequency of sexist discrimination itself—irrespective of women's subjective appraisals of/responses to it—contributes to women's symptoms. Thus we predicted that SSE-Recent or SSE-Lifetime (frequency of discrimination), rather than SSE-Appraisal, would be selected as the best predictor of women's symptoms. This hypothesis is based on Krieger's (1990; Krieger & Sidney, 1996) studies in which she found that women and Blacks who stated that they were not bothered by the gender or race discrimination they faced at work had as many symptoms (rates of hypertension) as those who were disturbed by discrimination and indeed had more symptoms. Hence, Krieger's (1990; Krieger & Sidney, 1996) data suggest that discrimination contributes more to symptoms than does the appraisal of that discrimination.

To test this hypothesis for Sample 2 as a whole, we conducted 10 stepwise regression analyses, one for each of these symptom outcome measures: (1) HSCL Total Symptoms Score; (2) HSCL Somatization scale; (3) HSCL Obsessive-Compulsive scale; (4) HSCL Interpersonal Sensitivity scale; (5) HSCL Depression scale; (6) HSCL Anxiety scale; (7) BDI scores; (8) CES-D depression scale scores; (9) PMTS-During Menses symptom scale; and (10) PMTS-Before Menses symptom scale. The content of these scales was detailed in Chapter 3. In each regression, we used these three predictors: SSE-Lifetime, SSE-Recent, and SSE-Appraisal scores.

Results of Hypothesis 1

Table 5.1 displays the results of the stepwise regressions. As shown, the best predictor of women's symptoms in 8 of the 10 regressions was SSE-Recent, which alone accounted for 10.19% to 15.63% of the variance. SSE-Recent was the best predictor of

- total symptoms (HSCL Total scores)
- somatic symptoms (HSCL Somatization scores)
- depressive symptoms (HSCL Depression and BDI scores)
- symptoms entailing feelings of inadequacy and inferiority (HSCL Interpersonal Sensitivity scores)
- anxiety symptoms (HSCL Anxiety scores)
- physical and psychiatric symptoms relating to menses (PMTS-During and PMTS-Before scores).

For the remaining two measures (depression measured by the CES-D scale and obsessive-compulsive symptoms measured by that HSCL scale), SSE-Appraisal was the best predictor, accounting for 12.46% and 8.72% of the variance, respectively, contrary to our predictions. In addition, in four of the eight regressions in which SSE-Recent was selected as the best predictor of symptoms, SSE-Appraisal was selected as the second-best predictor. In those cases, SSE-Appraisal added to the ability to predict women's symptoms but accounted for only an additional 1.39% to 2.65% of the variance on its own.

Discussion of Hypothesis 1

This analysis found that on the whole, the frequency of sexist events rather than the appraisal of those events best predicted women's symptoms, as hypothesized. Specifically, in 8 of 10 regressions, recent experiences with sexist discrimination were the best predictor of women's symptoms, and lifetime experiences were never selected as a predictor. The latter outcome is a logical one and suggests that recent sexist discrimination is a more acute stressor than lifetime experiences with sexist discrimination. This issue will be discussed in the next chapter, in which the data in Table 5.1 are used in an overall, theoretical model of the role of different types of discrimination in symptoms among women. In any event, however, this finding means that **it is the recent presence of sexist discrimination, rather than a woman's subjective appraisal of that discrimination, that**

TABLE 5.1 Stepwise Regressions Predicting Symptoms for Sample 2 With SSE-Lifetime, SSE-Recent, and SSE-Appraisal as Predictors

Symptom	Step	Predictor(s) Selected	R	R^2	SS	ANOVA F(df)	p
HSCL-Total (N = 470)	1	SSE-Recent	.36	.1305	39,818.58	60.32 (1, 402)	.00005
	2	SSE-Appraisal	.38	.1444	44,091.55	33.86 (2, 401)	.00005
HSCL-Somatization	1	SSE-Recent	.32	.1019	1,677.54	50.86 (1, 448)	.00005
HSCL-Obsessive	1	SSE-Appraisal	.29	.0872	886.94	41.76 (1, 437)	.00005
HSCL-Sensitivity	1	SSE-Recent	.39	.1506	1,164.24	82.06 (1, 463)	.00005
	2	SSE-Appraisal	.41	.1706	1,318.83	47.49 (2, 462)	.00005
HSCL-Depression	1	SSE-Recent	.37	.1339	2,383.83	69.59 (1, 450)	.00005
	2	SSE-Appraisal	.38	.1456	2,591.63	38.26 (2, 449)	.00005
HSCL-Anxiety	1	SSE-Recent	.32	.1037	489.67	53.12 (1, 459)	.00005
CES-D (N = 140)	1	SSE-Appraisal	.38	.1246	2,667.35	19.92 (1, 140)	.00005
BDI (N = 140)	1	SSE-Recent	.39	.1563	1,612.83	24.28 (1, 131)	.00005
	2	SSE-Appraisal	.43	.1828	1,885.98	14.54 (2, 130)	.00005
PMTS-During (N = 135)	1	SSE-Recent	.38	.1408	1,201.19	18.68 (1, 114)	.00005
PMTS-Before (N = 135)	1	SSE-Recent	.36	.1291	1,413.28	19.71 (1, 133)	.00005

NOTE: HSCL = Hopkins Symptom Checklist (Derogatis et al., 1974) and various subscales; BDI = Beck Depression Inventory (Beck et al., 1961); Center for Epidemiological Studies [...] PMTS = Premenstrual Tension Syndrome Scale (Condon, 1993) and two subscales.

best predicts women's symptoms. Whether a woman personally experiences and perceives a sexist event as stressful and upsetting or simply dismisses it as inconsequential (and says that it does not bother her), the events contribute to her symptoms nonetheless. This important finding is consistent with evidence indicating that a (generic) stressor need not be perceived or experienced as stressful to contribute to symptoms (Taylor, 1995). It also is consistent with Nancy Krieger's (1990; Krieger & Sidney, 1996) finding discussed previously.

In addition, this analysis found that appraisals of sexist discrimination also played a role in symptoms but a secondary and minor role (in terms of percentage of variance accounted for) relative to the frequency of sexist discrimination, as predicted. The exceptions to this were symptoms of depression only when measured by *one* of the three depression measures (i.e., by the CES-D), and obsessive-compulsive symptoms. The depression finding is no doubt an artifact of minor differences in the content of the CES-D versus the content of the HSCL Depression scale and the BDI, and thereby can be regarded as inconsequential. The finding for obsessive-compulsive symptoms cannot be dismissed in that manner, however, and suggests the clinically interesting possibility that the subjective appraisal of sexist events is specifically related to such symptoms—but not to other symptoms. Obsessive-compulsive symptoms are repetitive actions or thoughts that are experienced as uncontrollable intrusions. For example, the urge to repeatedly go back into one's place of residence to check that the stove and coffeepot are turned off or the constant intrusion of a melody or a thought that interrupts concentration are obsessive-compulsive symptoms.

Finally, this analysis found that sexist events accounted for a significant percentage of the variance in women's symptoms: Sexist events contributed as much to the symptoms of these women as they did to those of the women in Sample 1. These findings, based on a second independent sample of women, are consistent with those presented in Chapter 3 for Sample 1 and thereby confirm and validate that sexist stress plays a role in physical and psychiatric symptoms among women.

Before we can develop a general theoretical model of the role of sexist versus generic stress in symptoms among women, these two remaining questions require empirical investigation:

■ Is the role of sexist events in women's symptoms the same for minority and White women?

▓ What is the role of feminism in sexist events? Does feminism mediate the impact of sexist events?

The remainder of this chapter empirically addresses these two questions by posing specific hypotheses and then testing those statistically.

HYPOTHESIS 2: MINORITY VERSUS WHITE WOMEN

We hypothesized that sexist events would have a greater negative impact on the physical and mental health of women of color than on the physical and mental health of White women, simply because women of color experience sexist events significantly more often than do White women, as shown in Chapters 2 and 4 for Samples 1 and 2, respectively. Hence, we predicted that the R^2 between sexist events and symptoms for minority women would be larger than the R^2 for White women. In addition, we hypothesized again (as we did in Hypothesis 1) that it would be the frequency of sexist events (Lifetime or Recent), rather than the appraisal of those events, that would best predict symptoms for minority and White women alike. Hence, we also predicted that SSE-Lifetime or SSE-Recent would be selected as the best predictor of symptoms for both groups of women. We tested these hypotheses by repeating the set of stepwise regressions reported above but running them separately for White and minority women.

Hypothesis 2 Results

The results of the regressions are shown in Table 5.2. Sexist events were a stronger predictor of (had larger R^2 with) symptoms for minority women than for White women *for all 10 of the symptom outcome measures,* as predicted. For example,

▓ Past-year sexist discrimination accounted for 8% of the total symptoms (HSCL) of White women, but for 20% of the total symptoms of minority women.

▓ Past-year discrimination accounted for 5.98% of the depressive symptoms (HSCL-Depression scale) of White women, but 25.76% of those symptoms for minority women.

... regressions for White and Minority Women

Outcome	Group	Step	Predictor(s)	R	R^2	SS	ANOVA F(df)		p
HSCL-Total	White (N = 252)	1	SSE-Recent	.28	.0807	14,236.20	22.05	(1, 251)	.0005
	Minority (N = 247)	1	SSE-Recent	.45	.2057	26,190.59	38.58	(1, 149)	.0005
HSCL-Somatization	White	1	SSE-Recent	.27	.0735	642.87	21.66	(1, 273)	.0005
	Minority	1	SSE-Recent	.36	.1331	1,018.41	26.56	(1, 173)	.0005
HSCL-Obsessive	White	1	SSE-Appraisal	.27	.0727	416.69	20.85	(1, 266)	.0005
	Minority	1	SSE-Appraisal	.34	.1126	494.65	21.44	(1, 169)	.0005
HSCL-Sensitivity	White	1	SSE-Recent	.34	.1125	501.90	35.76	(1, 282)	.0005
		2	SSE-Appraisal	.36	.1324	590.45	21.44	(2, 281)	.0005
	Minority	1	SSE-Recent	.46	.2086	682.69	47.18	(1, 179)	.0005
		2	SSE-Appraisal	.48	.2264	741.12	26.05	(2, 178)	.0005
HSCL-Depression	White	1	SSE-Recent	.24	.0598	626.99	17.55	(1, 276)	.0005
	Minority	1	SSE-Recent	.51	.2576	1,863.64	59.67	(1, 172)	.0005
		2	SSE-Appraisal	.52	.2742	1,984.14	32.30	(2, 171)	.0005
HSCL-Anxiety	White	1	SSE-Recent	.22	.0475	122.72	13.97	(1, 280)	.00002
	Minority	1	SSE-Recent	.42	.1767	364.79	37.98	(1, 177)	.0005
BDI	White (N = 91)	1	SSE-Appraisal	.30	.0924	660.27	9.16	(1, 90)	.0032
	Minority (N = 43)	1	SSE-Recent	.68	.4607	1,461.02	33.32	(1, 39)	.0005
CES-D-Total	White (N = 96)	1	SSE-Appraisal	.26	.0683	936.23	6.97	(1, 95)	.0097
	Minority (N = 43)	1	SSE-Recent	.64	.4068	3,122.74	28.81	(1, 42)	.0005
PMTS-During	White (N = 96)	1	SSE-Recent	.24	.0566	329.34	4.68	(1, 78)	.0336
	Minority (N = 43)	1	SSE-Appraisal	.66	.4367	1,127.50	25.58	(1, 33)	.0005
PMTS-Before	White (N = 96)	1	SSE-Recent	.34	.1139	833.49	12.09	(1, 94)	.0008
		2	SSE-Appraisal	.42	.1789	1,308.45	10.13	(2, 93)	.0001
	Minority (N = 43)	1	SSE-Lifetime	.56	.3116	1,050.58	15.85	(1, 35)	.0003

NOTE: HSCL = Hopkins Symptom Checklist (Derogatis et al., 1974) and various subscales; BDI = Beck Depression Inventory (Beck et al., 1961); Center for Epidemiological Studies Depression scale = CES-D (Radloff, 1977); PMTS = Premenstrual Tension Syndrome Scale (Condon, 1993) and two subscales.

▒ Similarly, when using the BDI as a measure of depressive symptoms, sexist discrimination accounted for 9.24% of the symptoms of White women, and for 46.07% of the symptoms of minority women.

Thus the first part of Hypothesis 2 is supported.

Likewise, in the 20 regressions shown in Table 5.2 (10 for White and 10 for minority women), the frequency of sexist events (Recent or Lifetime), rather than the appraisal of those events, tended to be selected as the best predictor of symptoms for both groups of women, as we predicted. For White women, recent sexist events were selected as the best predictor in 7 of the 10 regressions, and appraisals were selected as the best predictor in only 3 regressions (HSCL Obsessive-Compulsive scale, BDI, and CES-D). For minority women, recent sexist events were selected as the best predictor in 7 of the 10 regressions, lifetime sexist events in 1 of the 10, and appraisals in 2 of the 10 regressions (HSCL Obsessive-Compulsive scale and PMTS-During Menses Scale). Thus **the frequency of sexist events was selected as the best predictor of symptoms in 15 of 20 regressions.**

Discussion of Hypothesis 2

We predicted that sexist events would have a greater negative impact on (i.e., be more strongly related to symptoms for) minority women than White women simply because minority women experience these events more frequently, as demonstrated in Chapter 4 for this sample. This prediction appears to be supported by the data in Table 5.2, insofar as R^2 was larger for minority women than for White women in every single regression. However, there are several alternative explanations for this finding that must be examined and ruled out before we can conclude that our hypothesis was supported.

One possible alternative explanation of the above finding is that more of the White women than of the women of color might be feminists (would classify themselves as such if asked), and feminist consciousness may decrease the negative impact of sexist events as theorized in Chapter 1. Thus ethnic differences in the role of sexist events in symptoms could be an artifact of ethnic differences in feminism: Sexist events could have a greater negative impact on minority women because minority women are not feminists (i.e., lack an understanding of sexism as a general response to women rather than to them personally).

To assess this possibility, all women in the current sample were asked "Are you a feminist?" to be answered yes or no, and were then classified as feminists versus nonfeminists based on their answers. A chi-square comparing the number of White versus minority feminists and nonfeminists (self-defined) was not statistically significant, $\chi^2(1) = 0.173, p = .678$:

- 31.8% of White women and 30.3% of minority women classified themselves as feminists.
- 68.2% of White women and 69.7% of minority women categorized themselves as nonfeminists.

Thus minority and White women did not differ in the percentage who considered themselves to be feminists, such that the greater negative impact of sexist discrimination on minority women's physical and mental health cannot be dismissed as an artifact of their lack of feminism.

One obvious concern about this analysis is that the self-labeling used to define feminist and nonfeminist groups could be meaningless insofar as such labels may have little relationship to feminist consciousness or participation in feminist work, and so little relationship to the negative impact of sexist discrimination on women. As shown later, however, these self-classifications were strongly related to the differential, negative impact of sexist events in a manner that was predicted a priori, suggesting that they were indeed related to some type of feminist consciousness.

Another alternative explanation for the finding that sexist events had a greater negative impact on minority women is that minority women might have more symptoms than White women: Sexist events could be more strongly related to symptoms for minority women simply because they have a greater range and number of symptoms. We tested this possibility in several ways:

- We conducted a t test that compared minority women and White women's scores on the HSCL Total Symptoms score, and it was not statistically significant ($t(df\ 411) = -1.42, p = .157$). The mean difference between minority and White women's scores on this scale was a mere 3.94 points.
- We also conducted a MANOVA comparing minority women and White women's scores on the PMTS-During Menses and PMTS-Before scales. This MANOVA was not statistically significant, $T^2 = .00855$, Exact $F(2, 109) = 0.466, p = .629$, and neither of the follow-up ANOVAs was significant.
- Finally, we conducted an additional MANOVA comparing minority and White women's scores on the CES-D and BDI; it was not significant, $T^2 = .00018$, Exact $F(2, 124) = 0.011, p = .989$, and neither of the follow up ANOVAs was significant.

These three analyses indicate that minority women did not have more symptoms than White women. Thus the finding that sexist events played a greater role in the symptoms of minority women than of White women is not an artifact of ethnic differences in feminism or in number of symptoms.

Hence, the most plausible explanation for the greater negative impact of sexist events on minority women is that minority women experience such events more frequently than do their White counterparts (as shown in Chapter 4 for Sample 2, and in Chapter 2 for Sample 1). In addition, however, we note that in Chapter 2, which we examined ethnic differences on the SSE in detail by looking at scores on the factors of the SSE, we found that minority women and White women did not differ in every type (factor) of sexist events. Instead, they differed in only two factors: Sexist Degradation and Its Consequences and Sexism in Close Relationships. When we combine that finding with the new finding—sexist events had a greater negative impact on minority women than on White women—we come to this new hypothesis:

> Of the many arenas and types (factors) of sexist discrimination, what hurts women the most is Sexist Degradation and Its Consequences and Sexism in Close Relationships. These two highly personal types of sexism (e.g., name-calling, and unfair, lesser treatment by family and lovers) are more harmful to women's physical and mental health than the more impersonal types of sexism (Sexist Discrimination in the Workplace and Sexist Discrimination in Distant Relationships).

This hypothesis also is consistent with the findings in the last chapter, namely, the highest appraisal ratings appeared to be on items in these two factors and that events found stressful by large percentages of the sample also seemed to be events in these two factors. We will test this logical, sensible hypothesis in the next chapter before formulating a general theory of the role of sexist discrimination in women's lives.

In any event, as predicted, we found that sexist discrimination had a greater negative impact on minority women than on White women. The irony in this finding is that the women most neglected by feminist psychology, feminist therapy, and women's studies—minority women—are the very women upon whom sexism has the greater negative effect.

An additional finding shown in Table 5.2 is that, on the whole, the frequency of discrimination rather than the appraisal of it best predicted symptoms for minority women and White women alike, as we predicted. Indeed, past-year sexist discrimination was the best predictor of symptoms for both minority women and White women, with lifetime experiences with discrimination and the appraisal of discrimination playing a lesser role. This finding supports the hypothesis and also replicates the findings shown in Table 5.1 for the sample as a whole. The data in Table 5.2 therefore also will be included in the general theoretical model of the role of various types of discrimination in women's symptoms that is presented in the next chapter.

The exception to this frequency-rather-than-appraisal rule was for obsessive-compulsive symptoms, in which the appraisal of discrimination was the best predictor for minority women and White women alike (Table 5.2), as it had been for the sample as a whole (Table 5.1). This finding again raises the interesting clinical possibility that different aspects of discrimination (frequency versus appraisal) play a role in different symptoms among women and that the subjectively experienced stressfulness of sexist discrimination is related to obsessive-compulsive symptoms specifically. In addition, however, appraisals of discrimination were also the best predictor of PMTS-During Menses symptoms for minority women and of BDI and CES-D scores for White women. These findings together suggest that appraisals of discrimination play an important role in a few specific symptoms, *if* those symptoms are measured with specific scales, for a specific ethnic group of women. Thus, on the whole, it was again the frequency of discrimination that best predicted symptoms.

HYPOTHESIS 3: FEMINISTS
VERSUS NONFEMINISTS

The last question concerns the role of feminism in the impact of sexist events. We had hypothesized in Chapter 1 that feminist consciousness is a unique personality variable that mediates and decreases the negative impact of sexist events on women. Specifically, we had hypothesized that feminism provides women with a schema for understanding sexist discrimination as an aspect of the reality of gender rather than as a response to women as individuals. Nonfeminists, lacking this schema, should (mis)understand sexist discrimination as a response to them as individuals and blame themselves for it. Thus, sexist discrimination should (ironically) have a greater negative impact on the health of nonfeminists (i.e., on women who might deny the existence of such discrimination or might fail to perceive it) than on feminists. Sexist discrimination should be a better predictor of the symptoms of nonfeminists than of feminists.

Hence, we offer the logical but counterintuitive hypothesis that the R^2 between sexist events and symptoms will be larger for nonfeminists than for feminists.

As noted earlier, women in the current sample classified themselves as feminists ($n = 199$) or nonfeminists ($n = 438$) and were divided into two groups based on that classification.[1] To test this hypothesis, we used SSE-Lifetime, SSE-Recent, and SSE-Appraisal scores to predict scores on the HSCL (total symptom score) and on the five symptom subscales of the HSCL (six outcome measures). Scores on the PMTS, CES-D, and BDI (total $N = 145$ for all three) were omitted from these analyses because the number of women who completed them *and* classified themselves as feminists (e.g., 7 of 145) was too small to analyze. To test Hypothesis 3, we conducted regressions on the six outcome measures separately for feminists versus nonfeminists. The results are shown in Table 5.3.

Hypothesis 3 Results

As shown in the table, the R^2 for nonfeminists was larger than for feminists, as predicted. Specifically, the percentage of variance in symptoms accounted for by sexist discrimination (i.e., R^2) was larger for nonfeminists than for feminists *in five of the six symptom measures* and appeared to be equal for the sixth measure. Sexist events accounted for:

- 8.42% of the variance in total physical and psychiatric symptoms (HSCL total) for feminists, but 19.68% of the variance for nonfeminists
- 5.07% of the variance in somatic symptoms for feminists, but 15.18% of the variance for nonfeminists
- 4.06% of the variance in obsessive-compulsive symptoms for feminists, but 14.75% of the variance for nonfeminists
- 13.16% of the variance in interpersonal sensitivity symptoms (e.g., feelings of inferiority and inadequacy) for feminists, and 21.41% of the variance for nonfeminists
- 9.57% of the variance in feminists' and 19.25% of the variance in nonfeminists' depressive symptoms
- 12.16% of the variance in feminists' and 10.48% of the variance in nonfeminists' symptoms of anxiety

---

1. The sample sizes of feminists versus nonfeminists in the analyses that follow are smaller than these, however, because only women who completed *every item* in each scale were included in the data analysis for that scale.

TABLE 5.3 Regressions for Feminists Versus Nonfeminists

Outcome	Group	Step	Predictor(s)	R	R^2	SS	ANOVA F	ANOVA (df)	ANOVA p
HSCL-Total	Feminists ($N = 142$)	1	SSE-Recent	.29	.0842	7,451.68	11.22	(1, 122)	.0011
	Nonfeminists ($N = 314$)	1	SSE-Appraisal	.42	.1720	36,589.77	56.31	(1, 271)	.00005
		2	SSE-Recent	.44	.1968	41,864.45	33.08	(2, 270)	.00005
HSCL-Somatization	Feminists	1	SSE-Recent	.23	.0507	236.21	7.32	(1, 137)	.0077
	Nonfeminists	1	SSE-Appraisal	.36	.1324	1,526.28	46.089	(1, 302)	.00005
		2	SSE-Recent	.39	.1518	1,749.39	26.93	(2, 301)	.00005
HSCL-Obsessive	Feminists	1	SSE-Recent	.20	.0406	128.18	5.71	(1, 135)	.0182
	Nonfeminists	1	SSE-Appraisal	.38	.1475	1,023.57	50.71	(1, 293)	.00005
HSCL-Sensitivity	Feminists	1	SSE-Recent	.36	.1316	340.26	21.37	(1, 141)	.00005
	Nonfeminists	1	SSE-Appraisal	.45	.2003	1,007.38	78.40	(1, 313)	.00005
		2	SSE-Recent	.46	.2141	1,076.65	42.49	(2, 312)	.00005
HSCL-Depression	Feminists	1	SSE-Recent	.31	.0957	572.61	14.61	(1, 138)	.0002
	Nonfeminists	1	SSE-Appraisal	.42	.1719	2,013.46	62.92	(1, 303)	.00005
		2	SSE-Recent	.44	.1925	2,254.12	35.99	(2, 302)	.00005
HSCL-Anxiety	Feminists	1	SSE-Recent	.35	.1216	175.49	19.51	(1, 141)	.00005
	Nonfeminists	1	SSE-Lifetime	.32	.1048	335.25	36.17	(1, 309)	.00005

NOTE: HSCL = Hopkins Symptom Checklist (Derogatis et al., 1974) and various subscales.

Thus, with the exception of symptoms of anxiety (where the R^2s seem to be equal), Hypothesis 3 was supported: Sexist discrimination accounted for a far larger percentage of the variance in the symptoms of nonfeminists than of feminists. Before concluding, however, that sexist discrimination has a greater impact on nonfeminists as we had theorized, several alternative explanations of the findings in Table 5.3 must be explored and ruled out:

1. One possibility is that nonfeminists reported more frequent sexist events (Lifetime and/or Recent) than did feminists. Sexist events could be more strongly related to their symptoms simply because they experience more of these events—like minority women.
2. Another possibility is that nonfeminists find sexist events to be more stressful than do feminists (perhaps because they do not expect them to occur, whereas feminists expect such treatment). Sexist events could be more strongly related to nonfeminists' symptoms because they *appraise* sexist events higher. This alternative hypothesis seems particularly likely because appraisals of sexist events were selected as the best predictor of the symptoms of nonfeminists in five of the six regressions for them, whereas appraisals were *never* the best predictor of the symptoms of feminists.
3. A third possibility is that nonfeminists have more symptoms than feminists, and this alone would increase the correlation between sexist events and symptoms for nonfeminists.

To test these three alternative explanations for the results, we conducted a MANOVA comparing feminists and nonfeminists on SSE-Lifetime, SSE-Recent, SSE-Appraisal, and the HSCL symptom subscales. This MANOVA was significant ($T^2 = .07388$, Exact $F(8, 395) = 3.648$, $p = .0005$), and the follow-up ANOVAs are shown in Table 5.4.

As shown in Table 5.4, feminists scored higher on the SSE-Lifetime, SSE-Recent, and SSE-Appraisal than did nonfeminists. In addition, there were no differences between feminists and nonfeminists on any of the five HSCL symptom scales (Fs), and no difference in their scores on the Total HSCL Symptom Score (t test). Feminists reported more frequent lifetime and past-year sexist discrimination than did nonfeminists, appraised sexist events as more stressful, and had a similar number of symptoms. Thus the finding that sexist events played a greater role in the symptoms of nonfeminists cannot be explained by the three alternative possibilities. This suggest that our theory—feminism mediates and decreases the negative impact of sexist discrimination on women—is the best explanation for the results.

TABLE 5.4 Feminists Versus Nonfeminists on SSE and HSCL Scales

Measure	Feminists (N = 126)	Nonfeminists (N = 280)	SS	F(df 1,402)	p
SSE-Recent	44.72	40.05	1,893.25	8.44	.004
SSE-Lifetime	56.34	48.01	6,013.99	23.11	.0005
SSE-Appraisal	53.89	46.67	4,528.53	11.51	.001
HSCL-Somatization	19.87	20.25	12.97	0.35	.553
HSCL-Obsessive	14.75	15.36	32.57	1.43	.233
HSCL-Sensitivity	13.93	13.94	0.009	0.001	.981
HSCL-Depression	19.67	19.73	0.30	0.001	.930
HSCL-Anxiety	9.39	9.52	1.44	0.14	.712

NOTE: HSCL = Hopkins Symptom Checklist (Derogatis et al., 1974) and various subscales. t test on HSCL-Total: Feminist Mean (σ) = 102.21 (26.72), Nonfeminist Mean = 103.45 (27.78), $t(df\ 404)$ = 0.42, p = .674.

OVERALL DISCUSSION

This study has four important results. The first is that (for White women, minority women, and the sample as whole) the frequency of sexist discrimination contributes much to women's symptoms (it was selected often as the best predictor and accounted for 5.66% to 46.07% of the variance, Table 5.2), whereas women's appraisals of that discrimination contribute far less (rarely selected as the best predictor and accounted for 0.9% to 9.24% of the variance, Tables 5.1 and 5.2). This means that **sexist discrimination plays an important role in physical and psychiatric symptoms among women, irrespective of women's individual appraisals of that discrimination**: Sexist discrimination contributes to physical and psychiatric symptoms among women, whether those women subjectively appraise sexist acts as stressful or dismiss them as inconsequential. **It is not a woman's high or extreme personal subjective appraisal of/response to sexist behavior but rather, the presence and frequency of that sexist behavior, that is related to symptoms among women.**

The second related finding is that subjective appraisals of sexist events, although generally contributing little to women's symptoms (i.e., for the sample as a whole), can however make a significant contribution to the symptoms of women *if the women are not feminists.* For nonfeminists, appraisals of sexist events were the best predictor of symptoms—even though their appraisals were lower than those of feminists.

The third important finding is that whereas sexist discrimination contributes to the symptoms of all women, it contributes even more to the symptoms of women of color. The reason for this is undoubtedly that women of color experience these events more frequently than do White women—something that we found in two studies (Chapters 2 and 4). Such consistent findings highlight (a) the need for research on the meaning and consequences of gender for minority women; (b) the need for new feminist advocacy for minority women where sexism is concerned; and (c) the need for new multicultural-feminist clinical interventions for women of color. These topics have received little attention in the history of feminist psychology, feminist therapy, women's studies, and feminist advocacy, and the need to finally address them fully and empirically cannot be denied (Landrine, 1995). How can research in feminist psychology justify studies of gender entailing samples of White women alone, when women of color experience sexist discrimination—the reality of gender—significantly more frequently than their White counterparts? How can feminist therapy focus almost solely on the mental health of White women when the mental health of women of color is far more seriously eroded by sexism—when sexism accounts for 46.07% of the variance in depression among women of color and only 9.24% of the variance in depression among White women? The answers are obvious and underscore the urgency of bringing cultural diversity to feminist psychology, therapy, and women's studies.

The fourth important finding is that while sexist events contribute to the physical and psychiatric symptoms of all women, they make an even greater contribution to the symptoms of the nonfeminist women who constitute (generalizing from our sample and from prior research) about 70% of all women in the nation. **Sexist events had a greater negative impact on nonfeminists than on feminists, even though feminists appraised such events as more stressful and reported more of such events.** Nonfeminist women, lacking feminist schema for understanding sexism as par for the course in a patriarchal society, may blame themselves for it, and this may contribute to physical and psychiatric symptoms, depression in particular. Specifically, feminists may find sexist events stressful *because they are inherently unfair,* and their appraisal ratings may increase with the degree of blatant injustice entailed in the sexist discrimination. Nonfeminists, on the other hand, may find sexist events stressful because they interpret them *as their own fault,* and their appraisal ratings may increase with the degree of self-blaming entailed in the sexist discrimination. This may be how and why appraisals of the stressfulness of sexist events played a major role in the symptoms of nonfeminists but no role whatsoever in the symptoms of feminists—despite feminists' having higher appraisal scores.

Thus these findings are consistent with our theory and suggest that feminism may be an important schema that mediates and decreases the negative impact of sexism on women and acts as a buffer protecting their physical and mental health. This, in turn, means that feminism, however much maligned in the popular press these days, is beneficial to women not only in the larger social arena, where it leads to changes in legislation that improve women's lives in the long run. Rather, feminism also may be beneficial to women in the smaller personal arena of a woman's everyday thoughts and feelings about herself, where it may entail causal attributions for sexist treatment that decrease the negative impact of that treatment, in the short run of the here and now. Feminism then may be a neglected resource for women, one that may play as important a role as social support and similar resources in mediating the negative impact of stressors but has yet to be sufficiently investigated. If this is the case, then the need to address the "backlash" against feminism, restore feminism's tarnished image, and attract more women to it also is pressing.

A final implication of these results is that feminist and nonfeminist women may be two very different populations of women—as different as minority and White women—for whom psychological and sociological principles and variables play different and perhaps opposite roles. It may be as important to ask women (in studies of every type) if they are feminists as it is to ask them about their age, social class, and ethnicity.

We now turn to a theoretical model of the role of various types of stressors in women's symptoms, a model that is based on all of the findings thus far.

Theoretical Model
and Interim Summary

Before formulating a theoretical model of the role of various types of discrimination in women's symptoms, one important empirical question remains: Which type (factor) of sexist discrimination plays the greatest role in women's symptoms? Answering this question will further clarify the nature of the relationships between sexism and women's symptoms and provide the final piece of data needed to formulate a preliminary but well-founded theory. Hence, in this chapter, we first examine the role of the types (factors) of sexist discrimination in the symptoms of Sample 2. We focus on Sample 2 because a larger number of women (470 versus 120 for Sample 1) completed the symptom outcome measures. Then, we combine these findings with all previous ones reported to propose a general theoretical model.

SSE FACTORS AND
SYMPTOMS FOR SAMPLE 2

In Chapters 2 and 4, we found that minority women in both samples had higher total SSE-Recent and SSE-Lifetime scores than White women. In Chapter 2, we analyzed these ethnic differences in detail and found that minority women's higher total SSE frequency scores were due to their higher scores on two of the four SSE factors, namely, Sexist Degradation and Its Consequences and Sexism in Close Relationships. Likewise, in the last chapter, we found that sexist events contributed far more to the symptoms of minority women than of White women. Hence, we hypothesized that this could be due to minority women's greater frequency of experiencing Sexist Degradation and Its Consequences and Sexism in Close Relationships—the factors that led them to have higher SSE scores than White women. This, in turn, suggests that these two types or domains of sexist discrimination are the most harmful to women: Sexist Degradation and Its Consequences and Sexism in Close Relationships might be more harmful to women because they are more personal forms of discrimination than are Sexist Discrimination in the Workplace and Sexist Discrimination in Distant Relationships. A review of the items in the factors (see Chapter 2) strongly suggests that Sexist Degradation and Its Consequences and Sexism in Close Relationships indeed are more personal or intimate than the other types or domains of sexist discrimination. Finally, in Chapter 4, we found that sexist events related to these two factors also appeared to be experienced as the most stressful by the sample, and this is consistent with the hypothesis.

Thus we hypothesized that two factors of SSE-Lifetime and SSE-Recent, Sexist Degradation and Its Consequences and Sexism in Close Relationships, would emerge as the best predictor of women's symptoms; this would mean that these are the domains or types of discrimination that are most hurtful to women.

ANALYSIS

To test this hypothesis, we conducted 10 stepwise regression analyses for the women in Sample 2 as a whole (irrespective of ethnicity), one for each of these outcome measures: (1) Hopkins Symptom Checklist (HSCL; Derogatis et al., 1974) Total Symptoms score, (2) HSCL Somatization score, (3) HSCL Obsessive-Compulsive score, (4) HSCL Interpersonal Sensitivity score, (5) HSCL Depression score, (6) HSCL Anxiety score, (7) Beck Depression Inventory (BDI; Beck et al., 1961) score, (8) Center for Epidemiological Studies Depression scale (CES-D; Radloff, 1977) score, (9) PMTS (Condon, 1993) Before Menses score and (10) PMTS During Menses score. In each of these regressions, we used the same eight predictors, namely, the four SSE-Lifetime and the four SSE-Recent factors.

RESULTS

The results of this analysis are shown in Table 6.1.

▨ Recent Sexist Degradation and Its Consequences was selected as the best predictor in 8 of the 10 regressions.

▨ Lifetime Sexism in Close Relationships was selected with it as the second-best predictor in 5 of those 8 regressions.

▨ Recent Sexist Discrimination in Distant Relationships was selected in one regression as the best, and in another as the second-best predictor.

▨ Sexist Discrimination in the Workplace was selected as the third-best predictor in one regression.

Thus, on the whole, Recent Sexist Degradation and Its Consequences and Lifetime Sexism in Close Relationships were the factors (types) of sexist discrimination most strongly related to women's symptoms. The highly personal, yet subtle events assessed by these factors have not been examined previously but appear to be important variables contributing to women's symptoms.

TOWARD A THEORETICAL MODEL

Thus far, our analyses have revealed

▨ Almost 100% of women report experiencing some type of sexist discrimination, in their lifetimes as well as in the past year (Chapters 1 and 4).

▨ Sexist stress (discrimination) is a better predictor of symptoms among women than is generic stress (Chapter 3).

▨ Sexist events account for a statistically significant and a large percentage (up to 46%) of the variance in women's symptoms (Chapters 3 and 5).

▨ Minority and young women experience sexist events more frequently than do their White and older counterparts (Chapters 2 and 4).

▨ The strength of the relationship between sexist events and symptoms varies with a woman's ethnicity and feminism, being larger for minority and nonfeminist women (Chapter 5).

▨ It is the frequency rather than the (high, extreme response or) appraisal of sexist events that contributes to women's physical and psychiatric symptoms for the most part (Chapter 5).

However, we also found the following:

TABLE 6.1 Stepwise Regressions Predicting Symptoms of Sample 2 Women from SSE-Lifetime and SSE-Recent Factors

Outcome	Step	Predictor(s)	R	R^2	SS	F(df)	p
HSCL-Total	1	Recent Sexist Degradation	.381	.1455	44,663.43	68.94 (1, 405)	.00005
	2	Lifetime Sexism in Close Relationships	.398	.1585	48,656.61	38.04 (2, 404)	.00005
HSCL-Somatization	1	Recent Sexist Degradation	.345	.1188	1,957.44	60.66 (1, 450)	.00005
HSCL-Obsessive	1	Recent Sexist Degradation	.266	.0709	705.0	433.48 (1, 439)	.00005
	2	Lifetime Sexism in Close Relationships	.292	.0854	849.99	20.45 (2, 438)	.00005
HSCL-Sensitivity	1	Recent Sexist Degradation	.368	.1357	1,051.07	72.84 (1, 464)	.00005
	2	Lifetime Sexism in Close Relationships	.392	.1536	1,189.64	42.00 (2, 463)	.00005
	3	Recent Workplace Discrimination	.403	.1621	1,255.32	29.78 (3, 462)	.00005
HSCL-Depression	1	Recent Sexist Degradation	.384	.1472	2,595.75	77.84 (1, 451)	.00005
	2	Lifetime Sexism in Close Relationships	.405	.1639	2,891.53	44.13 (2, 450)	.00005
HSCL-Anxiety	1	Recent Sexist Degradation	.336	.1130	529.68	58.66 (1, 460)	.00005
	2	Lifetime Sexism in Close Relationships	.352	.1242	581.52	32.54 (2, 459)	.00005
BDI	1	Recent Sexist Degradation	.408	.1664	1,602.52	26.34 (1, 132)	.00005
	2	Recent Sexism in Close Relationships	.443	.1964	1,892.02	16.01 (2, 131)	.00005
CES-D	1	Recent Sexist Degradation	.380	.1444	2,998.35	23.81 (1, 141)	.00005
PMTS-Before	1	Recent Discrimination in Distant Relationships	.309	.0955	1,036.81	14.15 (1, 134)	.0003
	2	Recent Sexist Degradation	.355	.1258	1,366.16	9.57 (2, 133)	.0001
PMTS-During	1	Recent Sexism in Close Relationships	.331	.1094	931.73	13.87 (1, 113)	.0003
	2	Recent Sexism in Distant Relationships	.374	.1402	1,194.12	9.13 (2, 112)	.0002

▓ Appraisals can contribute significantly to symptoms if the women are nonfeminists (Chapter 5).

▓ It was most often recent (past-year) rather than lifetime experiences with sexist discrimination that best predicted symptoms among women (Chapters 3, 5, and 6).

▓ The more personal types of sexist discrimination are more harmful to women (contribute more to their symptoms) than the more impersonal types (Chapter 6).

▓ Finally, all of these findings are consistent with data in the literature on discrimination against women (Introduction and Chapter 1).

From this wealth of evidence, we formed the general theoretical model of the role of sexist and other types of stress in women's physical and mental health, depicted in Figure 6.1. In this model, we theorize the following:

1. **Generic stressful life events and hassles, along with role-related gender-specific stressors (role overload, strain, or conflict) and lifetime sexist events (in particular, lifetime Sexist Discrimination in Close Relationships) operate as distal predictors of symptoms among women.** Distal predictors are background or contextual variables that function as a diathesis, and set the stage for, but do not lead to, symptoms. Hence, although the presence of the distal predictors may be said to characterize most if not all women's lives, most women do not exhibit significant physical or psychiatric symptoms. For example, studies of drug abuse and delinquent behavior among adolescents have found that lack of parental monitoring (leaving children alone, especially after school), poor grades in school, poverty, and family conflicts *set the stage for* drug abuse, cigarette smoking, and risky sexual behavior among youth but do not necessarily *lead to* such behaviors (Jessor & Jessor, 1977; Metzler, Noell, Biglan, Ary, & Smolkowski, 1994). Because distal predictors simply set the stage for symptoms, their role in symptoms is causal but indirect: Distal predictors are necessary but not sufficient to predict symptoms. An additional predictor, a proximal one, is needed to produce symptoms.

2. **Recent (past year) sexist events (in particular, Sexist Degradation and Its Consequences) and brutal/physical sexist discrimination (rape, battering, sexual harassment) operate as proximal predictors of symptoms among women.** A proximal predictor is a variable that is current or recent, salient, and has a direct, causal effect and role in symptoms or behavior. In the absence of a proximal predictor, distal variables alone produce no symptoms or mild ones at best. Thus, to

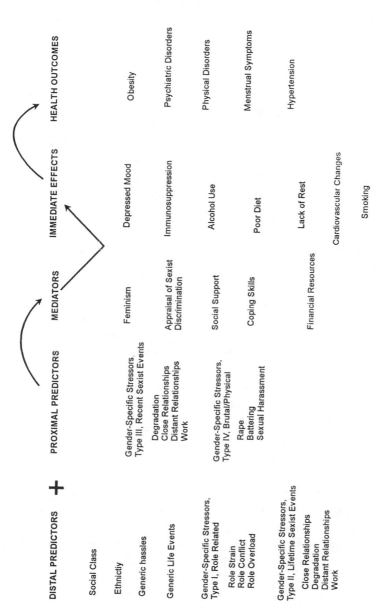

Figure 6.1. Theoretical Model of the Role of Various Stressors in Symptoms Among Women

continue the example, in problem behavior among adolescents, association with a group of deviant peers (who smoke cigarettes, take drugs, cut school, or break the law) is the *only* proximal direct predictor. Many children who live in poverty, are left alone after school, and whose parents have troubled marriages (distal predictors) do not exhibit significant or severe cigarette smoking, drug abuse, violence, or risky sexual behavior and do not join gangs because they do not associate with a group of (deviant) peers who engage in these behaviors (proximal predictor). Likewise, many women experience the distal predictors (detailed above), and indeed, the presence of these distal variables might be argued to be the definition of being a woman in most societies. These distal variables constitute a background level of chronic moderate to high stress that places women at risk for symptoms. Yet many women adapt to these distal conditions (via mediators such as coping skills and strong social support networks) and do not exhibit severe symptoms (but may exhibit mild ones) because of the absence of proximal predictors. We theorize that any one of the proximal predictors shown in Figure 6.1 (Recent Sexist Degradation and Its Consequences, Recent Sexism in Close Relationships, rape, battering, and other forms of violence) is sufficient to produce symptoms.

Likewise, many variables mediate the negative impact of sexist discrimination on women. Of the mediators, as argued in the previous chapter, feminism may be as important as social support. This is because feminism appears to decrease the impact of sexist events and also might determine the content and reason for the appraisal of sexist events.

This model is merely one hypothetical example of the types of causal models (consistent with the literature and data presented here) that are needed to elucidate the role of various kinds of stressors in women's symptoms. It is, however, a theoretical model that is consistent with all of our findings thus far and with the literature on sexist (and to some extent, racist) discrimination.

With the frequency of sexist discrimination demonstrated to be high for all women, and the role of that discrimination in women's symptoms demonstrated repeatedly to be a strong one, we can now turn to how women feel about and cope with sexist discrimination, and to things that women can do about it.

PART II

Remedies for Sexist Discrimination

SEVEN

Coping With Sexist Discrimination

Toward Recovery and Resistance

PHYLLIS BRONSTEIN

After reading the studies presented in this book, I found myself approaching the writing of this chapter from three different perspectives. As a researcher, I was first of all impressed by the magnitude and importance of the research that had been done, and elated about the findings. Here, at last, was solid, scientific documentation of the damaging effects of sexism on women's lives. However, as a woman, I could not help but be stirred by images and stories that came immediately to mind of past and recent encounters with sexism in my own life and in the lives of the women around me. Probably every woman reading this book will have that experience. Thinking back on just the past few weeks, I noted that:

AUTHOR'S NOTE: I am very grateful to Judy Breitmeyer, Judith Koplewitz, Jean Pieniadz, and Sondra Solomon for sharing their thinking and expertise, which I have incorporated into this chapter. In some instances, details have been modified slightly to disguise individual identities.

A 25-year-old woman at a large family dinner outing I attended had the temerity to ask the waiter to bring extra bread to the table. Her grandfather admonished her loudly for "having to take charge of everything" and lectured her later on how her assertiveness was the reason she didn't currently have a boyfriend.

A colleague at another university, who is on the committee to review all applications for reappointment, tenure, and promotion, shared with me that in the materials submitted, there were negative allegations made about character for 25% of the women, but for none of the men. These allegations ranged from complaints about being obstructive or "difficult" to insinuations about dishonesty and unethical behavior.

A 60-year-old neighbor, recently divorced, is having to deal with the criticism and resentment of her adult children because for the first time in her life, she is pursuing her own interests and is thus not available to baby-sit her grandchildren.

I had a visit from a friend, who is one of two female faculty in her university's chemistry department. Despite an outstanding record of publishing and receiving government funding for her research, she has just been denied tenure, ostensibly because student ratings of her teaching were lower than the average ratings received by faculty in her department. No account was taken of the fact that she has been assigned to teach the very large introductory courses, which students are required rather than motivated to take—and which almost invariably receive lower ratings than more advanced courses offered in more intimate settings. Nor was account taken of the disrespectful attitudes shown toward a young female professor by some of the male students, who scrawled comments such as "Great tits!" on the evaluation forms.

Finally, as a therapist, I found myself pondering several key questions:

1. How can women be helped to recover from the effects that sexism has had in their lives?
2. What are effective ways to deal with the everyday forms that they continue to encounter?

Knowing the kinds of obstacles and negative messages that women have experienced, I wanted to suggest some approaches that might help women in their efforts to recover their full sense of themselves, promote their individual development, and claim their rightful place in the world.

To better explore these issues, I decided to broaden my knowledge base by interviewing several feminist therapists. In my interviews, I asked them first to describe some of the experiences and feelings related to sexism that women clients have brought to therapy, and then to discuss how they helped their clients deal with them.

Following the aim of the research, I asked them to focus only on the effects of nonviolent forms of sexism and sexist discrimination. Although this seemed like a plausible limitation, one therapist pointed out that women's lives are so saturated with sexism that it is often difficult to know whether or not the more extreme forms, such as rape or battering, have occurred. Different women may label such events in different ways, depending on their life context and their level of self-awareness. Some women may uncover memories of violence or violation during the course of therapy—or come to relabel events that were not previously acknowledged as physically abusive. Thus, for each woman, it may be difficult to know where the line is between a coercive or menacing act such as grabbing her arm and propelling her to leave and what is most commonly regarded as physical or sexual assault.

However, given that the line between violent and nonviolent forms of sexism may be blurred, it is still useful to consider the ways that sexism takes hold of women's lives, on both conscious and unconscious levels. Understanding these processes is an important first step in overcoming the pain and limitations that they have imposed. After focusing on that aspect of the problem, I will present approaches and strategies that women may find useful as they strive to reclaim their full selves, broaden their view of what options are available to them, and deal with the challenges of living in a sexist society.

MAPPING SEXISM IN WOMEN'S LIVES

Sexism can occur in all areas and at all stages of women's lives, and it can take many forms. It can be as ordinary and unavoidable as a recurrent head cold, gradually undermining a woman's self-concept and weakening her resistance to the oppression she will encounter in the world. Or it can be as momentous and intimidating as a lightning strike—sometimes a single event does enormous damage to a woman's hopes and expectations, letting her know that to venture beyond certain boundaries is to risk serious loss, perhaps of her career, or of a central relationship in her life. Four domains where sexism frequently affects women's lives are within the family, in school, in the workplace, and within intimate partner relationships.

The Family. In a woman's family of origin, sexism can begin before she is born. Research tells us that most parents would rather have a boy, and this is especially true for fathers. Studies of parenting reveal differences throughout infancy and childhood in the ways parents interact with boys and girls. For example, parents (again, especially fathers) tend to show more interested attention to boys, allow boys more independence, and instruct and encourage boys more in both physical and intellectual activities.[1] This kind of differential treatment is likely to convey to girls the message that females are less interesting, less important, and less able to manage on their own, while also providing them fewer opportunities to develop their physical and intellectual capabilities.

One of the therapists I interviewed gave examples of family inequities described by many of her women clients who have brothers. She described a fairly typical scenario of parents saving up money for their sons, but not their daughters, to go to an Ivy League college—and perhaps not putting aside any money at all for their daughters' higher education. She also related a common family dynamic in which boys were allowed the freedom to demean their sisters, whereas if the sisters tried to retaliate in kind, their behaviors were noticed and punished. The messages girls receive from these kinds of differential treatment are that higher education is not an appropriate female pursuit (or that they, in particular, are not worthy of it) and that males may denigrate females with impunity, whereas females are expected to allow such treatment and never to respond with anger or aggression.

School. Much of the sexism that women encounter occurs in school. Studies of classroom interaction and teacher attitudes from preschool through high school have found that teachers tend to show more attention to boys than to girls and more effort in fostering boys' cognitive development. Studies of co-ed college classrooms have found that White male students, compared with White female students and students of color, volunteer sooner and more frequently in class and speak longer with fewer interruptions—and that male faculty encourage this pattern. Thus the messages that many girls have gotten at home—that they are less worthy of attention and education—are replicated throughout their years in school.

In addition, college entrance and scholarship exams can be very real barriers to academic advancement for women, as well as for students of color and those from low-income families. Not only do such tests exhibit gender and sociocultural bias in the content of their items, but they are biased in their predictions of academic performance. Average SAT scores are 61 points higher for males, making them appear to be better scholastic

---

1. For a review of this research, see Bronstein (1988).

prospects—yet the reality is that females receive higher grades than males throughout both high school and college. Also, because of their lower test scores on the PSAT, girls receive only about a third of National Merit Scholarships and lose out on many other scholarships from government and private agencies who rely on PSAT, SAT, or ACT results to select winners. Ethnic minority girls face double jeopardy, because similar gaps between male and female scores exist within every ethnic group, and ethnic minorities overall score lower than Whites. Thus female and ethnic minority students are less likely to be admitted to the more prestigious institutions and, as a result of receiving fewer scholarships, are more likely than White males to attend state and community colleges, rather than those private colleges and research universities that open the way to graduate school.[2] (For a discussion of this topic, see Bronstein, Rothblum, & Solomon, 1993.)

Finally, during the middle school and high school years, the social environment becomes a major source of sexism. Sexual harassment, both verbal and physical, becomes a fact of life. No girl gets through those years without being demeaned by comments on the adequacy or inadequacy of her physical attributes. Every girl experiences uninvited attempts at sexual touching, whether by an overeager date or a stranger on a crowded bus.

The Workplace. Sexism and sexist discrimination are common experiences for women in the workplace. There are certainly glass ceilings preventing women's advancement to higher levels of financial remuneration and power, and there are also glass walls limiting their access to particular professional specialties and higher-paying blue-collar jobs. There are different behavioral norms for women than there are for men, norms that demean and constrain women's behavior—for example, he's a go-getter, but she's a ball buster. There is sexual harassment, ranging from lewd jokes and innuendoes to coercive sexual advances. The therapists I interviewed related incidents in a variety of settings—a university, a business office, an elementary school, a religious order. One described a fairly typical work situation of women not feeling listened to:

> When anger comes up for women at work, they often feel their
> coworkers or bosses just want them to be a good girl. For one woman,
> a teacher, it came up around how decisions were being made. She

---

2.   This is so common that it has a name. It is called the "chilly classroom climate." See Hall and Sandler (1982).

would disagree about decisions about the children's care or about the curriculum, but instead of her message being heard, she would be scapegoated or just dismissed for being angry.

Another provided a more blatant example of a client who had worked as a nurse at a correctional facility. The woman came to therapy feeling depressed and humiliated because she had made two mistakes in administering medication and had been suspended from her job without any sort of hearing. It seemed to her that she was falling apart. The therapist described the stressfulness of her work environment:

> There were pornographic pictures all around her on the men's cell walls. She watched men masturbating and clutching their crotches, heard sexually explicit jokes shared between prisoners and male guards, was called "bitch" and "cunt" as she made her medication rounds. Everyone taunted her about her errors. She had also been written up for inappropriate behavior without a formal hearing for "inciting the inmate population," after she responded angrily to a male guard who yelled at her.

Intimate Relationships. A key finding of the research in this volume is that sexism in close relationships is one of the most damaging kinds. In intimate relationships with men, it is often manifested in the criticism, irritability, or anger that many men feel free to direct toward their female partners. Women may come to feel that they have to move about invisibly, on tiptoe, "walking on eggs." They may also learn that their own anger is unacceptable. One therapist described what usually happened when her women clients tried to express their anger to their male partners:

> They were told that they were hysterical, that they should shut up, that they were just flaky. They were put down for their ideas, they were put down for their mind. They were told they were stupid, they were dumb—"You're out of control!"—when they were just saying they were mad, and they might have used a loud voice. The men could not tolerate it, though at the same time, the men were also raising their voices. So it was really a double standard they were experiencing.

Another spoke of more subtle ways that women are controlled by their male partners:

> There is implication all the time with men that they will hurt you. When I work with heterosexual couples, one of the things men do with the

women is that they will begin to raise their voices in ways that women don't. And they start bracing their body as if they are containing a whole lot of physical tension. I work with a co-therapist, and it really comes across to everyone in the room. There is the implication that somebody is going to get hurt if they cross the line. Some men are aware, they've got it down to an art, but some are not. They're not aware of how much they've learned from their fathers and brothers over the years of how to hold their bodies so as to imply threat.

THE INTERNALIZING OF SEXIST MESSAGES

Although the kinds of sexist treatment described above can limit opportunities and cause pain and disappointment, the effects can end, theoretically, when a woman gets away from the situation that is causing them—perhaps by leaving home, graduating, quitting her job, or getting a divorce. In most cases, however, no matter how far she gets from that sexist treatment or environment, she will still feel its harmful effects because she has *internalized* its insidious messages. The messages, with some variation according to ethnicity or socioeconomic level, are that

1. She is not capable enough to succeed in a man's world.
2. In any case, it is best not to be very smart or successful, and certainly not to be outspoken or angry.
3. What she *should* strive to be is thin, sexy, nurturant, and a good listener.

The therapists I interviewed talked of a number of different ways that internalizing sexist messages affects the way women feel and act in the world. Most often mentioned was **loss of voice.**[3] Recent writers such as Carol Gilligan and Mary Pipher (see Table 7.1) have described this phenomenon in adolescent girls, and many women can look back to their early adolescence and remember both overt and subtle pressures to be quiet, good, and "ladylike," and to never be bossy or angry, never to "talk back." Women of color similarly have been silenced, not only by these social messages, but also by the long history of ethnicity-related oppression that denied them access to education and made it life-endangering for them to speak out about racism (see Landrine, 1995).

---

3. There are many studies on loss of voice or "self-silencing." See, for example, Gratch, Bassett, and Attra (1995).

TABLE 7.1 Suggested Readings With a Feminist Viewpoint

Author	Title	Publication Information
Maya Angelou	I Know Why The Caged Bird Sings	Random House: New York, 1970, c1969
Susan Faludi	Backlash	Crown: New York, 1991
Marilyn French	The Women's Room	Summit Books: New York, 1977
Betty Friedan	The Feminine Mystique	Dell: New York, 1964, 1963
Carol Gilligan	In a Different Voice	Harvard University Press: Cambridge, MA, 1993
Emily Hancock	The Girl Within	Dutton: New York, 1989
bell hooks	Talking Back	South End Press: Boston, MA, 1989
Maxine Hong Kingston	Woman Warrior	Knopf: distributed by Random House, New York, 1976
Ursula Le Guin	Left Hand of Darkness	Ace Books: New York, 1969
Audre Lorde	Sister Outsider	Crossing Press: Trumansberg, N.Y., 1984
Jean Baker Miller	Toward a New Psychology of Women	Beacon Press: Boston, MA, 1977, 1976
Kate Millett	Sexual Politics	Doubleday: Garden City, NY, 1970
Robin Morgan	Sisterhood is Powerful	Random House, New York, 1970
Toni Morrison	Bluest Eye	Knopf: distributed by Random House, New York, 1993
Tillie Olsen	Silences	Delacorte Press/Seymour Lawrence: New York, 1978
Marge Piercy	Woman on the Edge of Time	Knopf: New York, 1976
Mary Pipher	Circles in the Water	Alfred A. Knopf: New York, 1990
Adrienne Rich	Reviving Ophelia	Putnam: New York, 1994
Gloria Steinem	Of Woman Born	Norton: New York, 1986
	Outrageous Acts and Everyday Rebellions	H. Holt: New York, 1995
	Moving Beyond Words	Simon & Schuster: New York, 1994
Alice Walker	In Love & Trouble	Harcourt Brace Jovanovich: New York, 1973
Virginia Woolf	To the Lighthouse	Routledge: London, New York, 1994

One therapist described how these pressures have affected women by the time they reach adulthood:

> A lot of women talk about not knowing they're articulate, about not knowing that they know. As though they're not supposed to have access to the elements of their inner life. If they were to make those distinctions, they would get in touch with all the screams that are inside them. . . . Almost every woman I have worked with has said they do not have their voice. And that is not something my male clients come in with.

Another therapist, in thinking about women's difficulties in articulating their life choices, even to themselves, told this story about her own initial career direction:

> When I was applying for college, my minister wrote me a wonderful reference. But in it, and to my face, he talked about how I should never forget that my role as a woman had to do with being married and having children. It was his voice that I listened to—his voice and my parents' voice—about being a teacher, because you could always fall back on that if you got married. So I became a teacher, when I really wanted to be a psychologist.

Women's loss of voice affects many aspects of their lives. Within the family, it can prevent them from arranging a fair division of household responsibilities, from getting their sexual needs met, from standing up to intrusive in-laws, and from letting their children know they are not to be disturbed when the study door is closed. In the work world, it can prevent them from pursuing their ambitions, from speaking up so that people will notice their ideas and abilities, and from writing up and publishing their research and their opinions. On a personal level, not knowing their own feelings and not trusting their own voices can make women feel crazy.

One of the factors contributing to women's loss of voice is fear. Fear of verbal and physical abuse from men makes women tactful and apologetic in their interactions with men, even in situations and relationships where there is no likelihood whatsoever that abuse might occur. In intimate relationships with men, women learn to become careful and silent, out of fear that they will be cut off from love and affection. A therapist who works with heterosexual couples described the way that women are controlled through this fear:

Men imply that they will cut off everything, that the relationship is over if you cross a certain line. I've had men say, "I just can't do this anymore" if a woman tries to push back at him. If she tries to engage in a fight with him, truly engage as an equal, he'll say, "I'm out of here." This is particularly scary for a lot of women.

In moving through the wider world of school and work, women fear humiliation. They have internalized the sexist messages personally directed at them, as well as those absorbed from the culture. As a result, they are fearful that their inadequacies will be exposed should they attempt new challenges or put themselves forward in a visible way. Thus fear, in both the personal and professional domains, helps maintain women's loss of voice.

Another important area in which internalized sexism affects women is in their feelings about their bodies. The cultural messages are imparted early, not only by the thin, large-breasted cartoon images of women in Disney movies and Saturday morning television, but also in that girlhood icon of beauty and style, the Barbie doll. It is not uncommon for girls as young as 9 or 10 to be dieting, as they try to reduce themselves to the cornstalk images of the models in their older sisters' teen magazines. During the adolescent years, the leering, the pawing, and the approving or rejecting comments from the males around them make women extremely anxious about their bodies, and it is at this age that eating disorders become alarmingly common. By adulthood, the habit of fixating on their perceived imperfections has become a permanent way of life; women check mirrors constantly, they diet, they compare themselves with other women, they contemplate cosmetic surgery. Eventually, it may bring them to therapy. One therapist stated,

Lots and lots of women come in talking about their bodies, from catcalls and harassment that happen on an ongoing basis to women who are starving their bodies or using laxatives to an extreme because they hate their body. All of this has to do with all we see in this society, in magazines and on TV, about women's bodies and how they're sexualized.

The hurt that many women inflict on their bodies—dieting obsessively, bingeing and purging, augmenting their breast size, and even cutting themselves in hidden places—may also be a way of directing their rage toward a safe target—themselves—rather than risking expressing it toward the men in their lives and the patriarchal society that are oppressing them.

In sum, women take sexism very personally. They may reject it on a theoretical level, but unconsciously, they cannot help but absorb the messages that are everywhere in the air around them. The "reality" they live in is defined by the patriarchy, and that reality views women and people of color as less capable and valued than White males, and less entitled to power, resources, and respect. There have been many changes in society in the last 30 years, and the majority of adult women now work outside the home, increasingly in traditionally male domains. Yet, deep inside themselves, many women are weighted down by conflicts, doubts, and self-limits. They have internalized the patriarchy's constrictions of their role into sexual object, helpmate, listener, and caretaker, along with its devaluation of their worth.

DEALING WITH SEXISM: RECOVERY AND RESISTANCE

We return now to the original questions I asked myself as a therapist, of how to help women recover from sexism's harmful effects in the past and deal with the sexism they continue to encounter. The various approaches touched on by the therapists I interviewed can be grouped into four categories: education, psychological work, activism, and support.

Becoming Educated About Sexism. One of the striking findings about the research in the current volume was that although women who considered themselves to be feminists reported more sexism in their lives and appraised its effects as more damaging, their mental health was less affected by it than was the case for women who did not consider themselves to be feminists. As the authors point out, feminists are more likely to attribute the sexist inequities, denigration, and abuse they experience to social and political factors, whereas nonfeminists, lacking a broader political explanation, are more likely to believe sexist messages about their inadequacies, and to blame themselves for the inequitable, disrespectful, and abusive treatment they receive.

Thus it is not surprising that the therapists I interviewed stressed the importance of educating women about sexism, although they go about it in very different ways. One engages her clients in collaborative research to better understand the problems they are dealing with. Together, they contact feminist scholars, look for research articles, and if appropriate, contact state agencies to find out what data exist, how the problems can be analyzed from a feminist perspective, and what remedies may be available. She also recommends tapes and books by feminist authors such as Audre Lourde and Tillie Olsen that will expand clients' understanding of what it means to be a woman in a sexist society (see Table 7.1). In addition, she stresses the importance of networking as a way for women to gain a better political understanding of their situation, validate their own perceptions by comparing them with those of other women, and get help in developing strategies for dealing with the problem at hand.

Another therapist uses a psychodynamic approach, doing a kind of re-education of the psyche. She explained,

> The elements of the unconscious are, I don't believe, only constituted from parental dynamics. It tries to make sense of elements in the culture as well. I try to listen for sexist learning that's gone so deep inside the person it's second nature to them. I try to bring to light sexism or racism that has gone unanalyzed, so that people can learn from their own minds how insidious this stuff is in the culture, that it seeps into your own mind. . . . I stop people and say, "Let's talk about where you first got that idea. When did you first start saying this about yourself?" It may be true and it may not be true, but we've got to look very closely at where it came from. I try to track the history of that aspect of self-concept whenever I can.

If a woman wishes to educate herself further about sexism, there are many books available that explain or illustrate the topic. Such nonfiction classics as Betty Friedan's *The Feminine Mystique,* Kate Millett's *Sexual Politics,* Jean Baker Miller's *Toward a New Psychology of Women,* and Carol Gilligan's *In a Different Voice* are a good place to start. More recent works that women have found to be especially informative are Gloria Steinem's two collections, *Outrageous Acts and Everyday Rebellions* and *Moving Beyond Words,* bell hooks's *Talking Back,* Susan Faludi's *Backlash,* Emily Hancock's *The Girl Within,* Mary Pipher's *Reviving Ophelia,* and Maya Angelou's *I Know Why the Caged Bird Sings.* There are also many wonderful works of fiction that depict the effects of sexism in women's lives, such as Virginia Woolf's *To the Lighthouse,* Toni Morrison's *Bluest Eye,* Alice Walker's *In Love and Trouble,* Marilyn French's *The Women's Room,* and Maxine Hong Kingston's *Woman Warrior.* Science fiction fans will enjoy Marge Piercy's *Woman on the Edge of Time* and Ursula LeGuin's *Left Hand of Darkness.* For poetry that speaks to women's experiences in a sexist world, readers might sample Audre Lourde, Adrienne Rich, Marge Piercy, and Robin Morgan (see Table 7.1).

Doing the Psychological Work. Most of the psychological approaches the therapists mentioned for helping women recover from sexism have been developed for the therapy they do with their clients. The following descriptions of how they work may give women a sense of how feminist therapy can be helpful and also provide some ideas for approaches women can try on their own.

An important part of the psychological work feminist therapists do, along with the education process, is getting women to challenge their internalized sexism. For example, the therapist whose client was a nurse in a correctional facility explained,

> She perceived it as shame, that as a professional woman she had made two errors. What was going on? She could understand it once, but twice? "I think my mathematical ability isn't good. Maybe I really made an error because I'm not good in math. I know I have a terrible temper." Clients get worn out trying to do it alone, believing they have emotional and personal problems. Here, we get to work with that, because it's not the whole story.

Another therapist described the ways she tries to get clients to reframe some of their negative self-perceptions:

> Words like gossip, nag, bitchiness—when my clients call themselves that, I really try to get them to find other words. I think that gossip is a creative way of women trying to be together, to understand their oppressors. They're indirectly analyzing who are the power players here, who has what goods, who's in good with the oppressor, and what are we trying to get here? What we call nagging is really women hanging in there and persisting and trying not to disengage, in the face of incredible resistance or oppression or someone ignoring them. So I see that as determination and strength.

Another aspect of the psychological work is helping women reclaim their voices. To do this, women usually need to understand fully how they were silenced—when it first began to happen, and the ways that it continued throughout their lives. Some therapists encourage women to relate current instances when they feel voiceless to the suppression that happened in the past. This is based on the notion that when we find ourselves unable to deal effectively with present-day situations, it is often because they are reminiscent of unresolved incidents from the past, perhaps from childhood or adolescence, when we had insufficient knowledge or resources to deal with them. In reexamining the past from an adult perspective, women are often able to express the emotions that surrounded those incidents, and to gain a better understanding of how their efforts to contain the feelings of fear, shame, or anger may have contributed to their long-term self-silencing. Releasing the old feelings can free women up to react in new ways in the present.

Several of the therapists spoke of strategies to help women recognize their own feelings, to really allow themselves to hear their own voice. One teaches her clients to attend to themselves in a new way: She asks them to write down what they are feeling from one moment to the next, within a given hour, as a kind of journal-keeping exercise. Another stresses the importance of women really embracing and being proud of their anger. As a start, she suggests creative ways that they can begin to acknowledge their angry feelings to themselves and vent them—by writing letters that never get sent, shredding magazines, or stomping on paper cups, which makes a wonderful popping noise and leaves very little mess to clean up. She also helps women fine-tune their anger, coaching them to use "I" statements rather than accusations, and encouraging them to stop listening to the messages in the culture and in their personal lives that insist that they shouldn't be angry. As an example of her approach, she described her therapy work with a nun who was having difficulty expressing anger:

> The place we started was for her to notice it internally first. She would be in a meeting, and this rage would come up on how the meeting was going, or that she was not being listened to, or that issues weren't being addressed. The first step was for her to just acknowledge in her *head* during the meeting that she was angry. And that was a great relief to her. Another step was that she would let somebody else know, somebody she felt safe with. And eventually, she was able to talk about it out loud with some people in this meeting. Over a period of months, she found that she could have her voice. I encouraged her that in the meeting, she could be jotting notes to herself about her anger, and that was great fun for her to do. I think that being a nun, she probably had gotten the ultimate message about being a good girl.

Another therapist has devised a technique to help women begin to reclaim their voices in their personal relationships. When women feel locked into certain ways of responding to their partner, or perhaps to their mother or father on the phone, she helps them generate a list of things that the other person is likely to say, with alternative responses that are respectful but at the same time will enable them to hold their own. Then, for example, when they are on the phone with their parent, they can just go down the list, taking note of how predictable that person is—or they can try out some of their new responses and see whether that alters the typical patterns of conversation. The therapist noted that all her clients who have tried this have come back with some new insight or new distance, which has helped them break free of the feeling of being locked into a prescribed pattern of response.

An additional aspect of the psychological work involves women's feelings about their bodies. The therapist who talked the most about this felt that it was important for women to express fully the internalized hatred that many feel toward their bodies—so that they get it enough outside themselves to see it clearly and work with it. She described her work with a woman with an eating disorder:

> She's in a relationship, and the man puts her down a lot and is pretty abusive in the ways he does that. And when that goes on, she starts not liking herself, believing his words, and a lot of it gets focused on her body, and how she hates her body. And so sometimes I will encourage her in the session to talk to her body, like a Gestalt technique, talk to her body outside of herself. Often a woman can then express her anger and her sadness. And another part can then come out, which is compassionate. I also encouraged her to start drawing, and she would draw her body. And it was interesting to see the progression of drawings, from this self-loathing place to really loving. And we tried to find some strategies for when those bouts would come up with her partner—how not to internalize them, and how to express her anger to her partner in a safe way for her, so that she didn't start abusing laxatives. She would probably take 20 laxatives a day.

As a way for women both to work on feelings about their bodies and discharge accumulated rage at the sexism they have experienced, one therapist recommended self-defense training. In particular, she urged that women take the intensive course known as Model Mugging (or a similar version of it), which involves all-out physical contact with a heavily padded male "attacker." The training helps women connect with and release their anger in a very empowering way and provides them with a new respect for the strength and resilience of their bodies. In addition, discovering that they can successfully defend against and disable an attacker can greatly enhance women's self-confidence and their sense of safety and independence in the world.

One other aspect of the psychological work a therapist described that seemed particularly useful was a technique she referred to as "flaunting it."

By this, she meant a woman doing whatever she chose to do in a big way and making a fuss about herself in the process. She explained,

> When people have a tiny little light that they haven't been allowed to shine any bigger, something they really like doing, like art, or science, or mothering—something they were told they shouldn't do because it wasn't woman enough, it wasn't good enough, it wasn't *something* enough. . . . I encourage people to go after that tiny little light, sometimes at the expense of other things they were encouraged to do or expected to do because they're women. So people will take courses or start a project where they're exaggerating that light . . . so that light will have a bigger place inside them.

BECOMING AN ACTIVIST

One very important way for women to overcome the effects of sexism in their lives is to become activists. This means taking a stand against the oppression instead of going through life trying to be compliant and "good" in hopes of being treated fairly. Activism can take many forms. One therapist, in speaking of her clients, said,

> In my work, I would always encourage women from a place of empowerment to take some stands—to become politically active, to go to a speakout, or to work at a battered women's shelter or a rape crisis center. Even if they hadn't been raped or battered, they wanted to help other women. It helped them be more aware of the issues and helped their healing. A lot of healing happens in helping somebody else. In my work as a therapist, I benefit all the time from my clients' healing.

Activism can mean making a commitment to a larger movement. This is an effective way to help keep sexism externalized, and away from the personal realm. Women can then come to view themselves as fighters, and as a force for historical change, rather than as victims of oppression. They can connect with other women in this important struggle, and no longer have to feel the isolation and fear of having to struggle alone. And they can make a difference, in their own lives and in the society at large. Being part of a larger movement to end sexism does not necessarily mean formally joining an organization. Women can be activists in whatever sphere they operate in. They can do it at home by insisting on equitable relationships with male partners and by raising their sons to respect women and their daughters to respect themselves. They can do it in classrooms, and courtrooms, and boardrooms. Doing the research for this book is an example of activism. So is writing this chapter.

If women choose this route to recovery and empowerment, and it is highly recommended that they do so, there are cautionary factors to keep in mind. One is that they need to remember that it is not possible to change everything at once. In systems in which sexism is deeply entrenched, change may be slow in starting, and gains may be accrued slowly, with many setbacks. Thus, for example, as increasing numbers of women enter academia as junior faculty, greater numbers of them will get tenure even as many are still being denied. Eventually, some of these tenured women will become department chairs and deans, and they will then be able to assure that the doors keep opening wider for women.

Another precaution is for women to choose and time their battles carefully. For example, it may be more effective, when mounting a campaign for salary equity, not to deflect attention from the issue by demanding at the same time that the word *Ladies* be changed to *Women* on the firm's restroom door. Also, a therapist who is very supportive of her clients' activism provided this warning:

> It is important to assess the hazards. If women have not done the political analysis and are not aware of the kinds of pressures that come about when you talk about the truth—the institutional pressures—if they are politically naive, they're in danger. It's like women deciding to leave their abusive husbands. If they don't have a system set up the day they decide to leave, and an ongoing support system, they may end up dead.

A third precaution that activists need to keep in mind is to stay hopeful about people and avoid bitterness and resentment. It is very easy to view men, or some particular man, as permanently entrenched in the oppressor role and incapable of change. Ultimately, however, it may be more effective to believe and to act as if all people want to be fully caring and humane, even if they are not able to be that way at this moment. This seems to be an effective strategy for women to infuse their activism with a positive energy, and also a way of holding out that possibility for even the most sexist men they know. It does not mean that women should turn their backs on the dangers around them or that they should trust their oppressors. But it does mean taking the viewpoint that if society can change, each individual can change as well.

Getting Support

Support is an essential ingredient for women attempting to deal with sexism and its effects on their lives. Women can educate themselves about sexism through reading and research. But to be truly effective in counteracting the sexist messages inside their own heads and in the everyday world, they need people in their lives who can be counted on to remind them of their strengths, their accomplishments, and their potential. Such people may be friends, a partner, family members, colleagues, a mentor, or a therapist. One therapist, who referred to herself as a "cheerleader" with her clients, makes sure they know the importance of support—and provides an ample measure of it herself—particularly when she is helping them deal with sexual harassment in the workplace:

> I would help them find out if there were other people who could help verify it, and that they could turn to, because it might get nasty if they confront someone—especially if it's the boss, which it often is. I talk with them about where to get support in the state. My role is to support them in taking action. It could be scary, for their privacy and for the risk of losing their position. Or we talk about who in the environment could help them—or strategize about how to get out of that environment.

A therapist who frequently helps women experiencing sexist discrimination in the workplace mentioned that the filing of grievances and complaints is best done with others, to bring more weight to the complaint and to enable each complainant to feel supported throughout a difficult and intimidating process. She also stressed that it is almost impossible for one woman alone to achieve any sort of systemic change in trying to eliminate sexism. Even if she is the president of the corporation, she must have the support of the people who will implement her policies.

Although women are very skilled in providing emotional support for one another in the war against sexism, they need to provide other forms as well. Essentially, women need to do whatever they can to help open doors for other women. This means working to get women hired, promoted, appointed, and elected, and speaking up for women when they are being attacked. It means female managers advocating for higher salaries for their secretaries, and secretaries providing new women supervisors with useful knowledge of company politics. It means women faculty mentoring their female graduate students, and female graduate students writing letters to support the tenure and promotion of their mentors.

Women are moving into new roles, where no templates exist. We need to learn from one another and to be models for one another. Some of us who have grown up in the mainstream of U.S. culture may be better equipped to navigate effectively within traditional systems. Some us who have grown up feeling marginalized may be more comfortable being vocal and challenging. Both are important skills, which we can learn from watching each other in action. We need to teach and encourage one another to write and to model speaking out in public. And we need to wear our battle scars without shame, to remind one another that we have survived and gotten tougher and smarter in the process.

Women collectively have unlimited knowledge and skills to use in the fight against sexist discrimination, and to take our rightful places in the world.

EIGHT

Individual and
Collective Action

*Social Approaches and Remedies
for Sexist Discrimination*

BERNICE LOTT
LISA M. ROCCHIO

We begin this chapter by describing an investigation of women's responses to personal experiences of sexist discrimination (Lott, Asquith, & Doyon, 1997). This investigation is part of a continuing research program (Lott, 1995) concerned with interpersonal sexist discrimination, a program that has been derived from a social psychological analysis of sexism. Within this theoretical framework, sexism is defined in terms of three components: prejudice (negative attitudes toward women), stereotypes (beliefs about women), and discrimination. Discrimination may be institutional (as in employment, salaries, or access to positions of leadership), or it may be interpersonal as in responses to women of distancing, avoidance, exclusion, or belittling in face-to-face situations. It is with interpersonal discrimination that this chapter is concerned.

Anecdotal evidence of women's experiences of sexist discrimination in interpersonal situations abounds. Indeed, it is common for women to nod in recognition when others report having been turned away from, ignored, or put down by a man. Rowe (1973) has referred to incidents of everyday sexist discrimination as the "minutiae" of sexism, or as "microinequities," the "tiny, damaging characteristics of an environment" (Rowe, 1990, p. 155) that create and maintain subtle barriers. Thus a woman in conversation with a man may find him staring at her breasts, or her positive contributions to a discussion may be ignored or attributed to someone else. Piper (1990) has noted that a discriminator will often fail to acknowledge the presence of a member of a devalued group and will treat such a person in ways that would be clearly insulting if directed toward a recognized peer. To understand the behavior of discriminators, cautions Piper, "we must watch what they do, not what they say" (p. 299). An effort to do just that has found support, in varying settings, for the proposition that in relatively neutral situations, where men do not anticipate sexual pleasure or nurturance from a woman, they will tend to distance themselves from her, whereas women will not tend to distance themselves from a man (Lott 1987, 1989; Lott, Lott, & Fernald, 1990; Saris, Johnston, & Lott, 1994).

High status in income, education, or employment appears not to protect a woman from being the target of either subtle or obvious sexist behaviors. A study of women professors (Grauerholz, 1989) found that 32% of the professors reported sexist comments primarily from male students, and a study of women attorneys (Rosenberg, Perlstadt, & Phillips, 1993) found that two thirds reported being inappropriately addressed or on the receiving end of sexual or gender-specific remarks by other attorneys, clients, or judges. Studies of women (and girls) in other areas have yielded similar reports. Lee, Marks, and Byrd (1994) found that boys, in a sample of private co-educational schools, dominated class discussions or were more frequently recognized by teachers than girls. Fraternity "little sisters" in five public universities in the Southeast were found to receive consistent treatment requiring them to be subservient and dependent (Stombler & Martin, 1994). In addition, a study of Black women police officers (Martin, 1994) revealed that "inside the station, women face a hostile working environment filled with sexual propositions, pornographic material, and cursing" (p. 391). Similar findings came from a study of African American women firefighters (Yoder & Aniakudo, 1995).

A STUDY OF WOMEN'S RESPONSES
TO SEXIST DISCRIMINATION

The objectives of the study to be described (Lott et al., 1997) were to more systematically investigate experiences of interpersonal sexist discrimination among a sample of East Coast women in terms of the frequency of such experiences, the situations in which they occurred, the women's responses to them, and the gender of the discriminator. In this chapter, we will focus primarily on what the women told us they did in response to sexist treatment.

We asked our sample of women to respond to the Schedule of Sexist Events (SSE), described elsewhere in this book, which we modified to permit exploration of the ways that women handle incidents of sexist discrimination. This latter concern is not often the subject of careful investigation (but see Fitzgerald & Ormerod, 1993; Grauerholz, 1989). Our sample consisted of 262 participants (106 women of Color and 156 European American women). Analyses indicated that the four age × ethnicity groups were similar in student versus nonstudent status, hours employed per week, and education.

A nine-page survey included (1) a consent form, (2) a page requesting demographic information, and (3) 20 questions adapted from the SSE (Klonoff & Landrine, 1995; see Figure 1.1).[1] As a follow-up to the first 15 questions, we added a question about the gender of the people who behaved unfairly, to be answered on a 5-point scale from 1 = *mostly women* to 5 = *mostly men*. These questions ask about experiences in certain situations (e.g., unfair treatment by teachers). To each of these, we added a list of 10 specific ways that might have been used to respond to the unfair treatment, from ignoring it to confronting the person who had behaved in a sexist way. Each respondent was asked to check all of the ways that she had dealt with such experiences.

All 35 members of an upper division psychology class were asked to solicit survey information from 16 women (8 women of Color, and 8 European American women, and within each group, half to be 29 years old or younger and half to be 30 years old or older). The student investigators, all of whom were White, and 3 of whom were men, were instructed to approach acquaintances in school, neighborhoods, or jobs after being trained and given role-playing practice. Completion of this task was unre-

---

1.   The following SSE items were omitted from these analyses: Got into an argument, wanted to tell someone off, was angry, took drastic steps, and how different life would be now.

lated to the course grade. Each respondent, identified by a number, placed responses to Parts 2 and 3 of the survey in a sealed envelope before returning it to the student investigator. Hence the sample was a nonrandom convenience sample.

Frequency of Different Kinds of Sexist Treatment

Scores on each of the questions of the SSE ranged from 1 = *never* to 6 = *almost all of the time*. Table 8.1 presents the mean scores across all of our participants on each of these 20 SSE items for sexist treatment experienced during the past year and in one's entire life. The questions are grouped by the four factors identified by Klonoff and Landrine (1995): Sexist Degradation and Its Consequences, Sexist Discrimination in Distant Relationships, Sexism in Close Relationships, and Sexist Discrimination in the Workplace. Hearing sexist jokes was clearly the most frequently reported sexist experience both during the past year and over a lifetime. Being called sexist names and being subjected to unwanted sexual advances were also frequently reported.

Gender of the Discriminator

As described above, participants were asked to indicate the gender of the people who had been responsible for sexist treatment in the different kinds of situation. The means across the entire sample are given in Table 8.2. It is clear that those behaving in an unfair/sexist manner were generally identified as men, particularly on items from the Sexist Degradation and Sexism in Close Relationships factors; however, women also were identified (although less frequently) as responsible for sexist treatment on items from the Sexist Discrimination in Distant Relationships factor.

Responses to Unfair/Sexist Treatment

Table 8.3 presents the percentage of respondents in the total sample who indicated having responded to unfair treatment in each of 10 different ways across the 15 selected SSE items. These ways of responding are presented in rank order, based on the responses of the total sample. It can be seen that, across situations, the greatest percentage of women reported having ignored sexist incidents (39.3%). The next most-frequent responses were direct confrontation, leaving the place where the incident occurred, and avoiding interaction with the unfair/sexist person.

TABLE 8.1 Mean SSE-Lifetime and SSE-Recent Scores for an
East Coast Sample

Factor	Questionnaire Item	Lifetime	Recent
Factor 1: Sexist Degradation and Its Consequences			
	13. Wanted to tell someone off	3.04	2.60
	19. Heard sexist jokes	3.67	3.03
	16. Called sexist names	2.92	2.34
	14. Angry about sexism	2.70	2.15
	11. Sexually harassed	2.88	2.19
	17. Argued over sexism	2.25	1.75
	12. Got no respect	2.36	1.90
	18. Was picked on, harmed	2.02	1.46
Factor 2: Sexist Discrimination in Distant Relationships			
	4. Sexism by people in service jobs	2.38	1.92
	6. Sexism by people in helping jobs	1.83	1.42
	5. Sexism by strangers	2.02	1.67
	7. Sexism by neighbors	1.36	1.19
	1. Sexism by teachers	2.03	1.37
Factor 3: Sexist Discrimination in the Workplace			
	9. Sexism at work	1.66	1.29
	2. Sexism by employer	2.10	1.60
	15. Took drastic steps	1.26	1.11
	3. Sexism by colleagues	2.03	1.65
Factor 3: Sexism in Close Relationships			
	8. Sexism by boyfriend, husband, partner	2.21	1.72
	10. Sexism by family	1.95	1.60
	20. How different life would be	2.60	2.00

What These Findings Suggest

The results of this study suggest that sexist discrimination is a common experience. Given the pervasiveness of patriarchal institutions, practices, and assumptions in the United States, such findings should not surprise us. Highest on the list of common lifetime and past-year experiences were sexist jokes, being called sexist names, and unwanted sexual advances.

Although our sample was from the Northeast and that of Klonoff and Landrine (1995) was from the West Coast, the findings of the two investigations are very similar. Klonoff and Landrine also reported that "the most

TABLE 8.2 Mean Scores on Whether Mostly Women (1) or Mostly Men (5) Were Responsible for Sexist Treatment on 15 Selected SSE Items

Factor	Item	Mean Score
Factor 1: Sexist Degradation and Its Consequences		
	19. Heard sexist jokes	4.28
	16. Called sexist names	4.14
	11. Sexually harassed	4.94
	12. Got no respect	4.12
	18. Was picked on, harmed	4.31
Factor 2: Sexist Discrimination in Distant Relationships		
	4. Sexism by people in service jobs	3.78
	6. Sexism by people in helping jobs	3.85
	5. Sexism by strangers	3.97
	7. Sexism by neighbors	3.90
	1. Sexism by teachers	3.84
Factor 3: Sexist Discrimination in the Workplace		
	9. Sexism at work	3.87
	2. Sexism by employer	4.11
	3. Sexism by colleagues	3.83
Factor 4: Sexism in Close Relationships		
	8. Sexism by boyfriend, husband, partner	4.84
	10. Sexism by family	3.82

common sexist event was being forced to listen to sexist jokes" (p. 445). The means from our sample suggest a greater frequency of sexist/unfair experiences than those reported by the West Coast sample of Klonoff and Landrine. We do not know, however, if these differences are statistically significant and thus cannot say if the East Coast means actually are higher than the West Coast ones. What is clear, however, is that participants from both coasts report similar patterns of experiences with sexist discrimination.

How did the women we studied tend to respond to sexist discrimination? The most commonly reported response was to ignore sexist incidents, reported by more than one third of our participants. The next most common ways of dealing with sexist behavior were confronting the person, leaving the site of the incident, avoiding interaction with the person, joking about the incident, and seeking support from other women. With the exception of confronting the person, the other common responses (leaving the site,

TABLE 8.3 Mean Percentage of Respondents Who Reported Dealing
With Sexism in Different Ways Across the 15 Selected
SSE Items

Method of Dealing With Sexism	Mean Percentage Who Used Method
Ignored incident	39.3
Confronted person	26.2
Left site of incident	22.1
Avoided interaction with sexist person	20.9
Joked about incident	18.7
Sought support from women	15.0
Avoided site of incident	9.4
Reported incident	7.3
Changed own behavior	5.4
Avoided interactions with similar persons	4.5

avoiding the person, and joking) are unlikely to reduce sexist discrimination.

There is a paucity of other studies with which we can compare our findings. Grauerholz (1989) found that the most common response reported by a sample of women professors (presumed to be mainly White) to sexual harassment by their students was doing nothing, followed by direct confrontation. Yoder and Aniakudo (1995) found that the most common response to harassment reported by a small group of African American women firefighters was direct confrontation.

Our data, together with findings from other studies, lead us to conclude that sexist experiences are likely to be common to all women across the United States, that the discriminator is most often a man, and that the most frequent response by women to such incidents is to ignore them. Even when women do choose to directly respond to incidents of sexism or discrimination, they are most likely to do so on their own, that is, to use an individual strategy. Such individual strategies are known to be the most risky for women and to be the most likely to lead to retaliation or other negative consequences.

If the experience of unfair/sexist incidents is common to women in the United States, and if the most frequent ways of responding to such incidents are likely to be ineffective in preventing future incidents and are likely to involve risks, what other options are available to women? To illustrate the types of strategies women employ and to suggest which of those strategies may be most likely to be useful, we will focus on sexual harassment.

THE SPECIAL CASE OF SEXUAL HARASSMENT

The topic of sexual harassment[2] first appeared in the mid-1970s and has been the subject of increasing attention, as evidenced by the number of empirical and theoretical papers, books, workshops, and conferences on the topic. This vast quantity of material attests to the fact that sexual harassment has come to be viewed as a phenomenon of concern to government, law, business, and education, as well as the target of active pressures for social change. It has been the subject of far greater attention than other kinds of interpersonal discrimination. At the same time, however, a clear backlash is currently apparent in efforts to trivialize sexual harassment and to ridicule or pathologize those who are concerned with it.

Illustrative of such a backlash are two articles that appeared on the very same day in our hometown newspaper, the *Providence Journal Bulletin*. The first, a very brief news item, was headlined "All work, no play" (1996), and it communicated the presumably humorous report that "Asking someone you work with for a date can be dangerous" (p. G1). Why? Because federal and state laws permit a worker to file a grievance "if there's been an unwanted advance, an offer of work-related incentives, use of obscene or unwanted references to sex, or attempted unwanted physical attention." The implication of this item, as is clear from its headline, is that someone who is troubled by such commonplace and presumably innocuous behaviors is silly or mean.

In another section of the paper was a column entitled "Feminism and the Morality Police" by a sociologist from the Johns Hopkins University Institute for Policy Studies (Kelly, 1996). She warns the reader that there has been a dangerous expansion of the meaning of sexual harassment, so that "almost any behavior can be construed" as such. She argues that there is now a "new Inquisition" and "morality police," which enables people with "hurt feelings" to unfairly charge others with sexual harassment (p. B6). Such critics seem to us to be less concerned with the acts that define harassment than with protecting "misunderstood" perpetrators. Other critics of the attention given to sexual harassment (e.g., Paglia, 1994; Roiphe, 1993) have been given considerable media space. However, they do not seriously address questions about the antecedents, correlates, or consequences of sexual harassing behavior.

---

2. We recognize that men are sometimes the targets of sexual harassment, but our focus in this paper is on the more widespread situation for women and on possible strategies to reduce the sexual harassment experienced by women in academe.

Despite the enormous significance of the issue, a discussion of the complex, far-reaching consequences of sexual harassment is not often found in either the popular or scientific literature. If only sexually harassing behaviors were indeed trivial, as claimed in the new backlash, or easily ignored and shrugged off as "that's life," as girls and women have been taught to do, we could all stop talking about it. Unfortunately, that is not the case, as indicated by social science data and the reported experiences of women from varied backgrounds and in diverse situations.

Elsewhere, one of us (Lott, 1996) has proposed, using a social learning theory analysis, that experiencing sexual harassment has serious outcomes for women. Such experiences

- reinforce beliefs about personal vulnerability
- contribute to anxiety and self-doubt
- increase women's ambivalence toward heterosexuality by increasing the ambiguity of men's sexual behaviors as expressions of sexual interest or power
- encourage women to believe that they are not "good" (i.e., virtuous) or that they are not competent if they are not skillful enough to avoid harassment (Stanko, 1985)
- increase the likelihood that women will learn ways of avoiding or escaping from sexual harassing behaviors; such strategies may seriously conflict, compete, or interfere with going to classes, enhancing work status, earning a paycheck, or engaging in positive interpersonal relationships
- serve to maintain power inequalities between women and men

As noted by Fiske and Glick (1995), like stereotypes, "harassment similarly derogates, debilitates, and disadvantages the less powerful" (p. 110).

There are also reciprocal, serious, and far-reaching consequences for the men who engage in harassing behaviors. Those who get away with it (for whom there are no negative sanctions)

- are reinforced for their behavior, increasing the likelihood of its being repeated under similar circumstances
- learn that they are powerful, increasing the likelihood that they will continue to exert power in sexual and related situations
- become confused about the distinction between what is a "normal" expression of sexual interest (i.e., what is culturally acceptable) and what is deviant or aberrant (Stanko, 1985)

Such consequences for men affect their behavior toward women and how they feel about and interact with women. Because the outcomes for both women and men have widespread and complex social significance, it is essential to focus on ways of combating and reducing sexual harassment. Although proposing legal and organizational remedies to sexual harassment has increased, there is still enormous resistance to the subject among men and women.

As one of us has suggested elsewhere (Lott, 1996), we resist talking about sexual harassment because the subject taps the hidden experiences of so many women and men, because resolutions of the problems seem so out of reach, and because the behaviors we need to examine are so ubiquitous. We do not want to believe that our professors or colleagues or boyfriends want to hurt or demean us. Men do not want to see themselves as villainous harassers or insensitive louts. We women do not want to see ourselves as victims, or as losing the little power we may have by criticizing or threatening the more powerful. We fear there will be negative outcomes from identifying and countering incidents of sexual harassment. Such outcomes may include being perceived as a poor sport or complainer, losing a relationship, or being subjected to serious economic or professional reprisals.

STRATEGIES FOR CHANGE

Sexual harassment is generally regarded as a phenomenon that is inextricably tied to the power imbalance between women and men and to the existence of sexism.

> Sexual harassment is part of living in a sexist culture . . . in which women expect to be the targets of sexual jokes and innuendo as well as the receivers of positive sexual attention. Sexual harassment is deeply enmeshed in the relationships between women and men which we have been taught are natural. (Lott, 1996, p. 231)

Thus proposed solutions need to include all efforts to enhance or ensure gender equity. Riger (1991), for example, argues that "extensive efforts at prevention need to be mounted at the individual, situational, and organizational level" (p. 503). To answer the question of what women can do, we will examine three types of responses to sexual harassment: organizational strategies; individual strategies; and informal, collective strategies.

Organizational Strategies. The strategies for dealing with sexual harassment that are most often discussed are ones that focus on top-down organizational changes instituted by well-meaning or lawsuit-avoiding employers or supervisors. These include the development of policies and grievance procedures, educational workshops, and open discussions of differences between women and men in interpretations of, and attitudes toward, harassing behavior (e.g., Comer, 1992).

The law provides remedies for individuals, who can now bring suit against people and organizations on charges of sexual harassment. Sexual harassment is legally interpreted as a subclass of sex discrimination. What federal and state regulations have done with regard to sexual harassment is, as noted by Barak (1992), to "create a sanction system" that defines such harassment as "unacceptable conduct" and in this way sends a "philosophical and psychological message" (p. 818).

The story of how the courts have dealt with such suits is a fascinating and complex one (see, for example, Fitzgerald, 1996b; Chapter 9 in this book). One result of the legal actions that have been taken is that employers and educational institutions have been either encouraged or mandated to develop policies and procedures designed to prevent (or decrease) sexual harassment and also to punish transgressors (Fitzgerald, 1996a). To accomplish the latter, a woman who has been subjected to harassment must report the incident(s) to those able to provide negative sanctions. And therein lies the problem. All who have studied the current situation agree that bringing a harasser "to justice" through formal (or informal) grievance procedures is a strategy seldom adopted by women (Bingham & Scherer, 1993; Booth-Butterfield, 1991; Riger, 1991).

A woman who does consider using formal complaints, filing charges, and using the procedures available in her organization tends to be discouraged from doing so. She is likely to be very aware of the barriers to her attaining a successful outcome. Such barriers include (a) the anticipation of the time and energy such a response will entail; (b) the strong possibility of retaliation by the more powerful man she is accusing; (c) not wanting to be perceived as a victim; and (d) not effecting change in her general workplace environment even if she succeeds in having a single harasser punished.

Individual Strategies. Another group of strategies reported in the literature are those used by individual women attempting to respond to incidents of harassment on their own. One study (Bingham & Scherer, 1993) that surveyed faculty and staff at a midwestern university found, for example, that the most frequent personal response to sexual harassment was talking to the harasser. This response (if not in the form of an "aggressive" communication) was associated with the greatest satisfaction regarding outcome, and with greater satisfaction than talking with family or friends. Another finding from this study was that lower levels of satisfaction with situation outcome were associated with work climates that were perceived as "harassment-prone" or harassment encouraging.

Yount (1991) conducted a more anthropological study by spending over 5 months observing and examining, through interviews and group discussion, the strategies a sample of women coal miners had developed to manage sexual harassment on the job. Coal mines are settings in which interactions have typically been "highly sexual and jocular" (p. 399) and in which the presence of women workers was not welcomed. In addition, coal mines are settings where "stereotyped conceptions . . . were used by antagonistic bosses and workers to justify discrimination in training and assignment opportunities offered to women on the grounds that female workers were impediments to production, safety, and morale" (p. 401). In such a setting, women miners found sexual harassment to be a commonplace experience. Yount identified and categorized three dominant strategies that the women workers appeared to have developed: that of the "lady," the "flirt," and the "tomboy."

The ladies, by and large, were the older women workers. They tended to disengage from the men, to keep their distance, to avoid using profanity or engaging in any behavior that might be interpreted as suggestive, and to emphasize by their appearance and manners that they were ladies. The consequences for them were twofold: They were the targets of the least amount of come-ons, teasing, and sexual harassment, but they also accepted the least prestigious and remunerative jobs.

The flirts tended to be the younger single women. As a defensive measure, they feigned flattery when they were the targets of the men's sexual razzing. The consequences to them were significant. They became perceived as the "embodiment of the female stereotype, . . . as particularly lacking in potential and were given the fewest opportunities to develop job skills and to establish social and self-identities as miners" (p. 410).

The tomboys behaved differently. Also single but generally older than the flirts, they attempted to separate themselves from the female stereotype. They tended to focus on their status as coal miners and tried to develop a "thick skin." They responded to harassment with humor, comebacks, sexual talk of their own, or reciprocation. A major problem with their strategies is that the tomboys tended to be considered sluts or sexually promiscuous and as women who violated the sexual double standard. They were thus subjected by some men to intensified and escalated harassment. It is not clear whether the tomboy strategy was associated with better or worse job assignments and opportunities.

The results of this intensive study of women coal miners seem to us to be clearly applicable to other work settings—to factories, offices, and universities. What the findings suggest is that individual strategies are not likely to be effective. In addition, individual strategies may have unanticipated negative consequences for the workplace and may even lead to increased sexual harassment. Women who try to deal with sexual harassment on their own, regardless of what they do, seem to be in a no-win situation.

Informal, Collective Strategies. Strategies that are rarely mentioned are collective grassroots efforts. Such efforts mobilize women to work together to change the social climate of their immediate environments. We must work for widespread social and organizational changes in the direction of gender equity but, at the same time, we need to develop for ourselves collective strategies matched to our particular situations. Such collective strategies can effectively reduce the sexual harassment we experience in the everyday world at our places of work, training, and education. This type of approach was adopted by a group of women graduate students and faculty in a department of psychology, at a public university in the Northeast.

WOMEN AGAINST SEXUAL HARASSMENT (WASH): A CASE STUDY

Like other colleges and universities that receive federal dollars for any purpose, our university has a sexual harassment policy (Affirmative Action Office, 1988) that prohibits sexual harassment as a form of sex discrimination. Following the guidelines of the Equal Employment Opportunity Commission (EEOC), sexual harassment is defined in our university's policy as

> unwelcome sexual advances, requests for sexual favors, and other verbal or physical conduct of a sexual nature . . . when (1) submission to such conduct is made either explicitly or implicitly a . . . condition of instruction, employment, or otherwise full participation in University life; (2) submission or rejection . . . is used as a basis for evaluation

. . . ; or (3) such conduct has the purpose or effect of unreasonably interfering with an individual's performance or creating an intimidating, hostile, or offensive University environment.

The university promises to take "prompt action to investigate and redress sexual harassment" and prohibits retaliation against people who bring such complaints.

With respect to the steps to be taken by an individual wishing such "prompt action," our university, like others, is required to prepare and publish a set of procedures. Although the policy quoted above has remained the same since 1988, the complaint process has undergone revision. The current set of procedures is now generic. In other words, the rules apply to complaints of "discrimination/harassment on the basis of race, sex, religion, age, color, creed, national origin, disability and sexual orientation" (Affirmative Action Office, 1994), and the document describing the procedures consists of eight single-spaced pages.

In a pamphlet produced for campus distribution (*Sexual Harassment,* 1994), the final section is entitled "What Can You Do About Sexual Harassment?" This section advises the reader that the university has a pool of advocates "to offer support and provide information." In addition, those who believe they have been sexually harassed "are encouraged to contact an advocate." How to make such contact is not specified, but a list of relevant campus offices is provided. Clearly, the obstacles to effecting prompt action, to changing the behavior of individual harassers or the social climate of a particular workplace or educational environment, seem formidable.

The Formation of WASH

In the fall of 1991, allegations of sexual harassment against Judge Clarence Thomas were made public by Professor Anita Hill during the nationally televised Senate Judiciary Committee Hearings on his nomination to the U.S. Supreme Court. Although Judge Thomas was ultimately appointed to the Supreme Court, Professor Hill's testimony had an enormous impact on public awareness and concern about sexual harassment. Professor Hill's treatment by the Senate Committee and the media also made salient the powerful backlash that commonly occurs against any woman who publicly challenges her harasser. Efforts were made to denigrate Hill as a liar, as pathological, and as fantasizing about Thomas's attraction to her. The impact of the Thomas confirmation hearings could be observed within the Department of Psychology at our university. Class-room discussions were devoted to the topic, and students became more vocal about their own experiences with sexual harassment.

Two feminist women professors (both White) recognized that many students and faculty wanted to speak and act, and the two believed strongly in the potential power and necessity of collective action. Therefore, they posted signs around the psychology department that announced a meeting open to all "women faculty, graduate students, and staff interested in sexual harassment." The initial meeting (and subsequent meetings) took place at the University Women's Center, and the meeting time and place were printed in the psychology department newsletter as well as in signs in department corridors. This practice of open announcement of meetings was maintained for all meetings that followed.

WASH's Group Process

At the first meeting, we established important ground rules that were repeated at the beginning of each subsequent meeting. These rules were:

1. No one could disclose the identity of attendees to people who were not present at meetings (although each woman was free to disclose her own attendance).
2. No one could disclose the exact number of attendees or the graduate programs from which they came.
3. No one could repeat anything discussed at a meeting, even to women who had attended previous meetings.
4. If asked about a meeting, one should say that the meeting had been "well-attended and numerous incidents of sexual harassment were discussed" but should not provide any other information.

Our efforts to protect the identity of WASH members who did not wish to be identified reduced the fear of graduate students and faculty members that by speaking and acting openly in response to departmental incidents of sexual harassment, they might antagonize other students or faculty and thus potentially jeopardize their careers. The desire to avoid open disclosure reflects realistic awareness and fear of possible retaliation, as well as the damage done to self-confidence by personal experiences or observations of harassment. The confidentiality of our meetings and our focus on collective action worked together to emphasize that sexual harassment was a common experience for women and to reduce or eliminate risks to individuals. We believe that individual action is difficult to take, entails risks, and is often ineffective.

During the first meeting, in addition to establishing basic rules, we also articulated the general goals of the group and agreed upon our group name Women Against Sexual Harassment. WASH was to provide a safe and sympathetic forum in which to both discuss incidents of harassment and to plan collective preventive, educational, and direct action strategies. We wanted to focus particularly on changing the normative culture within our department, on changing the social, teaching, mentoring, and supervising environment. We shared the conviction that only by organizing and working together could we effect social change. We also agreed that all actions taken by the group would be legal, socially responsible, and respectful of the rights of others.

The number of student and faculty attendees at WASH meetings varied considerably across meetings. All attendees were White, reflecting the ethnic composition of the department at the time. Some members attended consistently, whereas others attended only one or two meetings, or attended sporadically. Attendance was never taken, either formally or informally, and the group remained open in both practice and spirit. Occasionally, openly identified WASH members were asked whether undergraduates or women from other departments could attend, and these decisions were made by consensus of the group on a case-by-case basis. In an effort to protect the confidentiality and boundaries of the group, it was generally limited to graduate students, faculty, and staff of the Department of Psychology.

Behaviors Discussed and Targeted by WASH

The incidents of harassment discussed were varied and covered a wide range of behaviors. With respect to clinical supervision, issues discussed by WASH members included: inappropriate personal disclosures by supervisors about sexual matters; asking supervisees for personal information not directly related to a client or issue being discussed; encouraging and enforcing sexist views of clients and their difficulties; encouragement by supervisors of flirtatious behavior with clients; making sexually suggestive or flirtatious remarks to the supervisee; and interpretation by supervisors of feminist viewpoints as indicative of "repression" or of being "uptight" or "conservative."

Research-related issues included professors asking undergraduate students in their classes for personal information under the guise of research without prior informed consent. Issues that were related to teaching included: the selection of course materials that presented a consistently negative view of women; the use of primarily women in examples of client "pathology"; sexually inappropriate or demeaning class examples and "jokes"; focus on a student's physical appearance or personal life in class; and the attribution of a student's or teaching assistant's complaints about any of the above as due to their pathology, discomfort with sexual material, or religious upbringing.

In addition, we discussed a variety of comments that were made "casually" as "jokes" or comments in the hallway, such as greeting women students with "hey baby" or full body hugs and frequent comments about a student's physical appearance. We also discussed incidents where professors spoke "out of concern" to other colleagues about particular students with openly feminist views who "seemed to have problems with men." A terrifying incident in which one of our members returned to her office and found that an unknown man had left semen on her desk was also the subject of considerable attention and discussion.

Strategies Used by WASH
at the Department Level

Our first group action was to publish a notice in the department newsletter stating that "the first meeting of Women Against Sexual Harassment (WASH) was well attended, and numerous incidents of sexual harassment were discussed." We announced the time and place of the next meeting and encouraged "all interested women faculty, graduate students, and staff" to attend. We specifically wanted to alert department members that sexual harassment within the department was being observed, discussed, and taken seriously.

Another early action was putting copies of the university's sexual harassment policy and procedures and related materials in student and faculty mailboxes and on a table in our department mailroom. In addition, we created a large "This Is Sexual Harassment" poster, shown in Figure 8.1, based on actual incidents that had occurred within our department. The approximately five-by-two-foot poster defined harassment by use of examples, and each item was printed in large black letters. The poster was pinned to our mailroom bulletin board and remained undisturbed for a year. When it was defaced and ripped by people unknown, we replaced it with a smaller version, which attracted a small piece of rude graffiti but, otherwise

THIS IS SEXUAL HARASSMENT

Asking questions about a student's, supervisee's, or employee's personal sex life

Refusing to stop sexual remarks when asked

Overusing sexualized content in teaching, such as frequent sexual examples to illustrate more general points in class

Making personal sexual comments to students, supervisees, advisees, or employees

Unwanted touching of students, supervisees, advisees, or employees

Making comments about a student's, supervisee's, advisee's, or employee's body parts

Using patronizing language or making hostile or derogatory comments about women

Using primarily women to exemplify negative constructs, including mental illness

Making sexual jokes that contribute to a hostile work/school environment for women

Characterizing women who object to sexual harassment as sexually repressed or conservative

Although men can also be victims of sexual harassment,
women are the primary targets.

Prepared and posted by
Women Against Sexual Harassment (WASH)
For more information, contact Bernice Lott (401) 792-4248, Fall 1991

Figure 8.1. Poster Developed and Displayed by Women Against Sexual Harassment (WASH)

remained undisturbed in the department mail room until a recent shift in the placement of mailboxes.

A small committee from WASH met with the department chair and requested that a sexual harassment workshop be conducted for faculty and graduate students (separately). The chair presented the proposal to the department faculty, who approved it, and two workshops were conducted by a university staff member who had never been asked to conduct such a workshop before (although it was part of her job description). The faculty workshop was well-attended, largely as a result of clear support from the chair of the department, who made a "strong recommendation" that faculty attend and who scheduled the workshop during a regular faculty meeting time. The graduate student workshop was less well attended. The suggestion that students with graduate assistantships be required to attend a sexual harassment workshop was supported by the department chair but never implemented.

Strategies at the Individual Level

One professor agreed to meet with a small group of past and present graduate student teaching assistants to discuss complaints about women-demeaning examples and comments in an undergraduate class that he taught. Prior to this meeting, the larger WASH group helped the teaching assistants develop an agenda and rehearse a respectful and reasoned presentation to the professor.

One graduate student who wished to speak privately with a professor about his behavior in interactions with her received support and advice from WASH. Several members offered to wait near the professor's office while she met with him and to knock on his door at an agreed-upon time to assist her in keeping the meeting from being prolonged. This plan was developed during a WASH meeting, and the student was supported in her decision to act individually.

Similarly, another student was supported in her desire to file a formal complaint against a professor for making remarks so demeaning to women that the student felt she could not continue taking the course. She wrote a letter of complaint to the professor and also filed a formal complaint that led to a hearing in the Affirmative Action office. Resolution of the issue was informal, and guilt was not established, nor was any corrective action taken. This incident is an example of the problematic nature of formal procedures for dealing with sexual harassment.

As a final example of individual strategies, a small group of WASH members met with a professor about his use of a textbook that the students felt was extremely sexist. As a result, the professor raised the question of the book's sexism in his graduate class and was convinced by the ensuing discussion not to use that book in subsequent semesters.

Strategies at the University Level

A letter was sent to the campus police department by WASH to communicate concerns regarding women's safety on campus. Soon after, several WASH members met with the new campus security director and, following that meeting, new policies were issued for improved lighting on campus and the publication of incidents of violence in the student newspaper.

A letter was also sent by WASH to the university president regarding a decision to disband the Affirmative Action Sexual Harassment Subcommittee. We expressed our concern that revised sexual harassment policies and procedures had not been communicated to the campus community. Unfortunately, we were not successful in our request that the Sexual Harassment Subcommittee be continued. Our concerns about policies and procedures were simply forwarded by the president to the Affirmative Action Officer without any direct response from him to us.

Strategies at the Community Level

Several members gave a presentation about WASH at a local psychiatric hospital. The meeting was attended by a number of women staff at the hospital, and the focus was on strategies they could develop and implement in their workplace. In addition, a workshop was conducted at a national conference of the Association for Women in Psychology on ways of eliminating sexual harassment within the academic community (Gregory, Minugh, Riedford, Rocchio, & Saris, 1993). The workshop presented WASH as a case study, emphasizing actions that were taken by members, problems that were encountered, and changes that were effected. Information about WASH has also been shared with wider audiences in a presentation to the higher education conference of the National Education Association in 1994 and in two published chapters (Lott, 1996; Lott & Rocchio, in press).

Responses to WASH

From the beginning, we heard "grumbling" within the department that came from a variety of sources. Some students and faculty were overheard in conversations deriding the objectives of WASH and talking about the "witch hunt" that was going on against men within the department. Graduate students were sometimes asked, "You're not one of them, are you?" Some men professors complained openly that the department "wasn't what it used to be" and that they had to be "so careful with what they said these days since so much could be misinterpreted." At a graduate student meeting, a male student asked the second author of this chapter (who was open about her membership in WASH) why men couldn't attend. He continued to push the issue and complained that WASH had "divided the department in two." In addition, the posted announcements of our meetings were occasionally torn down, or rude graffiti was written on them.

In general, however, these negative incidents and grumblings were few in number and did not appear to be representative of the feelings of the department. There was, however, one major incident that resulted from a single breach of confidentiality within our group. A woman who attended one meeting reported to a male graduate student whom she was dating information, that she claimed had been discussed, about his behavior. This graduate student wrote a lengthy letter of complaint against WASH and specifically against two of its members. He circulated this letter to the entire department faculty, the college dean, and an attorney. The matter was ultimately resolved satisfactorily at a meeting between the two named WASH members, the woman who breached WASH's confidentiality, the male graduate student, their respective advocates, the department chair, the clinical training director, and a third agreed-upon "impartial" faculty member who moderated the meeting. It is highly significant that we were able to use this meeting as an opportunity to address concerns raised by all parties, not just those raised by the male graduate student. In addition, we successfully affirmed WASH's right to maintain the confidentiality of its membership and discussions and refused to engage in any discussion that would jeopardize the confidentiality of our group.

Positive Impact of WASH on Individual Members

We recently asked five former student members of WASH to briefly tell us how their experience with WASH had changed or affected them, both at the time of their involvement and subsequently. We were particularly interested in how WASH had prepared them to deal with sexist experiences in academia and other work settings. Their complete verbatim responses can be found in Lott and Rocchio (in press). Here we can only summarize and provide a few examples of what they told us.

All said that their experience in WASH has made them more sensitive to incidents of harassment and less likely to confuse it with flattery (as noted by one of the respondents), stronger, less fearful of taking action, and more willing to discuss issues of harassment with their own students and colleagues. In the words of one respondent,

> We became a presence in the department. People took notice of "us."
> . . . The most valuable thing I've learned is that women must continue to support each other and challenge sexism. Individually, it's hard to take action. Collectively, it's hard to be ignored.

Another respondent talked about her "increased willingness to work for broader social change." A third wrote, "a veil of naiveté was lifted, never to fall again. WASH enabled me to label 'difficult' or 'uncomfortable' situations as sexual harassment and provided me with skills with which to handle such incidents." From another former WASH member came the following report: "As a junior faculty person . . . I am much more likely to 'speak up' when someone makes an inappropriate remark. . . . I am no longer afraid." Finally, another wrote, "The two most important lessons I learned . . . were the importance of labeling even subtle harassment as sexual harassment and the power of collective action."

Overall Accomplishments

We believe that WASH was effective in raising the level of awareness of sexual harassment within our department and in raising the consciousness of individual faculty members on such issues. We also educated ourselves and others in our community by discussing our objectives, actions, and strategies. During the course of an American Psychological Association (APA) site visit of the clinical program at our University, some faculty and students spoke openly about WASH and its activities. In the written site review, our APA visitors specifically mentioned WASH as a source of positive contributions to the department.

In our view, the general atmosphere of our department was significantly and constructively altered by the existence and activities of WASH. The overall incidence of sexual harassment appears to have decreased significantly, and the most overt examples of sexual harassment seem to have been eliminated. WASH's success can be measured in part by the fact that students no longer feel a need for it to exist. The group was active from the fall of 1991 to the spring of 1994, by which time there appeared to be no further need for the group. We will have to wait to see how long the "immunization" effect of WASH will last.

CONCLUSIONS AND RECOMMENDATIONS

Our review of women's responses to sexist discrimination lead us to the following conclusions. Most women across the United States continue to experience a significant number of sexist incidents across a wide variety of different situations. Highest in frequency are the hearing of sexist jokes and being subjected to unwanted sexual advances. Sexist acts are primarily performed by men with whom women interact in both close and distant relationships, and they do not seem to be reliably related to a woman's particular background or social category. These conclusions, as noted by Klonoff and Landrine (1995), are "perhaps consistent with what feminists might expect, that is, that the privilege associated with higher social class or education does not exempt women from their status as women in a patriarchal society" (p. 466).

The most common response of women to sexist behavior appears to be to ignore it. Women report frequently doing nothing, trying to avoid the situation or the sexist person, or making light of the incident. When women do choose to take action, they employ individual strategies that involve direct confrontation or discussion with the discriminator by themselves. Although Bingham and Scherer (1993) reported that women found this individual strategy to be the most satisfying, this strategy is the most risky where retaliation is concerned.

There are alternatives. In this chapter, we presented a case study of the formation and work of a group of women graduate students and faculty to illustrate the efficacy of informal, collective strategies for change. This group was formed to deal specifically with sexual harassment but clearly addressed sexism (e.g., in textbooks) more generally. Thus we believe that the collective strategies employed are broadly applicable to and are potentially useful for combating sexist discrimination in educational or work environments.

Some of the factors that we believe were crucial to WASH's success, and should be considered in the formation and work of any group of this type, are:

- Adherence to strict confidentiality regarding who attends meetings and what is discussed
- The use of strategies that are legal, ethical, and respectful of all people involved
- Respect for the right of each woman to decide how to respond (or not to respond) to her situation

Women forming groups for collective action will have to consider the specific features of their own educational or work environments, the probability of negative reactions, and so on. In some settings, it may not be wise to mix supervisory levels. For example, WASH was open to both graduate students and faculty, but not to undergraduate students. The presence of at least two strong feminist faculty women (who were tenured) contributed to WASH's success. In other settings, however, there may not be supportive women at the supervisory level, and group members may feel "safer" if all attendees are peers.

We have found that informal collective strategies can effect change. The specific strategies and the targeted goals will vary from setting to setting, but they are alternatives to "doing nothing" and to individual solutions that have low probabilities of success.

PART III

The Law and Sexist Discrimination

NINE

Legal Approaches
to Sex Discrimination

Lynne A. Wurzburg
Robert H. Klonoff

INTRODUCTION

In recent years, the topic of sex discrimination has become a major focus of public attention. This growing interest can be traced in large part to the October 1991 Senate confirmation hearings of then-Supreme Court Justice-nominee Clarence Thomas. The nominee had been accused of sexually harassing Anita Hill, a lawyer who had worked for him at the Department of Education and later at the Equal Employment Opportunity Commission (EEOC), the agency charged with enforcing antidiscrimination laws.[1]

The Thomas hearings resulted in public debate, not only over the credibility of Justice Thomas and Ms. Hill, but also over the nature of sexual harassment and the legal boundaries between acceptable and unacceptable behavior in the workplace. Increased public awareness of these

---

1. For readers with access to law materials, legal citations are included throughout this chapter. For collected essays and articles on the Clarence Thomas confirmation hearings, see "Gender, Race," 1992.

issues has resulted in a substantial increase in the number of sexual harassment claims. The year after the Thomas hearings, sexual harassment charges filed with the EEOC increased by 53%, the largest increase in the agency's history (Rubin, 1995). In the 5 years from 1991 to 1996, sexual harassment complaints filed with the EEOC more than doubled (Neuborne, 1996).

The impact of this heightened awareness can be seen in the 1991 Civil Rights Act, which for the first time made the Congress subject to antidiscrimination (and antiharassment) regulations. More recently, in 1995, when several former staff members of Senator Bob Packwood accused him of sexual harassment, the charges were extensively investigated,[2] and Senator Packwood ultimately resigned from office.

In addition to including Congress within its reach, the 1991 Civil Rights Act also authorized punitive damage awards against harassers, and employers who tolerate harassment. This means that juries can now award damages in excess of what is necessary to compensate the plaintiff in order to punish the defendant and to discourage similar behavior. Since punitive damages have become available, jury awards have escalated dramatically. A particularly notable verdict of $7.1 million (applying California state law) was awarded against the second-largest law firm in the world—Baker & McKenzie—for ignoring the complaints of a secretary who had been employed by the law firm less than 2 months.[3] Although the judge in the case subsequently reduced the award by half, the verdict nonetheless underscores the seriousness with which juries approach the issue of sexual harassment.

While awareness of sexual harassment has increased, so has confusion over its legal implications. Most people understand why the secretary at Baker & McKenzie was offended when her boss touched her breast, put M&M candies in the pocket of her blouse, then pulled her arms back and said, "let's see which [breast] is bigger" (Boennighausen, 1994, p. 76). However, many people remain confused over how courts and juries analyze those acts. Could the secretary have sued if the harasser were not her boss? Could she have won if he had not touched her? Is every offensive act grounds for a lawsuit? This chapter will address these questions by explain-

---

2. In the course of the investigation of Senator Packwood's behavior, the Senate Ethics Committee took testimony from hundreds of witnesses, reviewed thousands of pages of documents, and listened to several hundred audiotapes of Packwood's diaries (Kelly, 1995).
3. Weeks v. Baker & McKenzie (1994), filed less than 2 months after the Thomas confirmation hearings, was heard under California's fair employment practice statute, which allows larger punitive damage awards than does the 1991 Civil Rights Act. See Hartstein (1995).

ing the circumstances and the behaviors to which sex discrimination laws apply. In the process, this chapter will explore how the public understanding of discrimination continues to shape and be shaped by those laws.

FEDERAL LEGISLATION[4]

The first federal statute designed to remedy sex discrimination was the Equal Pay Act of 1963, which prohibits employers from paying men and women differently for performing the same work. Proof of discrimination under the Equal Pay Act focuses on whether the plaintiff (i.e., the person initiating the lawsuit) and her male comparables really are doing the same jobs and, if so, whether there is a legitimate explanation for the difference in pay. This legislation, limited to the issue of pay equality for men and women performing the same job, was soon eclipsed by the 1964 Civil Rights Act.[5]

Unlike the Equal Pay Act, the 1964 Civil Rights Act—as originally drafted—was directed not at sex discrimination, but at racial, ethnic, and religious discrimination. The prohibition of sex discrimination in employment emerged in an amendment designed to kill the legislation. Despite the controversial addition, the bill passed overwhelmingly.[6]

---

4. Sex discrimination in employment is addressed in federal statutes, their state and local counterparts, and the judicial decisions that interpret those laws. In the interest of brevity, this chapter focuses on federal rather than state law. It should be noted that state and local laws usually mirror their federal counterparts, with modifications that give the laws broader application. For example, the main federal antidiscrimination law, Title VII of the Civil Rights Act of 1964, applies only to employers with 25 or more employees (§2000e[b]). But the antidiscrimination statute for the District of Columbia, the D.C. Human Rights Act, applies to all employers regardless of size (D.C. Code Ann. §1-2502[10]).

5. The Civil Rights Act of 1964 prohibits discrimination in public accommodations, public facilities, public education, federally assisted programs, employment, and voting. The seventh section of the law, referred to as Title VII, concerns discrimination in employment (§2000e et seq.).

6. An amendment to Title VII prohibiting sex discrimination was proposed by Representative Smith of Virginia and backed by Southern Democrats. They argued that the amendment was necessary to keep White women from being pushed out of all employment opportunities by the protections that the legislation afforded Blacks. Representatives who opposed the amendment pointed out that many of its supporters had vigorously opposed the passage of the Equal Pay Act less than a year earlier. Representatives who had fought to pass the Equal Pay Act opposed the amendment that would afford equal employment opportunities to women, believing that the amendment jeopardized the bill's passage. The amendment was adopted over their opposition, but the larger plan backfired. The complete legislation, with its killer amendment, passed in the Senate by a vote of 76 to 18 after 83 days of debate. See *Legislative History of Titles VII and XI of Civil Rights Act of 1964*, U.S. Equal Employment Opportunity Rights Commission at 11, 3213-3232.

Far broader in scope than the Equal Pay Act, Title VII of the Civil Rights Act prohibits employers from basing any employment decisions on an employee's sex.[7] Under Title VII, an employer must refrain not only from discriminating against women in pay but also in decisions about hiring, firing, promotion, and any other area that might be considered a term or condition of work. There are several exceptions to the statute's application, the most interesting for purposes of sex discrimination being the *bona fide occupational qualification* (BFOQ) exception. The BFOQ exception allows employers to hire employees on the basis of sex where that trait is a "bona fide occupational qualification reasonably necessary to the normal operation of that particular business or enterprise." For example, because the normal operation of a movie studio requires character portrayals to be credible, hiring women to portray female characters and men to portray male characters is lawful (EEOC Guidelines, 1990). The application of this exception is discussed more fully in the next section.

The 1964 Civil Rights Act also established the EEOC, the agency charged with enforcing Title VII. No claim of discrimination under Title VII can be brought in court until the EEOC has had an opportunity to investigate the charge. The agency receives complaints of discrimination, investigates the complaints, and determines whether there is cause to believe that discrimination occurred. Where the agency finds such cause, it can sue on behalf of the charging party in federal court. Because the EEOC can litigate only a limited number of cases each year, however, it cannot sue, as a practical matter, on behalf of all parties for whom it finds cause to believe discrimination occurred. When the agency declines to sue on behalf of such a party, or when the agency finds no cause to believe that the charging party was discriminated against, the charging party can still hire her or his own lawyer and file suit in federal court.

In 1978, Congress amended Title VII so that the definition of sex discrimination now includes discrimination on the basis of pregnancy, childbirth, or related medical conditions.[8] Women experiencing any of

---

7. Title VII states, in relevant part, that it is,
   an unlawful employment practice for an employer . . . to fail or refuse to hire or to discharge any individual, or otherwise to discriminate against any individual with respect to his compensation, terms, conditions, or privileges of employment, because of such individual's . . . sex. (Civil Rights Act of 1964, §2000e-2[a])
8. The Pregnancy Discrimination Act of 1978 amended Title VII. The amendment responded to a 1976 Supreme Court decision (*General Electric Co. v. Gilbert*), holding that pregnancy was not equated with gender and therefore an employer did not discriminate on the basis of gender when it provided employees with disability benefits for all nonoccupational disabilities except those arising from pregnancy.

those conditions must be treated as people suffering from comparably disabling conditions. In other words, the law requires that an employer treat a woman disabled by pregnancy or childbirth as generously as he or she would treat a man disabled by a heart attack. To the extent that the employer makes medical insurance and disability leave available to one, the employer must make it available to the other.

In 1991, Title VII was further amended to make jury trials available and to expand the types of damages for which plaintiffs can sue.[9] Before 1991, successful plaintiffs suing under Title VII could only recover back pay for up to 2 years before they filed their charge, and that amount would be reduced by whatever money they earned or could have earned with reasonable diligence in that time. Successful plaintiffs also might have been awarded litigation costs and attorney's fees, at the court's discretion. Since the 1991 amendment, plaintiffs who prove a claim of intentional discrimination may receive a monetary award to compensate them for emotional pain, suffering, inconvenience, mental anguish, loss of enjoyment of life, and other nonfinancial losses, as well as for future financial losses and back pay. If plaintiffs suing under Title VII further prove that their employer engaged in discrimination with malice or with reckless indifference to their rights, they may also recover punitive damages. The total amounts of compensatory and punitive damages recoverable are capped by the statute at a maximum of $300,000 per plaintiff, with smaller caps established for smaller employers.[10]

It should be noted that federal legislation is not the only protection for victims of sex discrimination; state court decisions have created common law rights and remedies for many of the consequences of discrimination. Plaintiffs can sue in state court, where appropriate, for infliction of

---

9. Courts offer plaintiffs two types of remedies: ordering the defendant to do something or to refrain from doing something and requiring the defendant to pay money to the plaintiff. The first type of remedy is referred to as *injunctive relief,* as the order to do or not to do something is called an *injunction.* An order to reinstate the plaintiff in her previous job would be injunctive relief. The second type of remedy is referred to as *damages* or *monetary damages.* An order to pay a plaintiff wages that she lost because the employer unlawfully fired her would be an order of damages. *Back pay* is a payment equal to the wages that the plaintiff would have received if the employer had not taken an action to the plaintiff's detriment, for example, fired her or passed her over for a promotion.
10. Note that the $300,000 cap applies only to cases brought under the federal antidiscrimination law, Title VII, as amended by the 1991 Civil Rights Act. Awards in cases brought under state laws are not subject to the same limitation. Thus, the $7.2 million verdict in the *Baker & McKenzie* case was made possible by the fact that the case was brought under California's antidiscrimination statute (California Government Code § 12920 *et seq.*), which contains no limit on punitive damages.

emotional distress, interference with employment contracts, and wrongful discharge in violation of public policy. Such cases based in state common law (that is, law derived from court decisions rather than from legislation) avoid the statutory caps on damages imposed by the 1991 amendment to Title VII and the requirement that the employee first file her claim with EEOC.

THE COURTS' INTERPRETATIONS:
WHAT DOES IT MEAN "TO DISCRIMINATE"?

The word *discriminate* is often equated with hate, disdain, and assumptions about the inherent superiority of one group over another. And discrimination against women in the workplace has often been based on misogyny and on preconceived ideas about women's strength, intelligence, and abilities.[11] But must an employer be motivated by a negative view of women in order to discriminate? Do only misogynists discriminate against women? The answer from the courts is a resounding no.

Courts recognize two basic categories of employment discrimination. Discrimination of the first type involves an employer's intentional choice to treat women less favorably than men. This intentional type of discrimination is called *disparate treatment.* As the U.S. Supreme Court has noted (in *Teamsters v. United States,* 1977), it is "the most obvious evil Congress had in mind when it enacted Title VII" (pp. 335-336, n. 15). Discrimination of the second type—known as *disparate impact*—occurs when an employer, without any intention of disfavoring women, maintains policies and practices that fall more harshly on women than on men. This type of discrimination can be understood as the unintended consequences of a policy that appears to be sex-neutral on its face. Examples of each type of discrimination follow.

Examples of Disparate Treatment

When Title VII was enacted, airlines generally limited flight attendant positions to single women. This policy discriminated in hiring against all men and against married women. When a male applicant challenged the legality of such a policy at Pan Am, the airline asserted that the policy was

---

11.   See Posner (1989) for a brief survey of the main motivations, economically rational and otherwise, that can underlie sex discrimination.

justified by the fact that most women are better than most men at soothing passengers in flight and by the fact that customers preferred female flight attendants. A federal appeals court (*Diaz v. Pan American World Airways,* 1971) rejected both rationales, holding that Pan Am could not exclude *all* males just because *most* males might not perform the job adequately. Furthermore, the court held that customers' expectations and preferences could not justify sex discrimination, noting that "indeed, it was to a large extent, these very prejudices the Act was meant to overcome" (p. 389).

Similarly, a female flight attendant at United Air Lines challenged the no-marriage rule when she was fired after she married. At that time, United employed male flight attendants and did not require them to remain single. A federal appeals court (*Sprogis v. United Air Lines,* 1971) held that it was "clear that United had contravened [Title VII] by applying one standard for men and one for women" (p. 1198).

It is rare now to see such a transparent case of disparate treatment. Few employers maintain separate policies for men and women. Therefore, proving that an employer intended to treat men and women differently typically requires showing that the employer applied the same policy in a different manner to men and to women.

The case of Linda Stukey (*Stukey v. United States Air Force,* 1992), an applicant for a teaching position at the Air Force Institute of Technology (AFIT), is illustrative. Ms. Stukey claimed that the Air Force refused to select her for one of two open teaching positions because she was a woman. Ms. Stukey had no "direct evidence" (as opposed to circumstantial evidence) to prove her claim, such as an admission by school officials that they imposed higher standards on women.[12] She had to show that, in fact, AFIT imposed different hiring standards on female applicants and therefore the reasons AFIT gave for denying her the job should not be believed.

Ms. Stukey showed that the school unfairly suppressed female applicants' scores for teaching experience, veterans' preference points, and mock teaching sessions. Furthermore, before and during her interview, members of the selection committee asked Ms. Stukey improper questions about her divorce, her child care arrangements, and her ability to work and travel with men. No such questions were directed at male applicants. The trial court concluded that AFIT faculty members simply did not want

---

12. "Direct evidence" of discrimination demonstrates the employer's bias, usually through the employer's own words or policies. As courts have observed, "Direct evidence of intentional discrimination is hard to come by" (*Ang v. Proctor & Gamble Co.,* 1991).

female colleagues and that the reasons AFIT had given for not hiring Ms. Stukey were not true but were a pretext for sex discrimination.

A more subtle form of disparate treatment arises when an employer disfavors women who do not meet the employer's vision of how women should look and behave. In one widely publicized case that was ultimately heard by the U.S. Supreme Court (*Price Waterhouse v. Hopkins,* 1989), a female accountant at Price Waterhouse demonstrated that she was not advanced to partnership because of "sex stereotyping." Partners at Price Waterhouse stated in the accountant's evaluations that she was "macho" and that she "overcompensated for being a woman." She was counseled that she would improve her chances of making partner if she walked, talked, and dressed more femininely, and she was even advised to wear makeup and style her hair. The Supreme Court took these comments as "clear signs . . . that some of the partners reacted negatively to the accountant's personality because she was a woman." The Court reasoned that

> we are beyond the day when an employer could evaluate employees by assuming or insisting that they matched the stereotype associated with their group. . . . (p. 235)

> An employer who objects to aggressiveness in women but whose positions require this trait places women in an intolerable and impermissible catch 22: out of a job if they behave aggressively and out of a job if they do not. Title VII lifts women out of this bind. (p. 251)

It should be noted that employers can impose some sex stereotypes on their employees, if they do so even-handedly. For example, in the 1970s, men challenged dress codes that allowed women to wear their hair at any length while requiring men to wear short hair. Despite the EEOC's opposition to these grooming codes, the courts held that slight differences in appearance requirements for male and female employees did not offend Title VII if the requirements were part of a reasonable personal grooming code applied to male and female employees.[13] The *Price Waterhouse v. Hopkins* (1989) case is unlike the grooming cases, however, in that the company did not suggest that the accountant violated any grooming code. Rather, the partners resorted to criticizing the accountant's appearance as a reflection of her aggressive personality.

---

13. See, for example *Willingham v. Macon Telegraph Publishing Co.,* 1973: "Hair length is not immutable and . . . enjoys no constitutional protection."

The *Price Waterhouse v. Hopkins* (1989) decision implicitly invited the courts to reexamine gender roles and to rethink the question of what it means "to discriminate because of sex." Because the Supreme Court recognized that "masculine" qualities, such as aggressiveness, can distinguish one woman from another, some commentators have argued that the law's focus on biological sex is inappropriate and that the law should focus instead on discrimination based on masculinity or femininity.[14] Although no court has adopted such a reformulation of the law, courts have recognized that the rights protected by Title VII do not always fit neatly into a "male versus female" model.[15]

An Exception to the Prohibition on Disparate Treatment: Examples of Sex as a Bona Fide Occupational Qualification

The law allows that in some rare circumstances, a job applicant's sex can be a legitimate reason not to hire someone, that is, belonging to the required sex is a BFOQ. Diane Rawlinson's experience as an applicant with the Alabama prison system demonstrates how the BFOQ exception to Title VII applies.

The Alabama prison system required that guards in positions requiring continual close physical proximity to inmates be of the same gender as those inmates. The rule had the effect of excluding female applicants from about 75% of the guard jobs in the Alabama prison system. Thus the gender requirement explicitly discriminated against women. Nevertheless, the Supreme Court upheld the validity of the gender requirement in that case (*Dothard v. Rawlinson,* 1977).

In support of its decision, the Court cited evidence that the maximum-security male penitentiaries in Alabama were exceptionally disorganized and therefore dangerous. The penitentiaries failed to segregate sex offenders, which, according to Diane Rawlinson's own expert, made it unwise to use women as guards. There was a history of attacks on women visiting the prison, and the general level of violence made the prison, in the Court's words, "peculiarly inhospitable to human beings of whatever sex"

---

14. See, for example, Case (1995): "Gender [is] to sex what masculine and feminine are to male and female" (p. 1); and Franke (1995).

15. Courts disagree about whether sexual harassment between members of the same sex is cognizable as sex discrimination under Title VII. For a sample of recent cases on this topic, see the discussion later in this chapter. See also *Torres v. National Precision Blanking* (1996) for a discussion of the lack of legislative guidance on the question of same-sex harassment.

(*Dothard v. Rawlinson,* 1977, p. 334). The Court acknowledged that "in the usual case, the argument that a particular job is too dangerous for women may appropriately be met by the rejoinder that it is the purpose of Title VII to allow the individual woman to make that choice for herself" (p. 335). Nonetheless, the Court found that in the prison system in Alabama, which lacked the controls found in "normal, relatively stable maximum security prisons" (p. 336), the likelihood that Diane Rawlinson would be assaulted because she was a woman posed a threat to control of the prison and undermined her ability to provide security. So, under those exceptional circumstances, the requirement that guards be male was a BFOQ.

The decision in Diane Rawlinson's case has been limited by its unusual facts. Attempts to exclude women from jobs guarding male prisoners have failed when the employer's concern was not the safe operation of the prison, but protecting inmate privacy. In those circumstances, courts have held that by adjusting guards' work assignments, prisons could accommodate inmate privacy without excluding women guards.[16] On the other hand, male guards have been excluded from a women's prison where the prison's state-mandated goal of rehabilitating inmates was compromised by their presence. For example, in *Torres v. Wisconsin Department of Health & Social Services* (1988-1989), the superintendent of a female maximum-security prison made a professional judgment that the prisoners' rehabilitation would be better fostered by living in an environment "free from the presence of males in a position of authority" (p. 1530). The decision was based on the superintendent's expertise, her experience with female prisoners, and on the fact that 60% of the inmates in the prison had been physically and sexually abused by males. The federal appeals court reviewing that decision ultimately held that empirical research validating the superintendent's theory was not necessary to uphold it when such research was unavailable and when other penologists considered the program to be a reasonable approach.

More recently, the Supreme Court ended the debate over the controversial application of the BFOQ defense in the form of fetal protection policies. Employers had prohibited pregnant women or women of childbearing age from occupying jobs that were potentially hazardous to a

---

16. For examples of cases holding that women were qualified to guard male prisoners, see *Hardin v. Stynchcomb* (1982) and cases cited therein.

fetus.[17] The Supreme Court ended that trend, holding that such prohibitions explicitly discriminate against women on the basis of their sex (*Auto Workers v. Johnson Controls,* 1991). The Court stated that the only justification for such a policy would lie in an employer's ability to show that pregnancy actually interferes with the employee's ability to do the job. Only under those circumstances would being male (or female and infertile) be a BFOQ for such a job.

Examples of Disparate Impact and Bona Fide Occupational Qualifications

In contrast to disparate treatment cases, in which an employer intends to discriminate and makes decisions accordingly, in disparate impact cases, an employer may not intend to discriminate against women at all. Yet the employer maintains hiring or other policies that disproportionately exclude women from the workplace. In those circumstances, the employer's policies will be considered unlawful unless they are justified by a business necessity and there is no less discriminatory alternative policy available (see *Albemarle Paper Co. v. Moody,* 1975; *Griggs v. Duke Power Co.,* 1971).

For example, in *Dothard v. Rawlinson* (1977), described above, Diane Rawlinson's application for a job as an Alabama prison guard was rejected because she did not meet the job's minimum-weight requirement of 120 pounds. The job also required that applicants be between 5 feet 2 inches and 6 feet 10 inches tall. Those requirements, taken together, would exclude 41.13% of the U.S. adult female population, while excluding less than 1% of the U.S. adult male population. The job requirements, therefore, had a disparate impact on women applicants. The employer argued that the height and weight requirements were job related, because they related to physical strength, which was necessary to the job. Rejecting that reasoning, the Supreme Court observed that if the job really required strength, then the prison should use a test that measured strength directly. Thus the Court held that the height and weight requirements for the guard position were discriminatory.

---

17. See, for example, *Wright v. Olin Corp.* (1982), excluding all fertile women from jobs that would expose them to chemicals potentially harmful to a fetus; *Hayes v. Shelby Memorial Hospital* (1984), removing a pregnant x-ray technician to protect her "fetus from potentially harmful radiation and to protect the hospital's finances from potential litigation."

Sexual Harassment: What Does It Mean to Discriminate "Because of an Individual's Sex"?

A trial court first recognized that sexual harassment violates Title VII in 1976, in the case of *Williams v. Saxbe*. Diane Williams alleged that after she rejected her supervisor's sexual overtures, he gave her unwarranted reprimands, refused to communicate with her on necessary work matters, and eventually fired her. The court rejected the employer's argument that this conduct could not be discrimination on the basis of sex because either gender can be harassed. Instead, the court stated that "the conduct of the plaintiff's supervisor created an artificial barrier to employment which was placed before one gender and not the other, despite the fact that both genders were similarly situated" (p. 658). The court therefore found that Ms. Williams had established a claim of sex discrimination under Title VII.

Four years later, the EEOC (1990, 11[a]) issued guidelines that stated clearly that sexual harassment is a violation of Title VII. Furthermore, the guidelines adopted definitions for two different kinds of sexual harassment that had emerged through the courts' decisions: *quid pro quo* (Latin for "something for something"; here, an employer's demand for sexual favors in exchange for a work-related favor) and *hostile environment*.

The guidelines define quid pro quo sexual harassment as occurring in two situations. First, when submission to unwelcome sexual advances, or requests for sexual favors, or other verbal or physical conduct of a sexual nature is made either explicitly or implicitly a term or condition of an individual's employment. Second, when submission to or rejection of the above conduct is used as the basis for employment decisions. In either case, the harasser uses his power over the victim's employment to try to extort submission. Thus quid pro quo harassment can only occur between a superior and a subordinate.

The EEOC Guidelines (1990) define hostile environment harassment as unwelcome sexual conduct, as described above, that "has the purpose or effect of unreasonably interfering with an individual's work performance or creating an intimidating, hostile, or offensive working environment" (11[a]). Unlike quid pro quo claims, hostile environment claims can be based on the conduct of coworkers as well as superiors. In a hostile environment claim, there need not be any request for sexual favors or any adverse employment action taken against the employee; the theory is that just being subject to that environment has a negative effect on the employee. The right protected is the "right to work in an environment free from discriminatory intimidation, ridicule, and insult" (*Meritor Savings Bank v. Vinson,* 1986, p. 65).

In its 1986 decision in *Meritor Savings Bank v. Vinson,* the U.S. Supreme Court established unequivocally that hostile environment claims are valid causes of action under Title VII and clarified the nature of the wrong. Mechell Vinson, a new teller at Meritor Savings Bank, was asked out to dinner by a bank vice president. Throughout her training period, Ms. Vinson had felt that the vice president treated her in a fatherly way, but at dinner that night, he asked her to go to a motel to have sex. At first she refused, but out of fear of losing her job, she eventually agreed. Ms. Vinson testified that over the next 3 years of her employment at the bank, she had intercourse with the vice president between 40 and 50 times; that he fondled her in front of other bank employees, exposed himself to her, followed her into the restroom when she went there alone, made sexual demands on her, usually at the branch, and forcibly raped her on several occasions. The bank vice president denied ever having had a sexual relationship with Ms. Vinson.

Without resolving the conflict in the testimony, the trial court found that Ms. Vinson could not have been sexually harassed by the vice president, even if her version of the facts were true, because the alleged sexual relationship was voluntary and had nothing to do with her continued employment or advancement at the bank.[18] The court of appeals reversed the decision (*Vinson v. Taylor,* 1985), and the U.S. Supreme Court affirmed the reversal, with two significant clarifications.

First, the Court stated that in a hostile environment claim, there is no need to prove economic detriment; the plaintiff need not be fired, demoted, or unfairly compensated in order to suffer a detriment from the discrimination. As in racial harassment cases, the plaintiff is wronged by being forced to work in an environment "polluted with discrimination."[19] To rise to the level of hostile environment harassment, the conduct must be "sufficiently severe or pervasive to 'alter the conditions of [the victim's] employment and create an abusive working environment' " (p. 67, quoting *Henson v. Dundee,* 1982). Noting that the abuse to which Ms. Vinson was

---

18. Ms. Vinson worked at the bank for 4 years, and it was "undisputed that her advancement there was based on merit alone" (*Meritor Savings Bank v. Vinson,* 1986, p. 60). She was discharged for excessive use of leave after taking sick leave for over a month.

19. *Meritor Savings Bank v. Vinson,* p. 66 (quoting *Rogers v. EEOC,* 1971: employer created an offensive work environment for Hispanic employees by giving discriminatory service to Hispanic clientele).

subject was not only pervasive but criminal in nature, the Court found that her allegation was sufficient to state a claim for sexual harassment.

Next, the Court turned to the question of the plaintiff's voluntary participation in the sexual relationship. Noting that the "gravamen of any sexual harassment claim is that the alleged sexual advances were 'unwelcome' " (citing the EEOC Guidelines, 1985, 11[a]), the Court found that "voluntariness," in the sense of lack of physical coercion, is no defense to a claim of sexual harassment. Sexual conduct can be unwelcome even if the plaintiff gives her consent or voluntarily participates in the conduct, once solicited. Nonetheless, because the plaintiff's attitude toward the solicitation is relevant, evidence about Ms. Vinson's sexually provocative speech or dress became relevant to the inquiry on unwelcomeness. For this reason, the Supreme Court reversed the Court of Appeals' conclusion that evidence submitted about Ms. Vinson's "dress and personal fantasies" was irrelevant.[20]

The *Meritor Savings Bank v. Vinson* (1986) decision left unanswered several questions about hostile environment claims. For example, if a woman is subject to a hostile environment and neither suffers economic harm (which *Meritor* established is not necessary) nor manifests psychological injury, does she have a claim under Title VII? For example, Teresa Harris took a job as a rental manager at a forklift company, where she worked for more than 2 years under Charles Hardy, the company's president. During that time, he continually directed sex-based derogatory comments at Ms. Harris, such as calling her a "dumb ass woman," saying that the company needed "a man as the rental manager," and suggesting that Ms. Harris had offered a client sex to secure an account (*Harris v. Forklift Systems, Inc.,* 1991, p. 242). Hardy also engaged in what he described as jokes, such as throwing objects on the ground in front of Harris and other women employees, asking the women to pick the objects up, and then commenting on their attire. Although the other women at the company thought Hardy was just a joker, Teresa Harris experienced anxiety and strain in her family relationships and began drinking heavily. Eventually, she quit the job and sued the company.

---

20. Congress recently made it harder for employers to inquire into a sexual harassment plaintiff's sexual history. In 1994, Congress amended the Federal Rules of Evidence to give sexual harassment plaintiffs protection equivalent to that given rape victims. Before the Court will admit evidence of the plaintiff's sexual history, the employer must show that the probative value of that information will substantially outweigh the risk of harm or unfair prejudice to the victim. See Federal Rule of Evidence 412, as amended by The Omnibus Crime Control Act of 1994.

The trial court called it a close case, finding that Hardy was a vulgar man, but that the level of sexual hostility in the office was not "so severe as to be expected to seriously affect the plaintiff's psychological well being" (*Harris v. Forklift Systems, Inc.,* 1991, pp. 244-245). Therefore, the plaintiff did not establish a hostile environment claim. The decision was affirmed without an opinion by the appellate court (*Harris v. Forklift Systems, Inc.,* 1992), but the U.S. Supreme Court unanimously reversed, declaring that Title VII does not require a showing of psychological injury to make out a claim of hostile environment sexual harassment (*Harris v. Forklift Systems, Inc.,* 1993).

Instead, the Supreme Court established a test that is both objective and subjective. Objectively, the work environment must "reasonably be perceived . . . as hostile or abusive" (p. 22).[21] Subjectively, the plaintiff must perceive the environment as such. In other words, if the plaintiff actually is not bothered by the environment, then she has no claim. Thus the court must judge whether the plaintiff welcomed the sexual advances or off-color jokes. The inquiry requires a subjective examination of the plaintiff's behavior vis-à-vis the alleged harasser.[22]

For example, objectively it might be hard to imagine that a court would even ask whether a civilian jailer in a sheriff's office welcomed the following conduct:

> Plaintiff contends that she was handcuffed to the drunk tank and sally port doors, that she was subjected to suggestive remarks . . . , that conversations often centered around oral sex, that she was physically hit and punched in the kidneys, that her head was grabbed and forcefully placed in members' laps, and that she was the subject of lewd jokes and remarks. She testified that she had chairs pulled out from under her, a cattle prod with an electrical shock was placed between her legs, and that they frequently tickled her. She was placed in a laundry basket, handcuffed inside an elevator, handcuffed to the toilet and her face pushed into the water, and maced. (*Reed v. Shepard,* 1991,

---

21. Courts disagree over whether sexual hostility in a work environment should be measured from the perspective of a reasonable "person," a reasonable woman, or a reasonable man and a reasonable woman. See *Ellison v. Brady,* 1991, holding that conduct should be measured by the standard of a reasonable woman, as a sex-blind standard tends to ignore the experiences and concerns of women; *Radtke v. Everett,* 1993, arguing that the reasonable woman standard would entrench sexist stereotypes about female sensitivity and fragility; and *Lipsett v. University of Puerto Rico,* 1988, arguing that the fact finder must consider the perspective of each gender on the particular facts of the case.
22. In light of the test established in the U.S. Supreme Court's decision in her case, Ms. Harris's claim was sent back to the trial court for further fact finding.

quoting the unpublished opinion of the U.S. District Court for the Southern District of Indiana, May 25, 1990).

Although the court found that this conduct was, by any objective standard, repulsive, it was not so to the plaintiff: "[She] not only experienced this depravity with amazing resilience, but she also relished reciprocating in kind" (*Reed v. Shepard*, 1991, p. 486). Testimony from many witnesses painted a picture of the plaintiff as not merely a participant, but an instigator in the sexual horseplay.[23] Affirming the lower court's decision that this plaintiff was not sexually harassed, the court of appeals stated that the evidence that the plaintiff welcomed the activity was fatal to her claim.

Not every plaintiff who engages in sexual horseplay loses her ability to claim harassment, however. In *Zorn v. Helene Curtis, Inc.* (1995), the plaintiff admitted that she had written a flattering note to a male colleague;[24] she had kissed the shirt collar of another colleague, leaving a lipstick mark; she had passed raspberries and whipped cream from her mouth to that of a colleague; and when slightly intoxicated and trying "to be one of the boys," she had grabbed a colleague's pants near the crotch. Yet when the employer cited her behavior as "the only conduct of an arguably sexual nature," the Court refused to accept the defendant's implication that the plaintiff had welcomed the sexual overtures of which she had complained. Such overtures included continual remarks from three male colleagues on such topics as female anatomy, the plaintiff's body, and how the plaintiff could make herself look sexier, as well as discussions of sexual fantasies about particular female employees, references to women as "sluts" or "bitches," and inquiries as to whether the plaintiff had sex with anyone other than her husband (p. 1236). The court observed that the plaintiff's resentment of her treatment at the hands of her male supervisor was clear; there could be no comparison between her conduct and the "constant sexual banter, vulgarity, and insults reaped upon her by her male cohorts" (p. 1243, n. 17).

The courts presently are wrestling with the question of what to do when employees complain of sexual banter, vulgarity, and insults heaped

---

23.   *Reed v. Shepard*, 1991, p. 487; for example, the plaintiff was put on probation for her use of offensive language; she gave a colleague a softball warmer designed to resemble a scrotum; she gave another male colleague a G-string; she enjoyed showing male officers the abdominal scars from her hysterectomy; she told dirty jokes and was known as having one of the foulest mouths in the department.

24.   The plaintiff's note to her colleague read, "Roses are red, violets are blue, you're 35 and a real stud too."

upon them by colleagues of the same sex. Recently, one court stated that a male supervisor's harassment of a male subordinate could not present a claim under Title VII, even if the harassment had sexual overtones (*Garcia v. ELF Atochem N. Am., 1994*).[25] Yet another court has held that such same-sex harassment will not give rise to a hostile environment claim when the people involved are heterosexuals but will give rise to such a claim when the perpetrator of the harassment is a homosexual.[26] And yet another court held that a heterosexual male harassed by heterosexual males can state a hostile environment claim under Title VII (*Quick v. Donaldson Co., Inc.,* 1996). Resolving this issue will ultimately require guidance from the U.S. Supreme Court.

TRENDS AND EMERGING ISSUES IN SEXUAL HARASSMENT LAW

The increase in sexual harassment cases filed reflects more than women's increased willingness to confront harassment. To some extent, the numbers reflect the fact that women are making inroads into blue-collar jobs where they have not worked historically, and they are experiencing resistance—in the form of sexual harassment—from male colleagues (Neuborne, 1996).[27] For example, as this book goes to press, an auto manufacturing plant is the subject of the largest sexual harassment suit in the EEOC's history,[28] and

---

25.   See also *Oncale v. Sundowner Offshore Services,* 1996, following the Garcia holding and denying the claim of a man who was threatened with homosexual rape and physically violated by his supervisor and a coworker.

26.   Compare *Hopkins v. Baltimore Gas & Elec. Co.,* 1996, denying the hostile environment claim of a man harassed by his apparently heterosexual male supervisor and holding that when a male employee is harassed by other male employees, the plaintiff must overcome a presumption that the harassment was not "because of" his sex, that is, the plaintiff must show that the harasser acted out of sexual attraction, with *Wrightson v. Pizza Hut of America, Inc.,* 1996, a heterosexual male harassed by his homosexual male supervisor and five coworkers had a valid claim under Title VII.

27.   Neuborne was interviewing EEOC legal counsel Ellen Varyas. According to a *USA Today* analysis of 15,691 sexual harassment complaints filed with the EEOC in 1995, larger numbers of complaints were generated in predominantly male industries such as mining, construction, transportation, and manufacturing than in service industries, where women have a longer historical presence.

28.   The EEOC alleges that between 300 and 500 women may have been harassed since the Mitsubishi Motor Manufacturing plant opened in 1988 in Normal, Illinois. Allegations run the gamut from obscene graffiti to physical assault and group threats of rape. See Grimsley, Swoboda, and Brown, 1996.

the Army is investigating allegations of sexual harassment in its most egregious forms.[29]

Nonetheless, the increase in sexual harassment and discrimination claims filed is also attributable in part to tendencies in American society to resort to litigation quickly and to seek an expansion of legally protected rights. The greater popular awareness of sexual harassment law since 1991—in particular, the rise of hostile environment litigation—means that women are more inclined than ever to litigate harassment claims.

Several appellate courts have suggested that trial judges, juries, and plaintiffs are going too far, that the law of sexual harassment is being used for more than its intended purpose. In the case of *Baskerville v. Culligan International Co.* (1995), the court observed that "the concept of sexual harassment is designed to protect working women from the kind of male attentions that can make the workplace hellish for women. . . . It is not designed to purge the workplace of vulgarity."[30] The court observed that a "merely unpleasant working environment," even one that includes "occasional vulgar banter, tinged with sexual innuendo," will not support a claim of hostile environment sexual harassment (p. 430). Similarly, in *DeAngelis v. El Paso Municipal Police Officers Association* (1995), the court commented that the statutory ban on sexual harassment "cannot remedy every tasteless joke or groundless rumor that confronts women in the workplace."[31] The Court warned against juries' relaxing the legal standard for sexual harassment whenever there is some evidence of offensive conduct:

---

29. The Army brought charges alleging rape, sodomy and death threats, as well as less violent forms of harassment, against drill sergeants and a captain at a training camp in Maryland (Stolberg, 1996). As the scandal spread to other training facilities, Defense Secretary William J. Perry ordered the Secretaries of the Navy and the Air Force to examine their services' training programs ("Drill Sergeant," 1996). A Pentagon survey of 90,000 women in the armed forces revealed that 1 in 10 said she had been the victim of sexual assault in 1995; nearly 2 in 10 said that sexual favors were requested of or suggested to her in exchange for favorable treatment (Killian, 1996).

30. In this case, the plaintiff sued over nine comments that her boss made in the course of 7 months, most of which were no more crude than calling the plaintiff "pretty girl." As soon as the plaintiff complained to the human resource department, her boss was disciplined and the comments stopped. Based on that evidence, the Court of Appeals reversed the jury's award to the plaintiff.

31. In this case, a police department's first woman sergeant sued under a hostile environment theory when she was satirized by an anonymous columnist writing in the newsletter published by the police officers' association. Despite the misogynistic tone of the columns, the court held that four printed derogatory references to the sergeant in the course of $2^1/_2$ years was not conduct severe or pervasive enough to create a hostile environment.

A hostile environment claim embodies a series of criteria that express
extremely insensitive conduct against women, conduct so egregious as
to alter the conditions of employment and destroy their equal opportunity in the workplace. Any lesser standard of liability, couched in terms
of conduct that sporadically wounds or offends but does not hinder a
female employee's performance, would not serve the goal of equality.
In fact, a less onerous standard of liability would attempt to insulate
women from everyday insults as if they remained models of Victorian
reticence. (p. 539)

In addition, research shows that juries may be moderating their
verdicts in employment discrimination cases generally, voting more frequently in favor of defendants, keeping compensatory damages in line with
the plaintiff's lost earnings, and starting a trend toward decreasing punitive
damage awards (Jury Verdict Research, 1996, Charts E and P). Plaintiff
recovery rates in wrongful termination cases have dropped from 67% in
1988 to 48% in 1994 and 1995 (Chart F). Nevertheless, plaintiff recovery
rates for sexual harassment and sex-based discrimination averaged 53%
and 48% respectively, from 1988 to 1995, on par with age discrimination
claims (54% success rate) and race discrimination claims (47% success
rate) (Chart I).

Following the surge of public interest in sexual harassment, there is
some wariness over how sexual harassment lawsuits—particularly, hostile
environment claims—will affect workplace discourse. The fact that hostile
environment claims turn on subjective evaluations—by both plaintiffs and
courts—raises concerns that the hostile environment claim has become the
recourse of the thin-skinned and the weapon of the "politically correct."
Commentators cite examples from the far end of the subjective spectrum
to argue that sexual harassment laws have become a means of violating the
First Amendment right to free speech by banning words and pictures in the
workplace.[32] Such examples include the 1992 decision of Pennsylvania
State University officials to remove a reproduction of The Nude Maja by
Francisco de Goya after a teacher asserted that it made female students
uncomfortable and embarrassed her (Neal, 1995). Also cited is the 1993

---

32. The First Amendment to the Constitution generally prohibits the government from
regulating speech on the basis of its content, that is, on the basis of the ideas expressed. A few
exceptions to this rule exist for certain categories of speech, such as defamation, obscenity,
and "fighting words." Also, the government can regulate the time, place, and manner of speech
(for example, passing noise ordinances) and can regulate conduct that involves speech (for
example, prohibiting treason), so long as the regulations do not target particular ideas or
viewpoints.

decision by University of Nebraska officials to order a graduate student teaching assistant to remove the photograph of his wife which he kept on his desk. In the photo, his wife was clad in a bathing suit. The officials felt that the photo created a hostile environment for students, faculty, and staff.[33]

As the court deciding the *DeAngelis v. El Paso Municipal Police Officers Association* (1995) case observed, some applications of Title VII may violate the First Amendment. By prohibiting people from harassing others verbally, Title VII does regulate speech. To the extent that the prohibition focuses on verbal conduct[34] rather than on verbal expression of ideas, Title VII does not appear to raise First Amendment issues. Yet sometimes Title VII's prohibition can amount to regulating speech solely on the basis of the ideas expressed. As the *DeAngelis* court observed, these constitutional issues have not yet been resolved:

> Where pure expression is involved. . . . when Title VII is applied to sexual harassment claims found solely on verbal insults, pictorial or literary matter, the statute imposes content-based, viewpoint-discriminatory restrictions on speech. Whether such applications of Title VII are necessarily unconstitutional has not yet been fully explored. (pp. 596-597)

Thus, when an anonymous columnist in the *DeAngelis* case expressed his opinion that female police officers were not suited to patrol duty, he was exercising his First Amendment right to free speech. The courts have not yet resolved whether Sergeant DeAngelis's right to work in an environment "free from discriminatory intimidation, ridicule, and insults" (*Meritor Savings Bank v. Vinson,* 1986, p. 65) trumps the columnist's right to express his opinion.[35]

---

33. It should be noted that the cited decisions were made by universities, not the EEOC or the courts.

34. An example of verbal conduct would be a proposition by a supervisor to a subordinate, suggesting that the subordinate exchange sexual favors for continued employment. Although the proposition is verbal, it is treated as conduct. The supervisor is not expressing an idea but is acting coercively through words.

35. For an in-depth discussion of the conflict between the right to free speech and antiharassment law, see Browne, 1991, arguing that the First Amendment should protect all verbal or symbolic expression in the workplace; Volokh, 1992, arguing that the First Amendment should protect speech aimed at willing listeners, but not offensive speech directed at unwilling listeners.

CONCLUSION

In the more than three decades following the passage of the Civil Rights Act of 1964, the public and the courts have widened their understanding of sex discrimination. Concepts such as sexual harassment and hostile environment are now basic to the public's understanding of sex discrimination. With an expanded list of wrongs prohibited by Title VII, discussion turns to a refinement of rights.

Courts have begun defining limits to the rights created by Title VII, particularly, the right to work in an environment free from discriminatory intimidation. "Free" does not mean sanitized; an isolated remark will rarely support a hostile environment claim. Constant insults will not support a claim if the remarks do not offend the target. Some courts will not consider insults discriminatory if they are not directed at the opposite sex. Yet, neither the public nor the courts have defined limits to Title VII rights as they affect free speech rights. Whether the marketplace of ideas can—or should—operate freely inside an office building or manufacturing plant is yet to be seen. One thing is certain, however. The development of the law in the area of sex discrimination will continue to be fascinating and newsworthy, not only for employment lawyers but for the public at large.

Conclusions

Our Goals in This Book Were

1. to reveal the frequency and prevalence of a variety of types of nonviolent (i.e., excluding rape) discrimination against women
2. to examine—for the very first time—the extent to which that discrimination contributes to women's prevalent physical and psychiatric symptoms
3. to offer information on a few of the many things that women can do to reduce sexist discrimination in their lives.

Where the first goal is concerned, we found that the 631 women in our first study (Chapter 1) reported experiencing a variety of types of sexist discrimination in the past year as well as in their entire lifetimes, with

- 32% to 60% reporting being discriminated against by their employer
- 55% to 95% reporting unwelcomed sexual advances and sexist jokes
- 29% to 56% reporting sexist intimidation (being picked on, pushed, hit, shoved, or threatened with physical harm)

Likewise, the 652 women in our second study (Chapter 4) reported experiencing a variety of types of sexist discrimination in the past year and in their lifetimes, with

    ▓ 37% to 64% reporting being discriminated against by their employer
    ▓ 67% to 94% reporting unwelcomed sexual advances and sexist jokes
    ▓ 35% to 62% reporting sexist intimidation (being picked on, pushed, hit, shoved or threatened with physical harm)

Even though our second sample was a new group of women who differed statistically significantly from the first sample in terms of age and social class, their pattern of reports of the frequency of the various types of sexist discrimination matched those of the first sample. Thus the reports of the 1,283 women in our two samples were remarkably similar. In addition, we found with our 1,283 women that reports of various types of sexist discrimination did not vary with social class or education but instead were found among women of all groups (Chapter 2). Furthermore, we found that the 475 minority women reported even more frequent sexist discrimination than did the 808 White women in our two samples (Chapter 2).

Likewise, Lott and Rocchio's sample of 262 women (Chapter 8)—selected from a different geographical region a year later—reported experiences with sexist discrimination that closely matched what we found with our two samples. Hence the experiences of all 1,545 women were similar with respect to the frequency of various types of sexist discrimination in their lives.

From these data—as well as from the empirical evidence reviewed in the Introduction—we are scientifically justified in concluding unequivocally that

> **discrimination against women in America is rampant on the eve of the 21st century, irrespective of women's social class, age, ethnicity, or education.**

The above conclusion has many implications. First and foremost it means that

> **affirmative action programs for women are necessary and must continue despite regressive political efforts to undermine and dismantle them.**

Without such programs, women who are equal to men in job skills, experience, training, and education, and whose resumes are identical to men's, will *not* be hired, will *not* be promoted, or will be hired at a lower level and paid less than men, according to all of the scientific evidence in the Introduction and to the reports of the 1,283 women who participated in our studies. By discriminating in women's favor, affirmative action programs counteract and compensate for the ongoing, rampant discrimination against women, thereby giving qualified women equality of opportunity. Those who believe that such programs should be dismantled because they discriminate are ignoring existing discrimination against women (and minorities). Those who believe that quotas do violence to the American ideal of meritocracy are denying the violence entailed in relegating meritorious women (and minorities) to positions of lesser status through ongoing discrimination against them. Those who proclaim that affirmative action programs are "bad" because all people should be treated fairly and equally are denying the fact that all people are not so treated and never have been. Affirmative action programs are a necessary evil for combating the evil of rampant discrimination, and hence women—and men—must support them.

Although maintaining affirmative action programs may assist women (and minorities) in acquiring access to positions that they deserve, such programs cannot protect them from the subtle discrimination against them that continues once they acquire the positions in question. Instead, we found over and over again in these studies that women face ongoing unwanted sexual advances and comments and incessant sexist jokes and are treated with a lack of respect, ignored as inferiors by their coworkers, supervisors, and others on a daily basis. This subtle, ongoing sexist discrimination takes it toll on women, as evidenced by the case of famed neurosurgeon Dr. Frances Conley (for details, see Perrone, 1991). Conley, one of the few women neurosurgeons in the nation, had acquired the prestigious position of professor at Stanford University Medical School, only to resign in May 1991. In her resignation letter,[1] she explained that she was resigning because of the ongoing, subtle sexist discrimination she faced at work: If she disagreed with a male colleague, this was attributed to premenstrual syndrome or to "being on the rag." Likewise, one male colleague ran his hand up her leg during a professional meeting, and another once interrupted her to say, "Gee, I can see the shape of your breast even under your white coat." In her resignation letter, Conley wrote, "Those who administer my work environment at the present time have never been able to accept me as an equal person. Not because I lack professional competence, but because I use a different bathroom" (Perrone, 1991, p. 5).

---

1. For details of this case, see J. Perrone (1991). Sexism far from dead in medicine. *American Medical News*, p. 5.

The literature reviewed in the Introduction and the reports of our 1,283 women all indicate that Conley is not alone in such experiences. Likewise, the complaints that women bring to their therapists, as reported to Phyllis Bronstein (Chapter 7), match those of Dr. Conley. The treatment of women graduate students and faculty at the University of Rhode Island in 1991—treatment that necessitated the formation of WASH (Chapter 8)—consisted of the same subtle sexist come-ons, putdowns, and shutouts that led Conley to resign. The major court cases on sex discrimination reviewed by Wurzburg and Klonoff (Chapter 9) also indicate the prevalence of these experiences for women, showing that women can (and often do successfully) sue their employers for such treatment. The fact that Conley resigned and other women file lawsuits (Chapter 9), seek therapy (Chapter 7), or organize politically (Chapter 8) in response to subtle, sexist discrimination means that such discrimination is distressing to women. Hence, from all of this, we conclude that

the rampant sexist discrimination that women in America face includes acts both subtle and gross, blatant and pernicious, and that these acts are disturbing to women irrespective of their subtlety.

Our first goal—to reveal and highlight the prevalence and frequency of various types of nonviolent discrimination against women—was met.

Our second goal was to explore—for virtually the first time[2]—the extent to which such sexist discrimination contributes to physical and psychiatric symptoms among women. When we examined this issue for the 631 women of Sample 1 (Chapter 3), we found that sexist discrimination contributed to symptoms among women and was a stronger predictor of those symptoms than the ordinary (generic) stressors known to cause those symptoms. Sexist discrimination—sexist stress—alone accounted for 10% to 17% of the variance in the physical and psychiatric symptoms of the women in Sample 1. Likewise, when we examined this issue for the 652 women of Sample 2 (Chapter 5), we again found that sexist discrimination (sexist stress or sexist stressful events) contributed to symptoms among

2. To the best of our knowledge, there is only one other empirical investigation of the extent to which nonviolent discrimination contributes to symptoms among women, Nancy Krieger's (1990) study of workplace discrimination and hypertension among women. Although it is well-known that women face discrimination, no studies—except Krieger's and those reported in this book—have examined the possible impact of such discrimination on women's physical and mental health.

women and again was a stronger and better predictor of those symptoms than were ordinary generic stressors.

In addition (Chapter 5), we found that sexist events contributed even more to the symptoms of minority women than of White women and to the symptoms of nonfeminists more than feminists: Sexist events alone accounted for up to 46% of the variance in the symptoms of minority women, and for up to 21.47% of the variance in the symptoms of nonfeminist women. Finally, we found that the presence and frequency of sexist acts—rather than women's personal, subjective evaluations of those acts—predicted women's symptoms. Whether women found sexist acts to be personally upsetting and stressful or dismissed them as inconsequential made little difference: Sexist acts contributed to their symptoms nonetheless. From this, we are justified in the unequivocal, scientific conclusion that

> **the rampant sexist discrimination that women in America face—whether subtle (e.g., name calling) or blatant (e.g., discrimination in salaries) contributes to physical and psychiatric symptoms among women, irrespective of women's subjective appraisals of those acts.**

Furthermore, we can conclude that

> **Even subtle sexist treatment of women (e.g., telling women sexist jokes and treating them as if they were stupid) is not trivial because it contributes to women's physical and psychiatric symptoms.**

Precisely how sexist acts (sexist stress) contribute to women's symptoms then becomes the question. In the Introduction, we noted that studies have proven that ordinary stress contributes to women's symptoms (as well as to those of animals in laboratory studies) by *causing* them through well-known and documented mechanisms (e.g., suppression of immune functions). We argued that if ordinary (generic) stress contributes to women's symptoms because it causes them, and sexist stress contributes even more so to those very same symptoms, then sexist stress no doubt also causes those symptoms; **if stress causes symptoms, then the type of stress (generic v. sexist) is irrelevant to the causal relationship.** Hence, we have not proven but do strongly suggest that sexist discrimination (stress) was found here to contribute significantly to women's (stress-related) symptoms because it causes them. That suggestion is far from new—John Stuart

Mill suggested this in his 1869 book, *The Subjection of Women*—but nonetheless it needs to be proven scientifically.

Hence what is needed now is a series of laboratory studies demonstrating the causal relationship between sexist discrimination and immunosuppression. Likewise, studies that use the SSE and measures of symptoms (as we did here) along with sophisticated statistical procedures (e.g., structural equation modeling) that permit causal inferences (as we did not) also may elucidate the causal relationship that feminists have hypothesized and suspected to exist for many years. In the absence of such proofs, we can only *suggest* and *suspect*—but cannot conclude—that sexist stress causes the symptoms to which it so clearly and reliably contributes. Likewise, whether this ongoing sexism accounts for and explains women's higher rate (relative to men) of stress-related physical and psychiatric symptoms and disorders is something we *strongly suspect* to be the case, but similarly, it remains a question for further scientific study—and we have such studies currently under way.

Although the mechanism (the how) must be proven scientifically, what is clear in these studies is that sexist discrimination—sexist stress—does contribute significantly to physical and psychiatric symptoms among all women, and among nonfeminist and minority women in particular; exploring that possibility was our second goal. The question remaining then is, What should women do about this—what can women do about it? Exploring that issue was our third goal.

In Chapter 7, Phyllis Bronstein revealed that seeking counseling with a feminist therapist is one useful approach to surviving in a world replete with daily ongoing sexist discrimination. This is not only because of the social support and validation of experiences that therapists can provide. Rather, Bronstein suggested that feminist therapists also can assist women in attributing sexism to a patriarchal social order rather than to themselves and can encourage women to become politically active in efforts to reduce sexism in their relationships and workplace. Hence, Bronstein implied that seeking feminist therapy may be a necessary first step—something women must do before they can engage in collective action—because many women have internalized sexism. Women may need to first combat their own belief that they are inferior (a message inherent in the sexist discrimination against them) before they can use collective strategies such as those suggested by Lott and Rocchio (in Chapter 8) to create change.

Such arguments (resonated by the feminist therapists that Bronstein interviewed for her chapter) are not victim blaming; they simply acknowledge the sad fact that no one survives a destructive, patriarchal social order unscathed.

In Chapter 8, Bernice Lott and Lisa Rocchio highlighted an alternative strategy for combating and decreasing sexist discrimination; namely, taking collective action. They revealed that one effective strategy is for the women in a workplace or university to band together—even if informally—to discuss and validate each other's experiences, and then act *as a group* to change their environment. They argued that collective action is less risky and more likely to be effective than individual efforts to reduce sexist discrimination; in so doing, they resonate the views of a century of feminist activists. Lott and Rocchio also provided a detailed example of how such a group must be structured if it is to be successful.

Finally, in Chapter 9, Lynne Wurzburg and Robert Klonoff provided a detailed, objective (neutral) review of the major sex discrimination and sexual harassment suits that have appeared before the courts and demonstrated that the definition of both of these is widening. Such changes in the law are encouraging.

Thus the answer to the question, "What can women do?" is provided in Chapters 7 to 9: women can use any variety of individual, collective, and legal strategies to combat sexist discrimination. To the information and suggestions provided by those chapters, we add two suggestions of our own.

First, in our study of the women in Sample 2, we found strong empirical evidence indicating that being a feminist mediates the negative impact of sexist discrimination. Feminists were less harmed than nonfeminists by the sexist discrimination they experienced—even though feminists reported more frequent discrimination and found it more distressing. This suggests that feminism is a neglected resource for women, a resource that (like strong social support networks) can protect women—not from experiencing sexist discrimination, but from the more deleterious consequences of sexism. Hence, in addition to the individual, collective, and legal strategies available, another strategy for combating sexist discrimination is for each of us to elicit and nurture feminism in our women friends, students, colleagues, and children, in whatever way we can. Those ways might include (but are not limited to):

- Providing women and girls with feminist books as gifts
- Including feminist social science texts in our courses
- Making papers on feminist (and multicultural-feminist) readings an extra credit option for students

- Exposing colleagues and students to feminist lectures and meetings by taking them along
- Getting our departments to credit work in women's centers, rape crisis centers, and battered women's shelters for undergraduate internship
- Organizing informal book clubs to read and discuss feminist work
- Pooling our financial and other resources to create and run feminist summer camps, day care centers, and after-school programs for girls and boys

Increasing the prevalence of feminism among women and girls may not only partially protect them from the harmful effects of sexist discrimination but it may simultaneously increase the number of women who engage in collective strategies to create change.

Second, in the final analysis, decreasing sexist discrimination in women's lives is obviously contingent on a thorough analysis of the factors that maintain it. We know from thousands of psychological studies that behavior is maintained by its consequences—that is a truism. Hence, as behaviorists, we ask, "What maintains sexist behavior?" In the plethora of feminist writings on sexism in psychology and other social sciences, no one has attempted to answer that question either theoretically or empirically. Clearly, then, what is needed is a thorough functional analysis of sexist discrimination—careful, natural observation studies of the antecedents and the consequences of sexist behavior. Specifically, the antecedents—the internal and external events that prompt people to engage in sexist behavior—must be delineated. Likewise, the consequences—the internal and external events immediately following sexist behavior that reinforce and maintain it—also must be delineated. Although knowing both of these is important to changing—modifying—sexist behavior, delineating the consequences that maintain the behavior is crucial to reducing (extinguishing) it. What, then, are those consequences?

In their review of the literature, Lott and Rocchio (Chapter 8) found that women's most common response to sexist behavior is to ignore it. Likewise, in their own empirical study, these researchers also found that ignoring the behavior was women's most common response. Hence, ignoring sexist behavior and saying nothing about it is the typical consequence—the reinforcer for the behavior. In other words,

ignoring sexist behavior and saying nothing about it maintains the behavior and increases the probability of its future occurrence.

Although counterintuitive, this conclusion is a logical one that is consistent with everything psychology knows about the nature of behavior. Women's silent ignoring of men's sexist behavior clearly acts as a reinforcer, and may do so because it is understood by men as acceptance and approval. In any event, this means that

> **attending to sexist behavior (responding to it) will decrease the frequency of the behavior insofar as attending to the behavior constitutes withdrawal of the reinforcer.**

Support for this conclusion comes from many sources. First, Bingham and Scherer (1993) found that women who talked to sexual harassers were most satisfied with the outcome of that individual strategy—satisfied with the decrease in harassment that resulted. Talking to harassers about their behavior constitutes calling attention to—rather than ignoring—the behavior. Likewise, Yoder and Aniakudo (1995) found that African American women firefighters responded to harassment by confronting sexual harassers and that sexual harassment decreased. Similarly, Lott and Rocchio's WASH program (described in Chapter 8) entailed calling attention to sexist behavior by publicly announcing meetings on that topic, posting signs describing sexist behavior, and confronting individuals about their sexist behavior. In addition, the therapists that Phyllis Bronstein interviewed (Chapter 7) also (inevitably) suggested that women speak to the perpetrators of sexist discrimination and engage in political action. Thus each of these strategies entails calling attention to sexist behavior—and taking legal action is also a form of calling attention to sexist behavior. Alternatively, the Yount (1991) study found that women's responses (playing "the lady," "the flirt," or "the tomboy") did not decrease sexist discrimination. We suggest that this is because none of those three strategies entailed calling attention to the behavior and instead, all represented different forms of silence about the behavior—tacit approval.

Hence, along with the other strategies suggested in Chapters 7, 8, and 9, we suggest that

> **women speak up about and call attention to sexist behavior whenever they can. This can consist of simply stating, "What you said/did was really sexist" or "What you said/did offends me."**

Although these responses constitute a simple change, they may decrease the frequency of sexist behavior by removing the reinforcer for it. By this, we do not mean to suggest that women are responsible for the sexist discrimination that they experience *because they are not.* We mean instead to suggest that women have the ability to change their immediate environments and the world that they live in.

Appendix

Understanding the
Statistics Used in This Book

In this appendix, we discuss the statistics used throughout this book and then turn to the issues regarding psychological scales or tests (psychometrics) that are raised in this book. Experimental, psychometric, and statistical terms and symbols used throughout this book are shown here in **boldface** and are explained. Because this overview is brief, issues are simplified; they are more complex than this discussion indicates, but knowledge of that complexity is not necessary to understand the statistics in this book.

STATISTICS

Statistics is a branch of mathematics used to describe and analyze **data,** the information collected from and on people. The people who participate in scientific experiments or surveys are called the **sample** to differentiate them from the entire **population** of the United States. Three types of statistics are used in this book to examine data from the samples we studied: descriptive statistics (to describe), inferential statistics (to analyze), and data-reduction statistics (to reduce and simplify).

I. Descriptive Statistics

Descriptive statistics are used to describe scientific samples and are important; they give us a sense of what the people studied were like and how similar they were to us, thus highlighting the extent to which what was found for the sample might be true for us as well. Descriptive statistics also summarize the sample's data so that they can be analyzed. The major descriptive statistics are the **mean, median, mode,** and **standard deviation.**

The *mean* is the average for the group and is calculated by adding all of their scores and dividing by the number of scores (symbolized by N or n). For example, rather than list the incomes of the 652 women in Sample 1, we report the mean income for all of the women by adding their incomes and dividing that total by 652. The mean describes what the group as a whole (on the average) is like and is a useful descriptive statistic. Hence, the mean is the major variable analyzed in statistical proofs; as will be shown here, statistical proofs consist of comparing the means of groups, or trying to predict the mean of a group. In scientific tables, the mean is presented by the actual word mean or by the symbol M or the symbol $\overline{X}$.

The mean, however, can be misleading because it is pulled in the direction of extreme scores: one extremely low or extremely high score changes the mean and can render it a poor description of the group. For example, suppose we wanted to know the average (mean) income of a group of three people: you, your best friend, and the basketball star Shaquille O'Neill. We would add your income, your friend's income, and Shaq's income (about $25 million per year) and then divide by three. The resulting mean would be extremely high (about $8.4 million per year) and a poor description and representation of the group's income because it is pulled in the direction of Shaq's extreme income. Thus other descriptive statistics are used as well to give an accurate portrait of a group or sample. Because of this problem with the mean, economists (e.g., on the evening news) almost never report annual means (mean U.S. income, mean number of homes or automobiles purchased). Instead, they tend to report medians.

The median is an alternative way to describe a group or sample. It is the score (or value) in the exact center of all of the scores when these are put in order from lowest to highest: exactly one half of the people score above and one half score below the median. For example, consider a sample of five people whose ages are 20, 25, 28, 29, and 62 years. The mean (20

+ 25 + 28 + 29 + 62 ÷ 5) is 32.8 and says that, on the average, the whole group is about 32.8 years old. The mean is pulled in the direction of the 62-year-old (the extreme score) and so is higher than the ages of everyone except the 62-year-old. The median, the score in the middle, is 28: half of the people are younger than 28, and half are older than 28. The median says that, on the average, the whole group is about 28 years old. It seems a better description than the mean for this set of data because it is not, and cannot be, influenced or affected by the presence of extreme scores—this is why economists prefer medians. In professional research articles, scientists often report both statistics (mean and median) to give a clearer sense of what a sample is like. The word *median* is written out in scientific tables, or the median is represented by the symbol *Md*.

The *mode* is yet another way to describe what a group or sample in general—on the average, on the whole, and for the most part—is like. It is the most frequent score in a set of scores. For example, consider this sample of $N = 17$ people whose ages are:

18, 19, 20, 20, 20, 20, 25, 25, 26, 28, 32, 44, 45, 47, 62, 75, 82

The mean age is 35.76 years; the median age is 26; and the mode (or **modal**) age is 20 (the single most frequent age seen). Either of these is a more or less accurate description of what the sample of 17 people—as a whole, on the average—is like. Note that the mode is the most frequent score in the sample and *is not* the score that most people (the majority) received. A sample can have one mode (unimodal), two modes (bimodal), many modes (multimodal), or no *mode*. The word mode is written out in scientific papers.

The issue of variance. Even knowing the mean, median, and mode for a sample (e.g., for a sample's income, age, and number of years of education) still does not provide enough detail about the sample for one to judge the extent to which the sample of research participants was *representative* of the entire population—and so of you. This is because the mean, median, and mode do not provide any information on how the scores of the sample are **dispersed,** how they **vary.** Obviously, everyone in a sample does not receive the same score on a psychological test, and the people in the sample also are not all exactly the same age, do not all have exactly the same income, and the like. The participants in research samples typically differ from each other on every dimension studied. Indeed, if you treat your own family as a sample, they will no doubt vary in age, income, shoe size, height, weight, attitudes, physical symptoms—and nearly everything else, as well. The differences—the **variance**—within a random sample of people in a mall is even greater than the variance within one's own family. Without knowledge of these differences—of this variance—one cannot truly understand the nature of the sample and judge if those included are representative enough of us all to *generalize from them to us all*.

The best proof that the mean, median, and mode for a sample do not provide any information on the variance within that sample is the fact that one cannot predict or reproduce a sample's scores from knowledge of these three descriptive statistics. For example, knowing that a sample of $N = 17$ had a mean age of 35.76 years, a median age of 26, and a modal age of 20 (the hypothetical group above) does not tell us anyone's age. At most, we can say that at least two people were 20 years old (the mode), and that eight people (half) were older, and eight people (half) were younger than 26 (the median age). But we cannot say what the first person's age was, or the second's, or the third's: all of these are free to vary (this is called **degrees of freedom** and symbolized as *df*). Hence, to understand a sample, a measure of the sample's variance is needed.

The *standard deviation* (symbolized by σ *SD*) is the best measure of the variance in a sample. It is the average (standard) distance (difference) between each of the scores and the mean. The standard deviation is the typical, standard, or average (mean) amount by which each person's score differs (or deviates, hence: deviation) from the mean for the group. For example, a sample's ages can be described as having a mean of 20 and a standard deviation of 2. This means that the average age was 20 years, and that most people's ages deviated from that mean by 2 years—most people's ages were within 2 years of 20: the bulk of the sample was between 18 (2 years below 20, or −1 standard deviation) and 22 (2 years above the mean of 20, or +1 standard deviation) years old. Without knowing the median, or the mode, or how many people were in the sample, we still know a great deal about the sample from knowledge of the mean and standard deviation alone.

In fact, from the mean and standard deviation alone, we know even more than this about a sample. This is because, in general, just about anything and everything one wishes to study about people is distributed among those people in a specific manner that is so common (or normal) that it has come to be called **a normal distribution.** In a normal distribution, 68% of the people score within one standard deviation of the mean (+1 above, and −1 below), and 95% of the people score within 2 standard deviations of the mean (+2 above, and −2 below). Thus, from the mean and standard deviation, we know ahead of time what a sample's scores (and the population's scores) are like.

For example, if we took a random sample of American adults' heights, we would find a national mean of 5 feet 6 inches, and a standard deviation of 3 inches. Heights also would be found to be normally distributed: 68% of all people's heights are within one standard deviation (above or below) this mean—68% of all people are somewhere between 5 feet 3 inches (−1 σ) and 5 feet 9 inches (+1 σ) tall. In addition, 95% of all people—almost all of any group of people—would be found to be between 5 feet (−2 standard deviations, or −2 × 3 inches), and 6 feet (+2 × 3 inches) tall. The remaining 5% of all people (not many people) would fall at the extreme short end (2.5% would be found to be shorter than 5 feet) and at the extreme tall end (2.5% would be found to be taller than 6 feet).

Again, almost everything about people is normally distributed: height, age, income, number of years of education, number of children, shoe sizes, personality traits, specific life experiences, skills of various types, behaviors, attitudes, intelligence, and physical and psychiatric symptoms are all normally distributed. Hence, if we know the mean and standard deviation for any **variable** (anything measured and studied), then we know ahead of time that 95% of all people will score within +2 and −2 σ of the mean for that variable, with the remaining 5% scoring at the extreme high and low ends.

Thus the mean and the standard deviation together provide a clear picture of a what a sample is like because the mean describes the average, the standard deviation describes the variance around that average, and because whatever is being studied is probably normally distributed. Because of these three facts, the mean and standard deviation are used to make psychological decisions and judgments. For example, the SAT and GRE tests both have a mean of 500 and a standard deviation of 100. We know ahead of time that this means that 68% of all people who take these tests score between 400 and 600 (+1 and −1 σ). Hence a score higher than 600 is desired by colleges; a score of 700 or higher is the most desirable because few people receive such a score (95% receive scores of 300 to 700—± 2 σ). Likewise, IQ tests have a mean of 100 and a standard deviation of 15: The bulk of Americans (68%) score between 85 and 115, and 95% score between 70 and 130. Thus, a score above 130 (2 σ above the mean, 2 × 15) is the psychological definition of being "bright," and a score 2 σ below the mean—a score below 70—is part of the psychological definition of mental retardation. Similarly, the MMPI is a personality test that measures the presence of psychiatric symptoms, and it contains 11 subtests. Each symptom-subtest has a mean of 50 and a standard deviation of 10. One scientific definition of having a psychiatric disorder is to receive a score of 70 or higher on three or more MMPI subtests: a person must score two standard deviations above the mean (higher than 95% of all normal people) at least *three times* to be judged mentally ill.

A *percentile rank* or a **percentile** is another way to examine scores of an individual relative to those of a sample. A percentile is the percentage of the sample whose score is below a particular score. For example, if you scored 89 on a test in a course and were given a percentile of 70, this means that 70% of the sample (your classmates) scored below your score of 89. Alternatively, if your score of 89 was given a percentile rank of 20, this means that only 20% of the class scored below 89—and that the rest scored higher than you. From this perspective, a score has no inherent meaning (is neither high nor low in and of itself), and instead, its meaning stems from its position relative to the scores of the rest of the sample. A score of 89 can have any percentile rank—20, 50, or even 100 (if it was the highest score for a group, and so 100% of the sample scored below it)—depending on what the group's scores are like. Clearly, however, the higher your percentile rank the better.

Throughout this book, we often use the 33rd and the 66th percentiles to divide a sample into three groups of equal numbers. Scores below the 33rd percentile are the one third of the sample with the lowest scores, because 33% of the sample scored below this score (whatever it might be). The 34th to 66th percentile is the middle third of the sample, and the 67th to 100th percentile is the upper third of the sample.

Categorical data from a sample, however, cannot be described by use of the mean, median, standard deviation, or even percentile ranks. Categorical data are qualities such as people's sex, ethnic group, political party, or smoking status (smokers versus nonsmokers). These qualities, unlike age and income, do not exist naturally as quantities and cannot be represented by numbers indicating how much of them one has. Hence, these qualities cannot be added, subtracted, or averaged. One can calculate a mean age for a sample but not a mean sex, race, or marital status. Thus the mean and standard deviation are useful (as detailed above) only for **continuous variables,** variables that naturally exist as quantities in a series ranging from low to high and can be represented by numbers. Categorical (or **discrete**) variables are not continuous or sequential—smoker is not higher or lower than nonsmoker, and male is not higher or lower than female, the way that age 32 is higher than age 22. The only descriptive statistic that can be used for categorical data is the mode—one can report that the most frequent ethnic group was White, for example.

Nonetheless, categorical data are interesting and sometimes are what one wishes to examine. For example, one might wish to know if children of alcoholic fathers tend to become alcoholics themselves, whether they are male or female. The variables to analyze are all categorical and are not numbers or quantities: (1) father was alcoholic versus was not, (2) the person is alcoholic versus is not, and (3) the person is male versus female. Alternatively, one might wish to know if people who smoke tend to be of a specific sex, ethnic group, and the children of smokers, in order to predict who to target with a smoking prevention program. The variables are male versus female, White versus minority, and parent did versus did not smoke. Similarly, health researchers often want to know the sex and ethnic group of people most likely to contract a disease (AIDS, hypertension, cancer) in order to decide how to tailor health promotion campaigns. Each of these is an example of **epidemiological data** (where epidemiology is the study of the distribution of disease or disease-related behavior by status character-istics), and such data clearly are important. Because categorical data are scientifically important despite not being numbers, special statistical equa-tions exist for analyzing them, as shown later here.

The descriptive statistics above are the only ones used in this book. Before turning to the next type of statistics used in this book (inferential statistics), we need to consider variance further, because it is the central issue in inferential statistics.

Why Variance Is the Key

It has been noted that variance refers to the differences among people, whether in age, income, or physical and psychiatric symptoms. In the final analysis, statistics—and science—is about variance: both are about analyz-ing variance, predicting variance, and explaining variance. For example, suppose we want to understand why some people are depressed whereas others are not. Another of way of saying this is that we want to understand why there is variance in depression—why there are differences among people on this symptom. If we want to know why some people commit crimes, or commit suicide, or abuse drugs, or smoke cigarettes, or have some specific psychiatric disorder or physical illness, in the final analysis, we want to understand the variance among people on each of these variables or problems: We want to predict the variance (predict who will and won't develop the problem) and **account for** (explain the reasons behind) **the variance.** Variance then is the heart of the matter.

The total variance, *all* of the differences among a sample of people on a variable of interest, can be thought of as **100% of the variance.** For example, if we measure depression in a sample of people, using the Beck Depression Inventory (BDI; a well-known scale), all of the differences among the sample on the BDI (some people scoring high, others low/non-depressed) can be conceptualized as 100% of the variance on the BDI. Scientists then seek to predict and explain ("to account for" is the phrase used) as much of this variance as possible. To account for 50% of the variance is better than accounting for 5% of variance, in that more of what is going on with people (more of the differences among them) is being predicted and explained. As shown below, then, many inferential statistics are equations for calculating **the percentage of variance** in the variable of interest (called the **outcome variable**) that is accounted for by some other variable.

For example, if we wanted to know if being physically abused as a child (explanatory or **independent variable**) is related to adult amount of alcohol use (the outcome or **dependent variable** we want to explain), we would use inferential statistics to calculate the percentage of variance in adult alcohol use that is accounted for (predicted from and explained by) early childhood physical abuse. The larger the percentage of variance in adult alcohol use accounted for, the better we can predict and explain the differences among people in the amount they drink—and so the better we can predict and explain who will versus won't drink a lot and why. Outcome or dependent variables are the problems (e.g., drug abuse, depression, hypertension, poor school grades) that we want to predict, understand, and explain. They are called dependent because we assume and theorize that their variance is *dependent on* (caused by) other factors. Those other factors, the presumed causes of the problem, are called independent variables.

Predicting and explaining the variance in human behavior is not easy because people are extraordinarily complex. On the whole, no matter what behavior we wish to predict and explain (so that we can prevent or change it), more than one independent variable is involved—many factors are the cause of the behavior rather than a single factor. For example, some people who were abused as children become abusers themselves, but many more do not; early abuse by itself only accounts for a small percentage of the variance in later violence among adults, and other independent variables must be involved, to account for the remainder of the variance. Thus most research on human behavior takes a **multivariate** approach: Most researchers investigate many (multi) variables (variates) in their efforts to account for the outcome behavior, instead of taking a **univariate** approach.

How Much Variance Is Accounted for?

Because of the inherent complexity of human behavior, sadly, the typical social or psychological independent variable tends to account for 5% to perhaps 10% of the variance in the human behavior being studied—no matter what that behavior is, and no matter what the independent variable is: Whether the independent variable is physical abuse as a child, sexual abuse as a child, alcoholism among parents, or poverty, it probably accounts for 5% to 10% of the variance in behavior—no matter what that outcome behavior is (e.g., delinquency, drug abuse, violence, depression). Because 5% to 10% isn't much of the variance, many variables are needed to truly predict and explain human behavior. Hence, to be able to account for 10% of the variance in the outcome behavior with a single independent variable (IV) is good, and that IV is regarded as a powerful one: five or six of such IVs (predictors) together would account for 50% to 60% of the variance, and the latter is enough to be able to predict behavior and design interventions to prevent or change it.

In light of this, we can say that an independent variable that accounts for *less than 5% of the variance* isn't much of a predictor, cause, or explanation for the behavior under investigation.

Finally, you will find in our studies that sexist discrimination (as measured by our scale) accounted for more of the variance in symptoms among women than did ordinary life stress—sexist treatment was a better predictor and explanation of physical and psychiatric symptoms among women. Most important, you also will see that **sexist discrimination alone accounted for up to 46% of the variance in women's symptoms.** Given that a typical social-psychological variable accounts for 5% to 10% of the variance, our findings are astounding and highlight the enormous importance of discrimination against women in women's lives.

With the centrality of variance explained, we can turn to inferential statistics.

II. Inferential Statistics

Inferential statistics are a separate type of statistics whose purpose is to permit one to infer (hence: inferential) what scores and events for the

population are like, based on the scores and events of the sample studied. No scientist in any field can study the entire population of interest (e.g., all American women, all people in the United States, all people who have cancer or AIDS). Instead, all scientific research (necessarily) is based on gathering and studying a **sample** (a small group) from the population of interest, and then generalizing to the population. Because inferential statistics permit generalization to the population from the sample, they are the most important statistics used in all scientific research, no matter the type:

- A cure for a specific type of cancer is not based on all cancer patients in the country (let alone in the world) but only on those in a clinical-trials sample.
- The proof that HIV causes AIDS is not based on all people in the world who are HIV-positive but on a sample studied.
- Likewise, a scientist studying the extent to which cigarette smoking causes lung cancer cannot possibly study every single smoker in the country—let alone in the world. Hence, the researcher gathers a sample, and uses inferential statistics to generalize from the causal relationship found for that sample to a causal relationship for the entire population of smokers.

Inferential statistics are the heart and soul of scientific research because, without them, scientists would only be able to draw conclusions about their own samples (about the specific small groups of people they studied) and would be able to say nothing about the populations they wish to help. The size of the sample is not the issue here because even a large sample (e.g., $N = 20,000$) is still puny relative to a population of 260 million Americans, and inferential statistics are still needed to generalize to the population. Such generalizations are not "bad" science and are not unusual in science but instead *are science*. Generalizations from a sample to a population also are not sly, devious, bogus, wild, or unfounded. Rather, inferential statistics are equations that permit highly precise estimates of the probability that what is true for a sample is true for the population as well. Hence, whereas generalizations about people almost always are "bad" in that they are unfounded, baseless, and probably false, those based on inferential statistics are not unfounded or baseless, are probably true, and therefore are not bad.

In this book, then, we focus on the experiences of two samples of women (one sample of 631, and another of 652 women) with sexist discrimination. We examine the extent to which that discrimination accounts for the variance in the symptoms of these 1,283 women—the extent to which discrimination harms the women—and we use inferential statistics to generalize to all women in the country.

Limits of Generalization. Generalizations to a population from a sample can be made by use of inferential statistics, however, if and only if the sample is **representative** of the population to which one wishes to generalize. If one wishes to generalize to all Americans, then the sample must represent the diversity among Americans in terms of age, sex, income, geographical region of residence, religion, and ethnic group. If one wishes to generalize to all American women, the women in the sample must represent all women in the country; only then are inferential statistics valid. A major problem in research on women (in psychology of women, women's studies, etc.) is that samples tend to be White, middle-class college students. Such samples clearly do not represent all women in the country in terms of age, social class, ethnicity, or education. Inferential statistics used to generalize from such samples can only generalize to all White, middle-class, college-student women in the country, and no statements can be made about other women. Most people would evaluate generalizing from a sample of poor (welfare) Black mothers to all women in the country as bogus; generalizing from middle-class, White, college students (nonmothers) to all women in the county is equally bogus.

Hence, because most scientific research on women uses such samples, it cannot make valid claims about minority women, poor women, or older women, such that we in fact know very little about these groups of women (Landrine, 1995). Likewise, many—in fact most—medical studies that seek cures for health problems (e.g., heart attacks), as well as health and psychological studies, are based on samples composed entirely of men—and usually, entirely of White men. Generalizations from such samples to all people (to women) cannot be made and can be dangerous (e.g., a recent news report on a treatment for heart attacks—based on a sample of White men—that did not help, and even harmed, women heart attack victims). Courses on the psychology of women—and on Black psychology and cross-cultural psychology—exist because most psychological (and almost all medical) research is based entirely on samples of White men; separate courses, covering the (relatively little) research on women and minorities are necessary to compensate for this bias.

In summary, then, generalizing from a sample to a population is not bad, bogus science *unless* the sample in question does not represent the population in question. It is imperative that samples be representative of the population to whom one wishes to generalize—and inferential statistics assume such a match. This often means that the researcher must have a large sample (500 instead of 50) in order for it to represent the diversity of the population. A study based on 50 White college students should be dismissed because it can make statements about very few Americans through its inferential statistics. In this book, our samples *are* representative of the population of American women: Our samples include women on welfare and rich women; Black, Asian, and Latina women, as well as Whites; older women and young ones; married women, divorced/ widowed women, and single women; and secretaries, administrators, lawyers, businesswomen, and housewives from the community, as well as some college students.

Types of Inferential Statistics. The many types of inferential statistics can be classified into two broad categories, **group-differences statistics** and **prediction statistics.** These are shown in Table A.1 below, where we list *only* the statistics used in this book. As shown, these statistics differ in terms of the number of variables and the number of groups being studied (IVs is used for independent variables, and DVs for dependent variables, in the table). When the statistic is a group differences statistic, column 2 (second from left) indicates the number of groups in the study, whereas, when the statistic is a prediction statistic, column 2 indicates the number of independent variables.

Group Differences Statistics

The *t test* is the simplest group differences statistic, and it is used to compare two groups on one dependent variable to see if the groups differ. If we wanted to know if minority women and White women (two groups) differed in their scores on a measure of sexism, and that measure gave a single score (dependent variable), we would conduct a *t* test.

Analysis of variance (ANOVA) is used to compare two or more groups on one dependent (outcome) variable; it can be thought of as the multigroup generalization of the *t* test. If we wanted to know if Black women, Latinas, and Asian women (three groups) differed on an outcome measure, we would conduct an **ANOVA.** Notice that ANOVA and a *t* test could both be used to analyze differences between two groups on one dependent variable; which a scientist uses is a matter of whim.

TABLE A.1 Types of Inferential Statistics Used in This Book

			Prediction Statistics	
Dependent Variables	Independent Variables or Groups	Group Differences Statistics	Continuous Data	Categorical Data
1	2	t test Tukey HSD test	Bivariate correlation	Chi-square
1	2 or more	Analysis of variance (ANOVA)	Multiple correlation	Logit-loglinear
2 or more	2 or more	Multivariate analysis of variance (MANOVA) Cluster analysis of cases	Multiple correlation	Logit-loglinear

Multivariate analysis of variance (MANOVA) is used to compare two or more groups on more than one dependent variable; it can be thought of as the multivariate generalization of ANOVA. If we wanted to compare minority women and White women (two groups) on a whole set of symptom measures, we would use MANOVA. MANOVA is the analysis used most often in this book, because we have more than one dependent variable for our groups—we measure many types of physical and psychiatric symptoms at once and many experiences with discrimination at once. For example, in Chapter 2, we compare women of four different age groups to see if they differ in their experiences with two types of sexist discrimination (their scores on our Lifetime Sexist Events and Recent Sexist Events scales—two DVs) using MANOVA.

Cluster Analysis of Cases

A cluster analysis is a MANOVA (with two or more groups and multiple dependent variables) in which the computer program, rather than the researcher, determines the groups (called **clusters**). For example, suppose we wanted to know if women who have high depressive symptoms versus those with low depressive symptoms differ in the frequency with which they experience sexist discrimination, ordinary stress, and financial problems. One way to answer the question would be to conduct a MANOVA comparing these two groups of women on the three dependent variables. To do so, however, we would have to decide how to define high versus low depressive symptoms and could choose any criteria we want.

Thus we could (unconsciously) choose a criterion that would guarantee the desired result—that the groups differ on sexist discrimination.

The alternative and more objective analysis is a cluster analysis of cases. In that analysis, we would instruct the computer program to generate two groups of women (two clusters) who differed on depressive symptoms, sexist discrimination, ordinary stress, and financial problems. The program then groups the women (the **cases**) into clusters that differ on as many of these DVs as possible. There is no guarantee that the clusters will differ on sexist discrimination (the variable we are interested in) and no way to control how high and low depressive symptoms will be defined. The program instead selects cases that naturally differ as much as possible from each other on as many of the DVs as possible to create clusters. The program then yields a MANOVA (cluster) F, follow-up ANOVAs, and post-hoc tests (see below). In cluster analysis, researchers can request as many clusters as they like. We use cluster analysis in Chapter 2 as an objective, unbiased test of whether ethnicity is associated with experiencing highly frequent sexist discrimination, requesting first two and then three clusters.

What Do These Group Differences Statistics Do?

Notice that the word variance appears in the title of the group differences statistics and recall the prior discussion of how variance is the heart of the matter. This is because all inferential statistics analyze variance—and that is the only thing they do. In group differences statistics, groups of people are compared to see if they differ from each other or not by comparing their variance. The logic behind these analyses is this: For two groups of people to differ from each other, there must be more differences between them (between-groups variance) than within either group (within-groups variance). For example, in order for Black women and White women to be said to differ from each other in their attitude toward abortion, they must differ more *from each other* in their opinion than they do *among themselves*. If Black women differ so much among themselves in their attitude toward abortion that one cannot even say exactly what their attitude *as a group* is, then they surely cannot be said to differ *as a group* in their attitude from White women *as a group*. Hence, all group differences statistics simply compare the variance between groups to the variance within groups; the between-groups variance must be larger than (must exceed) the within-groups variance for groups to be said to truly differ from each other. The ratio of the between- to the within-groups variance is the test of whether the groups differ from each other or not. In the t test, this ratio is t, in ANOVA, this ratio is F, and in MANOVA this ratio is given twice as T^2 and as F. In the many statistical tables in this book, t, F, and T^2 appear repeatedly; these simply are tests of the extent to which groups differ on the dependent variable(s). All group differences statistics use the means and standard deviations for groups to arrive at a ratio of the between- to the within-groups variance (t, F, or T^2). In the process of calculating this ratio, the **Sums of Squares** (indicated in our tables as SS), a comparison of group variances, is calculated first.

Post-hoc Tests. When two groups are compared on a single dependent variable through a t test or ANOVA and are found to differ from each other as described above, it is clear that Group 1 differs from Group 2. However, in an ANOVA with more than two groups found to differ from each other on a single dependent variable, the F value tells us only that the groups differ, but it does not tell us which group differs from which group: Group 1 could differ from Group 3, or Group 2 from Group 3, or all groups from all other groups. In the multigroup ANOVA then, an additional set of group differences statistics is required to reveal which groups differed from which groups and thereby led to the F. Because these additional analyses are conducted only *after* the F has shown that groups differ (just not which ones), these analyses are called **post-hoc** (Latin for "after the fact") tests. Post-hoc tests (sometimes called **pairwise comparisons**) are a special form of the t test: After F indicates that 3, or 4, or 5 groups differ, each group is compared to every other group in pairs (hence: pairwise comparisons) by a special t test to find out where the differences were. The post-hoc t test we use in this book is called the **Tukey HSD,** where Tukey is the last name of the statistician who devised the equation, and HSD means *honestly significant difference.*

Post-hocs in Two-Group MANOVA. When two groups are compared on more than one dependent variable (e.g., Black women and White women are compared on four types of symptoms) in a MANOVA, the T^2 and F values tell us that Group 1 differed from Group 2, but they do not tell us on which of the dependent variables they differed; they could have differed on only the first or the third of the dependent variables. Again, additional analyses are needed, but this time to figure out the variable on which groups differed. The additional analyses here are ANOVAs (called **follow-up ANOVAs**) comparing the two groups on each dependent variable, one DV at a time.

Post-hocs in Multigroup MANOVA. Finally, the most complex case is the MANOVA with more than two groups (say, four groups) and multiple dependent variables (say, five symptom measures). In this case, the T^2 and F values tell us that the groups differed—but not which groups—on some of the dependent variables—but not on which ones. Hence: first the follow-up ANOVAs are conducted to figure out which DVs the groups differed on; this is done first because there's no point to conducting all pairwise comparisons (Tukey HSD tests) on a DV that the groups did not differ on. Next, the pairwise comparisons (post-hoc tests) are calculated to see which groups differed from others on the DVs highlighted by the follow-up ANOVAs.

The above statistical tests must be conducted in precisely this order— from MANOVA to ANOVA to post-hocs, from general to specific to highly specific. A set of ANOVAs comparing groups on each of the specific DVs (one DV at a time) cannot be conducted **without first conducting the MANOVA on the entire set of DVs.** To do so would be like having a series of highly specific, medical tests on each of your bodily systems (blood tests, urine analyses, chest X-ray, gynecological exam, neurologic exam, endocrinological exam, immune function exam) without first having a general physical that indicated you are sick—that there's a problem. There is no point to follow-up medical tests without the general physical first, and consequently, most physicians would refuse to conduct them. Worst still, if you had all of these specific medical tests in the absence of a general physical that revealed a problem, at least one of these specific tests would come back abnormal purely by chance—**even though you are not sick (do not have a problem of any significance).** The abnormal result could be due to a trivial problem you have (such as an allergy causing an abnormal blood test), or it could be an error (**a false positive**) on the part of the lab. Furthermore, the more of these specific medical tests you have, the greater the chances that one of them will come back abnormal **even though you are not sick**; the more tests you have (100 tests vs. 4), the higher the chances that they'll find something wrong with you—trivial or erroneous, but wrong with you. The same is true for statistical analyses:

A series of specific ANOVA tests (one on each DV) conducted without first conducting the general MANOVA can (and often do) reveal a difference between groups on one of the DVs that is purely by chance— when the groups do not in fact differ in any major way. Such a finding is called a **spurious result** and is analogous to a false positive medical test: it is a result that says there is something present (a difference between groups, an illness) when there is not. Likewise, the *more* statistical tests run on a set of data (*t* tests, *F* tests, Tukey tests, or any combination)—like the more medical tests run —the higher the probability that at least one of them will indicate a difference between groups that is, in fact, purely spurious. Throughout this book, we conduct many statistical analyses of interesting questions that are important for women. In many instances, we raise other important questions but then **fail to run any more statistical tests** to answer them (and instead, invite other researchers to do so). In the text, we state that we are trying to reduce (and hold to minimum necessary) the number of consecutive statistical tests. The reason is to avoid spurious results—false positives that are not true and are misleading.

So Where's the Inference in These Inferential Statistics?

Group differences inferential statistics do more than compare the groups within a sample; they also simultaneously make inferences to the population. For example, a t test comparing White and minority women on depression not only reveals whether these two sample groups differ from each other but also estimates the precise probability that this finding for the sample of White and minority women is true for the entire U.S. population of White and minority women as well; this is the inference, the generalization to the population from the sample, in all inferential statistics.

The statistic alpha (symbolized as the letter p or by symbol α) is given along with **every inferential statistic** (group differences statistics such as F, t, T^2, and HSD and prediction statistics such as r, r^2, R, and R^2). Alpha is the probability that the sample groups differ *but that the population groups do not.* Alpha is the probability (the chances) that what is true for the sample *is not true* for the entire population. Hence, researchers desire for alpha to be as small as possible because the smaller the p value, the lower the chances that what is true for the sample *is not* true for the population—and hence the higher the probability that what is true for the sample *is also true* for the population.

Thus a scientist might report that White and minority women's attitude toward abortion scores differ at $p = .01$. This means that the chances are less than one in 100 that the White and minority women in the sample differed while the White and minority women in the country (the population) actually don't. As will be seen in this book, our group-differences statistics are reported at $p = .00001$. This means that when we find differences between young and older women, or White and Latina women in our samples, the chances are less than 1 in 100,000 that those differences *do not* also exist in the population. In other words, the differences we find in our samples are highly likely to exist in the population as well—and hence findings from our samples are important.

Statistical Significance. The p or α value is called **the level of significance**: to say that a finding is **statistically significant** (or simply, "significant") is to say that the differences between the sample groups are not chance but are systematic (insofar as the variance between groups exceeds the variance within) *and* it is to say that what was found for the sample represents the state of affairs for the population at p (α) level of probability. This is how scientists generalize—on very good grounds—from samples to populations.

As a general rule, a statistical result (difference between sample groups) must be **significant at** $p < .05$ to be considered statistically significant: The chances must be less than 5 in 100 that what was found for the sample *does not exist* in the population for the result to be generalized to the population (if the chances are less than 5 in 100 that sample findings *don't exist* for the population, then the chances are more than 95 out of 100 that they *do* exist for the population). A $p < .05$ is the absolute minimum criterion for statistical significance and generalization to the population; we prefer higher levels of significance ($p = .001$ or more).

In summary then, the various group differences statistics all compare the between- to the within-groups variance to test if sample groups differ from each other. All such statistics simultaneously test the probability that what is true for the sample is also true for the population, with this probability indicated as a p value written near t, F, and other group-differences tests. Another value also appears along with F and p in all statistical tables, namely *df*, the degrees of freedom. This, as noted earlier, is the number of values in the equations that are free to vary. Understanding why the *df* is important is not necessary for comprehending the statistical analyses and tables in this book, and hence we do not discuss degrees of freedom here. What is important to understand in group differences statistics is the concept of variance, the meaning of F, t, and other tests, the meaning of p and of statistical significance, and of the purpose and proper use of ANOVA, MANOVA, and post-hoc tests.

Finally, earlier we noted that, the more statistical tests run, the higher the chances of finding a spurious result (a false positive). More precisely, what we meant is that the more **significance tests** run (on a t, F, or HSD), the higher the probability of **spurious significance**—of getting a spurious $p < .05$ indicating that the sample results hold for the population *when in* *fact they do not.* This problem of spurious significance due to running too many tests is so common that it has a name in statistics, namely, a **Type 1 error.**

We turn now to the prediction-type of inferential statistics.

III. Prediction Statistics

The Bivariate Correlation

The **bivariate correlation** (also called simple **regression**), symbolized as *r,* is the simplest of the prediction statistics. A correlation is a measure of the extent to which the variance in one variable (e.g., frequency of early childhood abuse) predicts (because it matches) the variance in another variable (e.g., amount of alcohol use in adulthood). It is a measure of the degree to which highs and lows (variance) in one variable (the predictor variable, symbolized as x) match and so predict highs and lows (variance) in the outcome variable (symbolized as y), a measure of how variables change together, in concert. Thus it is a measure of the co-relationship (hence: co-relation) of two variables.

When two variables are highly correlated, the variance in one can readily be predicted from the variance in the other, but this does not mean that the relationship between the variables is a causal one. For example, a strong correlation between early physical abuse (x, predictor) and amount of alcohol consumption in adulthood (y, outcome variable) *does not necessarily mean* that physical abuse in childhood (x) *causes adult alcohol consumption (y)—it could mean that, but it doesn't have to mean that. Instead, the two variables could be highly correlated because they are both* caused by a third variable—poverty, economic hardship. Correlations do not prove causation; causation must be proved through direct, experimental evidence. Thus a strong correlation between various types of stress and physical or psychiatric symptoms *does not prove* that stress causes those symptoms. Rather, the proof that stress causes the symptoms comes from experimental studies in which increasing the stress that animals are subjected to (e.g., the noise) causes immunological changes that then cause symptoms. One cannot reach a causal conclusion based on a correlation alone but instead must have direct, experimental proof of causation— where the latter is the *only* way to prove causation.

The fact that correlations do not prove or demonstrate causation does not make them useless however. Rather, correlations are highly precise measures of the extent to which one variable predicts another and are thereby important in and of themselves. This is because, if one variable predicts another, then changing the predictor variable *will change* the outcome variable whether the relationship between the two is a causal one or not: If stress (e.g., number of daily hassles) is (positively) correlated with (predicts) depression, that means that the variance in the two match— that low stress is related to low depression and high stress to high depression. Hence decreasing stress to a low level should (and does) decrease depression, whether stress causes depression or not. With the ability to predict a problem behavior comes the ability to change that problem behavior, irrespective of why the correlation exists.

Direction of Correlation. Correlations can represent two kinds of relationships between variables that are called **positive** and **negative.** A positive correlation (relationship between the predictor x and the outcome y) is one in which increases in x are related to increases in y, and decreases in x are related to decreases in y. The examples given above (the stress-depression correlation and the abuse-alcohol use correlation) are of **positive correlations**; in both cases, increases in the predictor are associated with increases in the outcome variable. The **direction** of the relationship between the variables is called positive because both variables change together in the same manner. Alternatively, a **negative correlation** is one in which increases in x are related to decreases in y, and increases in y are related to decreases in x. The direction of the relationship is called negative because the two variables change together in the *opposite* manner. For example, income and frequency of exposure to violence are negatively correlated: as income *decreases* (from middle-class suburban life to life in an urban slum), the amount of violence people observe around them *increases.* The terms negative and positive refer *only to* the nature of the relationship between x and y. To indicate that the direction of a correlation is negative, a minus sign (–) appears before the correlation. If the correlation is positive, no sign appears.

Strength of Correlation. The strength of a correlation refers to how well the outcome is predicted from the predictor—to how well the variance in the variables match. Correlations can be weak, moderate, strong, or perfect. The strength of a correlation is represented by a number, and the larger this value, the greater the variance in the outcome predicted and accounted for by the predictor. For all correlations, this number or value ranges from zero (no correlation at all) to 1.00 (a perfect correlation in which y is perfectly predicted from x), as shown in Table A.2. Again, a negative sign in front of any of the numbers indicates the direction (not the strength) of the correlation. Hence, $r = -.50$ is stronger than (greater than) $r = -.30$.

Table A.3 depicts a positive (top of table) and a negative (bottom) correlation. The actual scores on the two measures are shown on the right, and a graph (called a **scatter plot**) of the relationship between the variables on the left. The positive correlation shown at the top of the table is $r = .87$, a very strong correlation that approximates a straight line. The negative correlation shown at the bottom of the table is weaker ($r = -.68$) and does not approximate a straight line as well as the correlation at the top. A perfect correlation—positive or negative—*is* a straight line on which the samples' scores (dots shown in the scatter plots) lie.

Variance Accounted for by r. The correlation squared (r^2) is a measure of the precise degree of overlap or match between the variances of the two variables. Thus, r^2 ($\times$ 100%) is the exact percentage of variance in the outcome predicted by (accounted for by) the predictor. For example, for $r = .25$, $r^2 = .25 \times .25 = .0625$—meaning that 6.25% of the variance in the outcome is accounted for by the predictor (this is how much they overlap). Because 6.25% is not much of the variance, rs of this level (.20-.30) are weak. For an $r = -.73$, on the other hand, $r^2 = -.73 \times -.73 = .5329$, meaning that 53.29% of the variance in the outcome variable is accounted for by the predictor.

Statistical Significance of r. When a correlation between two variables is calculated for a sample, a significance test (with a p or α value) also is calculated. If a correlation is statistically significant, this means that the relationship between the variables for the sample is not by chance or random (but due to the matching of the variances) *and* that this is probably true for the population as well. The p value of a correlation is a test of the probability that a correlation exists for the sample but *does not exist* for the population. An $r = -.69$ with $p = .00001$ means that the predictor variable accounts for 47.61% of the variance in the outcome variable (which decreases as the predictor increases), and that the probability that this relationship *is not* true for the entire population as well is less than 1 chance in 100,000—and hence the sample correlation probably holds for the population too.

TABLE A.2 Strength of Correlations

0.00	.10	.20	.30	.40	.50	.60	.70	.80	.90	1.00
none	weak		moderate		strong		very strong			perfect

The Multivariate (Multiple) Correlation

The bivariate correlation is called bivariate because it is the relationship between two variables, a single predictor and an outcome variable. Given how complex people are, scientists rarely attempt to predict their behavior or problems from a single predictor and instead use many predictors. The **multiple correlation** (symbolized by R) is the multivariate generalization of the bivariate correlation and examines the extent to which two or more predictor variables can predict and account for the variance in an outcome variable. Thus, for example, instead of attempting to predict depression among women (y) from marital problems alone, most scientists would use a package of predictors including marital problems ($x1$), economic problems ($x2$), lack of social support ($x3$), and other variables. Multiple correlations, like bivariate correlations, can be positive or negative, range from zero to 1.00 in terms of their strength, and their statistical significance is tested in the same manner as bivariate correlations. Thus, an $R = -.69$ is larger than $R = .30$, and the former relationship is negative, whereas the latter is positive. Likewise, R^2 is an indication of the degree of overlap between the set of predictors and the outcome variable and so indicates the amount of variance in the outcome that is accounted for by the set of predictors. Multiple correlation is often called **multiple regression,** which means precisely the same thing.

One common procedure for calculating R is called **stepwise regression** or stepwise multiple correlation. In this procedure, the multiple regression computer program selects the one predictor (from the whole set of predictors) that has the single strongest bivariate correlation with the outcome. This predictor is selected first on what is called the **first step** (or step 1) because it is the best predictor of them all. Then the program proceeds to select the next best predictor of the outcome variable (on step 2); this is a predictor that increases the size of R (that assists the first variable in predicting the outcome), even though it is not as strong a predictor as the variable selected on the first step. Together, the two predictors account for more variance in the outcome than any one of them alone, and so the program increases the size of R to show the amount of

TABLE A.3 Examples of Types of Correlations

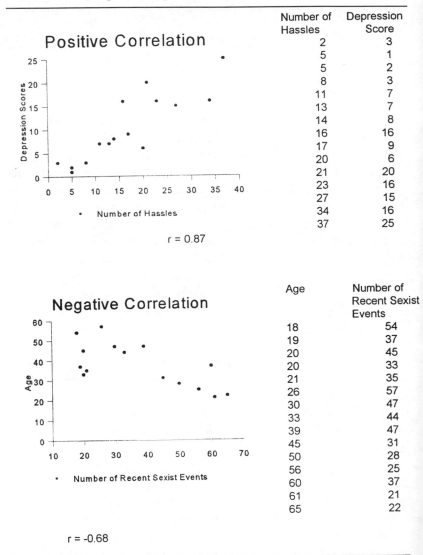

	Number of Hassles	Depression Score
	2	3
	5	1
	5	2
	8	3
	11	7
	13	7
	14	8
	16	16
	17	9
	20	6
	21	20
	23	16
	27	15
	34	16
	37	25

r = 0.87

Age	Number of Recent Sexist Events
18	54
19	37
20	45
20	33
21	35
26	57
30	47
33	44
39	47
45	31
50	28
56	25
60	37
61	21
65	22

r = -0.68

variance in the outcome accounted for by predictor 1 and predictor 2 together. This procedure continues until all of the good predictors (those that increase the size of R) have been selected. The program then gives a **regression equation,** a recipe for the outcome variable, that says (for example) that a high score on predictor 1 plus a low score on predictor 2 plus a high score on predictor 3 is the best way to predict the outcome behavior being studied. Most important here is that:

- ▓ The predictor selected on the first step is the single best predictor of the outcome (if one could only use a single predictor of the behavior, this is it), and it is better than the others.
- ▓ If the program selects only one predictor and no others, then the remaining variables failed to increase R appreciably and were poor predictors of the outcome relative to the predictor selected on the first step.

In this book, we present many stepwise multiple regressions.

Analyzing Categorical Data

The group differences and prediction statistics presented thus far are all based on the assumption that the variables being studied are continuous variables. Alternative analyses for categorical data are needed. In this book, we use two such statistics: chi-square and the phi-coefficient. Because we use each of these rarely, our description of them is brief.

Chi-square (symbolized as χ^2) is a measure of the strength of association between two or more categorical variables (e.g., male v. female and smoker v. nonsmoker). It indicates the extent to which membership in one category (e.g., male v. female) can predict membership in another (smoker v. nonsmoker). An example of the kind of data that would be analyzed through χ^2 is shown in Table A.4, where it is clear that there is a strong association between sex and smoking (more men than women are smokers). Each box in Table A.4 is called a **cell** (e.g., the women nonsmoker cell is shaded) and indicates the number of people (called the **cell count**) who fall in the intersection of the two categories.

The value of χ^2 ranges from zero to any number, like the value of t and F. The statistical significance of χ^2 is also tested; a significant χ^2 (one with a p value $< .05$) means that the association between the categories found for the sample probably exists for the population as well. When chi-square is statistically significant, the cells tend to have **matching diagonals.** That is, if we look diagonally from men smoker down to women nonsmoker, and up from women smoker to men nonsmoker, we see that the cell counts along these diagonals are nearly identical.

The phi coefficient (symbolized as ϕ) is a bivariate correlation for categorical data. All of the rules that apply to r apply to ϕ as well. Phi is

TABLE A.4 Examples of Cell-Frequency Data Used in Chi-Square
Analysis

	Smokers	Nonsmokers	Totals
Men	62	38	100
Women	35	65	100
Totals	97	103	200

usually reported alongside a significant χ^2 to give an indication (in corre-
lation-type language) of the strength of the χ^2 and of the percentage of
variance in membership in one category that is predicted from and accounted for by membership in the other.

IV. Data-Reduction Statistics: Factor Analysis

Factor analysis is a type of statistics whose purpose is to reduce either
a set of IVs or a set of DVs to a smaller set that is easier to understand,
analyze, and discuss. There are many types of factor analysis. The one most
commonly used in research and used in this book is called **principal
components analysis** (PCA) and so only it is described here.

PCA reduces a set of variables to a smaller number by examining the
bivariate correlations among them. PCA assumes that a set of IVs (or a set
of DVs) that have large (strong) correlations are related to each other—a
reasonable assumption. Specifically, however, PCA assumes that highly
correlated variables in a set are highly correlated *because* they all reflect
or are part of a single, underlying (unifying) dimension that they have in
common. This hypothetical unifying dimension is called a **factor** or **principal component.** A factor or principal component is an underlying,
theoretical dimension, one not measured or assessed but assumed to be
there and to explain why a set of IVs or DVs are highly correlated. The
variables that one actually measures are called **manifest** variables, where
this term means obvious, on the surface. Factors or principal components
are **latent** variables, hidden, beneath the surface dimensions that explain
why and how the IVs or DVs are highly correlated.

For example, suppose we wanted to predict and explain adult criminal behavior from these IVs:

1. Was a low-birthweight infant
2. Did not reach developmental milestones (sitting up, talking, walking)
   on time

3. Grew up in poverty
4. Grew up in a broken home
5. Father had criminal history
6. Was physically abused as a child
7. Had poor grades in elementary school
8. Has a history of truancy throughout Grades 2 to 12
9. Smoked cigarettes at age 13
10. Fought with peers throughout grade and high school
11. Uses alcohol
12. Uses marijuana and other drugs
13. Assaulted at least one adult when age 14 to 16
14. Caught stealing at age 12
15. Belonged to a gang when a teen
16. Spent free time with "bad" kids

Because 16 IVs is too many to discuss, we'd conduct a PCA to reduce them. This set of 16 IVs is likely to be highly correlated, with some variables having stronger correlations than others. PCA would examine these correlations and then put them into groups (factors) based on that. Three factors might be found:

	Factor 1		Factor 2		Factor 3
Variable 1	.80	Variable 9	.90	Variable 6	.99
Variable 2	.75	Variable 11	.87	Variable 5	.81
Variable 7	.70	Variable 12	.84	Variable 10	.71
Variable 3	.64	Variable 14	.76	Variable 13	.58
Variable 4	.63	Variable 15	.61		
Variable 8	.62	Variable 16	.59		
Factor Eigenvalue:	6.305		4.51		1.49
Factor Percentage of Variance:	43.00%		7.15%		5.85%

The variables that fall into these factors (**load** on these factors) seem to have something in common. Those on the first factor seem to be early childhood variables suggestive of underlying neurological problems. A researcher might call this factor *distal childhood variables* because a distal variable is one that sets the stage for problems. Or one might call it *early childhood variables* or *neuro-behavioral influences*—a researcher can name a factor whatever he or she likes. The variables in the second factor are about substance use (9, 11, and 12), whereas the remainder are about associating with deviant peers. One might call this factor *early deviant behavior* or *early law-breaking*. Finally, the variables in the third factor are all about physical violence on the part of others and on the part of the adult criminals we are trying to understand through this PCA; this factor might be named *violence*.

Hence, the PCA reduced 16 variables to a mere 3: It is easier to examine the relative influence of three factors (three underlying variables) on criminal behavior than it is to examine the role of 16 variables. One can readily examine which of the 3 factors accounts for the most variance in later criminal behavior (through a multiple regression) whereas it would be more difficult to use all 16 variables.

The statistical procedures involved in PCA are as follows. First, the computer program calculates bivariate correlations among all of the variables. Then, it pulls out (called **extraction**) the small set of variables that are highly correlated *and account for the largest percentage of the variance* in the sample's scores on the whole package of variables being analyzed and calls this subset the first factor or first principle component. The statistic **eigenvalue** is a measure of how strong a factor is, or how much of the variance in scores on all of the variables in the analysis is accounted for by this subset of variables alone. The general rule is that the eigenvalue of a factor must be at least equal to 1.00. Hence researchers instruct the computer program not to **retain** any factor whose eigenvalue is not at least 1.00 because such a factor accounts for too little of the variance to attend to. The program then extracts a second subset of highly correlated variables that account for the second-largest percentage of the variance in scores on all of the variables; this second factor does not account for as much variance as the first one, and its eigenvalue is therefore smaller. The program continues to extract factors until all of the variables have been included in the factors, or until the next factor has an eigenvalue less than 1.00, at which point it stops. All of the variables may not have **loaded** (fallen) on the factors that were extracted *and* retained—some variables could have loaded on additional but weak factors (with eigenvalues < 1.00) and so will not appear in the printout.

Next to each variable's name, the PCA prints a number called a **factor loading. This is the bivariate correlation between that variable and the factor,** between the variable measured and the hypothetical, latent dimension. The variable that loads the highest on the factor (the strongest *r,* the first variable in the list) provides a hint regarding what the factor is about—what the dimension beneath the variables is.

Finally, when instructing the program to create factors, researchers are free to choose the kind of relationship they would like the factors to have to each other. One common preference is for **orthogonal factors,** factors that are not correlated with each other. Another common preference is for **oblique factors** that are highly correlated. The program is instructed to try and retry the variables by moving them about (called **rotating a factor**) until it can find orthogonal or oblique factors.

In summary, factor analysis is simply a data reduction technique. It does not alter the data but only simplifies them so that one can better analyze and discuss them. By yielding information on the dimensions beneath variables, however, it can assist us in understanding the true nature and function of variables—how they are related in people's lives. Indeed, sometimes the factors on which variables load are a surprise to researchers and provide amazing insights into the underlying structure of people's beliefs or experiences. For example, in a recent study, we examined people's beliefs about the variables that cause physical illnesses. We examined 30 possible causes ranging from biomedical ones such as viruses and bacteria, to psychological ones such as stress, to mystical or supernatural ones such as punishment from God. To our surprise, genetic causes of illness did not load with other biomedical causes, but instead loaded on the Mystical Retribution factor with punishment from God, payback for things one did wrong previously, and hexes and curses (genetic causes correlated with these causes). This told us that people understand genetically caused diseases as an a priori (before the fact) punishment from higher forces.

In this book, we conduct PCAs of the 40 items in our Schedule of Sexist Events. We do so in order to understand the dimensions (or types) of sexist discrimination that women face. The PCA allowed us to reduce all of the DVs to four factors or types of sexist discrimination and then to examine which type harmed women the most. In our PCAs, we conduct an **orthogonal rotation** or a **rotation for orthogonal factors.** This means that we tried to find uncorrelated underlying dimensions of discrimination against women. We failed in that: The correlations among the factors were high despite orthogonal rotations, which means that the various types of discrimination women face are related to each other.

The above discussion has addressed every type of statistical analysis used in this book. Thus we turn now to a few technical terms and analytic strategies regarding psychological tests or scales that also appear in this book.

PSYCHOMETRICS

The scales and tests that we use in this book to measure depression, anxiety, or sexist discrimination are important in and of themselves because they are the data—the source of the data—we analyze. These psychological and social measures must be **reliable** and **valid** or they cannot be used as data. The analysis of the integrity, the "goodness" of a scale or test is called psychometrics (psycho = psychological or social, metric = measures). The integrity of the symptom and stress measures that we use in this book has been established through prior studies. Our own new scale measuring sexist discrimination (The Schedule of Sexist Events), which is the heart of the studies reported here, must be proven to have similar psychometric integrity. Hence, a portion of this book is devoted to statistical analyses to assess the reliability and validity of our scale, and those are explained here.

Reliability

Reliability is the extent to which a scale, instrument, test, or interview measures whatever it measures in a consistent, stable (i.e., reliable) manner; it is one assessment of the "goodness" of a measure. There are several types of reliability, and we discuss only those used in this book.

Test-retest reliability is the extent to which people receive the same score on a scale when they fill out that scale more than once. Theoretically, if the scale is a good (stable, consistent) measure, people's scores on it should be basically the same, no matter how many times they take it. If a scale measures generosity, a person's scores today should pretty closely match their scores next week or 2 weeks from now. If their own scores are not similar to their own scores, something is wrong with the scale, for example, the items or questions could be so ambiguous that people interpret them differently each time they fill out the scale and so receive a vastly different score. To assess the test-retest reliability of a scale, people complete the scale or measure once (test) and then again (1 week to 1 month later; re-test). A bivariate correlation between the two scores is taken and is called the **test-retest reliability coefficient** or the **stability coefficient.** For a test that has no implications for a person's life, this coefficient should be $r = .60$ to .80. For a test that could alter a person's life (e.g., a job qualification test, an IQ test), the reliability coefficient should be .80 to .90;

this assures that a major decision made based on a test score is not a mistake insofar as those tested no doubt would receive the same score if they took the test again.

One problem with using test-retest reliability as a measure of the reliability of a scale is that some attributes or experiences should not be stable over time. Personality traits should be stable over time, and so test-retest reliability is a good way to assess the reliability of a trait scale. But moods should not be stable over time (one would hope a person is not in the same bad mood this month as last month). Likewise, experiences with sexism should not be stable over time but, rather, should increase as more sexist things happen to women. Thus a woman's scores next month (unfortunately) should be higher than her scores this month; the test-retest reliability of the sexism measure consequently might be low, but that would not necessarily mean that the measure was not reliable. When the attribute being measured is not meant to be stable over time, other procedures must be used to establish the reliability of the test. Hence, although we do provide an examination of the test-retest reliability of our scale, we view it as of lesser importance than other types of reliability.

Internal-consistency reliability is the extent to which all of the items in a scale or test measure the same thing. Theoretically, if a scale is a good (stable, consistent) measure, then all of the items in it ought to measure the same thing. Thus, if a scale measures sexist discrimination, all of its items should measure that *and nothing else.* To assess internal consistency, a **correlation matrix,** a table displaying the bivariate correlations between each item and every other item, is calculated. Then, a grand, average intercorrelation of all of the items with each other is calculated, and it is called **Cronbach's alpha** (it has nothing to do with alpha from significance tests). Like other correlations, Cronbach's alpha can range from 0 to 1.00. A Cronbach's alpha of .70 or above is considered high. We report many Cronbach's alphas in this book.

Split-half reliability is similar to internal consistency. The logic again is that, if a test is a consistent measure of something, than all of the items ought to measure that same something. Thus, a person's score on half of the test should be the same as their score on the remaining half—and if it's not, then there's something wrong with the questions. To assess split-half reliability, a person's scores on the even-numbered items and on the odd-numbered items are calculated and the bivariate correlation is used to assess the strength of the similarity in scores.

In this book, we use split-half and internal consistency to assess the reliability of our scale and use test-retest only once.

Validity

Validity is more important than reliability. It is the extent to which a test, scale, or instrument measures what it claims to measure; it is the proof that the test measures what it purports to measure rather than measuring something else. For example, we could use your shoe size as a measure of your intelligence and would find that it is a very reliable (consistent, stable) measure of intelligence: the size of your left and right shoes would be highly correlated (internal consistency, split-half reliability), and your shoe size this week will be highly correlated with your shoe size next week (test-retest reliability). But shoe size would not be a valid measure of intelligence—it does not measure intelligence. In general, it is preferable to take a valid but unreliable test than to take a reliable but invalid test. Typically, when people complain that a test was not fair or was bogus, they mean that it was not valid—that the questions did not actually measure what they claimed to and were supposed to measure but instead measured something else (something silly or irrelevant). Validity, as we discuss briefly, is not easy to prove.

There are many types of validity, and we discuss only those two used in this book. We can think of the types of validity as falling into two categories, **test-related** and **criterion-related** validity.

Convergent validity is one type of test-related validity. Here, one proves that one's own test measures what it claims to measure by showing that scores on it correlate well with scores on other tests that claim to measure the same thing; one seeks to show that such scores **converge.** For example, to prove the convergent validity of a test that claims to measure stress, scores on that test would need to correlate with scores on other tests that similarly claim to measure stress.

The obvious problem with this procedure is that the other tests with which one's own test correlates may not be valid measures either. Hence, convergent validity is useful *only* if the validity of one of the tests has been established through criterion-related validity procedures. Likewise, many tests that have criterion-related validity do not necessarily correlate well with each other (do not have convergent validity), as discussed below.

Concurrent validity is one of the three types of criterion-related validity. Criterion-related validity refers the relationship between scores on a test and a concrete behavior (called the criterion) that represents and reflects what the test measures. To prove the criterion-related validity of a test that claims to measure stress, for example, scores on that test would have to exhibit strong relationships to concrete behaviors that everyone regards as signs of stress—for example, depression, anxiety, tension, disturbed sleep, decreased immunological functioning. To prove the criterion-related validity of a test that claims to measure anxiety, scores on that test would need to exhibit strong relationships to concrete behaviors that everyone regards as signs of anxiety—heart rate, sweating, and other physical symptoms. This is the best proof of validity because a criterion (a behavior) must be involved in the proof.

When scores on the test are used to predict the criterion behavior in the present, the validity established is called **concurrent** (both current) criterion-related validity; when scores on the test are used to predict the criterion behavior in the future, the validity established is called **predictive** criterion-related validity; and when scores on the test are used to distinguish between known groups that represent the criterion behavior, the validity established is called **group differences** criterion-related validity. Thus, to prove the concurrent validity of a stress scale, scores on the scale would need to be related to the current stress-related symptoms of a sample. For predictive validity, scores on the stress scale today would need to be able to predict who will develop stress-related symptoms in the future. For group differences validity, scores on the stress scale would need to be able to distinguish between and correctly identify mental patients diagnosed with a stress-related disorder (e.g., anxiety disorder) versus normals— groups that differ on the criterion. **Criterion-related validity, in the end, is the only way to prove that a test measures what it claims to measure and so is valid.** Convergent validity is useful only if one of the tests used in the correlations has criterion-related validity.

In this book, we establish the convergent validity of our measure of sexist discrimination (sexist stress) by examining correlations between scores on our measure and on other measures of stress, the PERI-LES and Hassles scales. The latter two scales have criterion-related validity (it was long ago proven that they are related and can predict symptoms and disorders that are known to be the result of stress). The PERI-LES and Hassles, however, were found in this book not to correlate well with each other (lack of convergent validity), *even though* both have been proven to be valid. In addition then, much of this book is devoted to analyzing the relationship between women's current stress-related symptoms (e.g., anxiety, depression) and our measure of sexist stress. Thus much of the book is a demonstration of the concurrent validity of our measure. In the process, however, we do not observe women for symptoms but instead measure those symptoms with scales that have well-established, concurrent, group-differences, *and* predictive validity. For example, to prove that our measure of stress is a measure of stress, we analyze how well it can predict scores on the Beck Depression Inventory (BDI). The BDI scale is a paper-and-pencil measure of depression that can distinguish between people hospitalized for depression and normals (group differences validity).

Validity is difficult to establish, and yet it is the most important feature of a test. For some tests, it is impossible to prove that they are valid—that they measure what they claim to measure. Intelligence tests are one such example: How does one establish the criterion-related validity of an intelligence test? What behavior can be used as the criterion for intelligence? Most studies have used grades in school, but obviously such grades do not necessarily measure intelligence. The criterion-related validity of intelligence tests has never been demonstrated. For our test, the Schedule of Sexist Events, we use many different types of symptoms **known to be caused by stress** as criterion behaviors, but we use valid scales to measure those symptoms instead of actually observing the symptoms ourselves. Our next step in proving the validity of our scale is to measure the stress-related symptoms without a scale—to measure blood-pressure or cigarette smoking directly and to examine how well scores on our scale predict those behaviors. Such studies are already under way.

References

Affirmative Action Office. (1988, September). *Sexual harassment policy.* Kingston: University of Rhode Island.

Affirmative Action Office. (1994, August 2). *The discrimination complaint process.* Kingston: University of Rhode Island.

Albemarle Paper Co. v. Moody, 422 U.S. 405 (1975).

All work, no play. (1996, July 25). *Providence Journal Bulletin,* p. G1.

Aneshensel, C. S. (1986). Marital and employment role-strain, social support, and depression among adult women. In S. Hobfoll (Ed.), *Stress, social support, and women* (pp. 99-114). Washington, DC: Hemisphere Publishing.

Aneshensel, C. S., Frerichs, R. R., & Clark, V. A. (1981). Family roles and sex differences in depression. *Journal of Health and Social Behavior, 22,* 379.

Ang v. Proctor & Gamble Co., 932 F.2d 540 (6th Cir. 1991).

Atkinson, D. R., Morten, G., & Sue, D. W. (1993). *Counseling American minorities: A cross-cultural perspective.* New York: Brown & Benchmark.

Auto Workers v. Johnson Controls, 499 U.S. 187 (1991).

Ayanian, J. Z., & Epstein, A. M. (1991). Differences in the use of procedures between women and men hospitalized for coronary heart disease. *New England Journal of Medicine, 325,* 221-225.

Barak, A. (1992). Combating sexual harassment. *American Psychologist, 47,* 818-819.

Baruch, G. K., & Barnett, R. (1986). Role quality, multiple role involvement, and psychological well-being in midlife women. *Journal of Personality and Social Psychology, 51,* 578-585.

Baskerville v. Culligan Int'l. Co., 50 F.3d 428 (7th Cir. 1995).

Beck, A. T., Ward, C. H., Mendelson, M., Mock, J. E., & Erbaugh, J. (1961). An inventory for measuring depression. *Archives of General Psychiatry, 4,* 561-571.

Beck, L. E., Gevirtz, R., & Mortola, J. F. (1990). The predictive role of psychological stress on symptom severity in premenstrual syndrome. *Psychosomatic Medicine, 52,* 536-543.

Belle, D. (1990). Poverty and women's mental health. *American Psychologist, 49* 384-389.

Bennett, J. C. (1993). Inclusion of women in clinical trials: Policies for population subgroups. *New England Journal of Medicine, 329,* 288-292.

Betz, N. E., & Fitzgerald, L. E. (1987). *The career psychology of women.* New York: Academic Press.

Billings, A. G., & Moos, R. (1981). The role of coping responses and social resources in attenuating the stress of life events. *Journal of Behavioral Medicine, 4,* 139-157.

Bingham, S. G., & Scherer, L. L. (1993). Factors associated with responses to sexual harassment and satisfaction with outcome. *Sex Roles, 29,* 239-269.

Boennighausen, M. (1994, October). $7.2 million secretary. *The American Lawyer,* p. 76.

Booth-Butterfield, (1991, February). *Information seeking, sexual harassment, and notification in organizations.* Unpublished manuscript, West Virginia University, Department of Communication Studies, Morgantown, WV.

Bronstein, P. (1988). Father-child interaction: Implications for gender role socialization. In P. Bronstein & C. P. Cowan (Eds.), *Fatherhood today: Men's changing role in the family.* New York: John Wiley.

Bronstein, P., Rothblum, E. D., & Solomon, S. E. (1993). Ivy halls and glass walls: Barriers to academia for women and ethnic minorities. In J. Gainen & R. Boice (Eds.), *Building a diverse faculty* (New Directions in Teaching and Learning series). San Francisco: Jossey-Bass.

Browne, K. R. (1991). Title VII as censorship: Hostile environment harassment and the first amendment. *Ohio State Law Journal, 52*(1), 481.

Case, M. A. C. (1995). Disaggregating gender from sex and sexual orientation: The effeminate man in the law and feminine jurisprudence. *Yale Law Journal, 105,* 1.

Civil Rights Act, 42 U.S.C. §§ 2000a through 2000h (1964).

Civil Rights Act, § 102(b), 42 U.S.C. § 1981a(b) (1991).

Clancy, C. M., & Massion, C. T. (1992). American women's health care: A patchwork quilt with gaps. *Journal of the American Medical Association, 268,* 1918-1920.

Cleary, P. D., & Mechanic, D. (1983). Sex differences in psychological distress among married people. *Journal of Health and Social Behavior, 24,* 111-121.

Cohen, S. (1986). Contrasting the Hassles Scale and the Perceived Stress Scale: Who's really measuring appraised stress? *American Psychologist, 41,* 716-718.

Cohen, S., Kamarck, T., & Mermelstein, R. (1983). A global measure of perceived stress. *Journal of Health and Social Behavior, 24,* 385-396.

Cohen, S., & Wills, T. A. (1985). Stress, social support, and the buffering hypothesis. *Psychological Bulletin, 98,* 310-357.

Colastosti, C. (1992). Making 65 on the dollar. *Labor Notes,* 7435 Michigan Ave., Detroit, MI 48210.

Comer, D. R. (1992). Exploring gender-based differences to combat sexual harassment. *American Psychologist, 47,* 819.

Condon, J. T. (1993). Investigation of the reliability and factor structure of a questionnaire for assessment of the premenstrual syndrome. *Journal of Psychosomatic Research, 37,* 543-551.

Corea, G. (1985). *The hidden malpractice: How American medicine mistreats women.* New York: Harper Colophon.

Coughlin, P. C. (1990). Premenstrual syndrome: How marital satisfaction and role choice affect symptom severity. *Social Work, 35,* 351-355.

Council on Ethical and Judicial Affairs of the AMA. (1991). Gender disparities in clinical decision making. *Journal of the American Medical Association, 266,* 559-562.

Darlington, R. B. (1990). Log-linear models. In R. B. Darlington, *Regression and linear models* (pp. 462-501). New York: McGraw-Hill.

DeAngelis v. El Paso Municipal Police Officers Association, 51 F.3d 591 (5th Cir. 1995), *cert. denied,* 116 S.Ct. 473 (1995).

De Maio-Esteves, M. (1990). Mediators of daily stress and perceived health status in adolescent girls. *Nursing Research,* 360-364.

DeMaris, A. (1991). A framework for the interpretation of first-order interaction in logit modeling. *Psychological Bulletin, 110*(3), 557-570.

DePalma, A. (1993, January 24). Rare in Ivy League: Women who work as full professors. *New York Times,* pp. Y-1, Y-11.

Derogatis, L. R., Lipman, R. S., Rickles, K., Uhlenhuth, E. H., & Covi, L. (1974). The Hopkins Symptom Checklist (HSCL): A self-report symptom inventory. *Behavioral Science, 19,* 1-15.

Diaz v. Pan American World Airways, 442 F.2d 385 (5th Cir. 1971), *cert. denied,* 404 U.S. 950 (1971).

Dohrenwend, B. S., Krasnoff, L., Askenasy, A. R., & Dohrenwend, B. P. (1978). Exemplification of a method for scaling life events: The PERI Life Events Scale. *Journal of Health and Social Behavior, 19,* 205-229.

Dothard v. Rawlinson, 433 U.S. 321 (1977).

Drill sergeant at Fort Leonard Wood pleads guilty in sex scandal. (1996, November 13). *The Detroit News.*

Eccles, J. S. (1987). Gender roles and women's achievement-related decisions. *Psychology of Women Quarterly, 11,* 135-172.

EEOC Guidelines on Sex Discrimination, 29 C.F.R. § 1604.2(A) (1990).

Ellison v. Brady, 924 F.2d 872 (9th Cir. 1991).

The Equal Pay Act, 29 U.S.C. § 206 (d)(1) (1963).

Falicov, C. J. (1982). Mexican families. In M. McGoldrick, J. K. Pearch, & J. Giordana (Eds.), *Ethnicity and family therapy* (pp. 134-163). New York: Guilford.

Feagin, J. R., & Feagin, C. B. (1978) *Discrimination American style: Institutional racism and sexism.* Englewood Cliffs, NJ: Prentice Hall.

Fidell, L. S. (1970). Empirical verification of sex discrimination in hiring practices in psychology. *American Psychologist, 25,* 1094-1098.

Fiske, S. T., & Glick, P. (1995). Ambivalence and stereotypes cause sexual harassment: A theory with implications for organizational change. *Journal of Social Issues, 51*(1), 97-115.

Fitzgerald, L. F. (1996a). Institutional policies and procedures. In B. Lott & M. E. Reilly (Eds.), *Combating sexual harassment in higher education* (pp. 129-140). Washington, DC: National Education Association.

Fitzgerald, L. F. (1996b). The legal context of sexual harassment. In B. Lott & M. E. Reilly (Eds.), *Combating sexual harassment in higher education* (pp. 110-128). Washington, DC: National Education Association.

Fitzgerald, L. F., & Betz, N. E. (1983). Issues in the vocational psychology of women. In W. B. Walsh & S. H. Osipow (Eds.), *Handbook of vocational psychology* (Vol. 1). Hillsdale, NJ: Lawrence Erlbaum.

Fitzgerald. L. F., & Ormerod, A. J. (1993). Breaking the silence: The sexual harassment of women in academia and the workplace. In F. L. Denmark & M. A. Paludi (Eds.), *Psychology of women: A handbook of issues and theories* (pp. 553-581). Westport, CT: Greenwood.

Fogel, C. I., & Woods, N. F. (1995). *Women's health care: A comprehensive handbook.* Thousand Oaks, CA: Sage.

Franke, K. M. (1995). The central mistake of sex discrimination law: The disaggregation of sex from gender. *University of Pennsylvania Law Review, 144*(1), 1.

Futternman, L. A., Jones, J. E., Miccio-Fonseca, L. C., & Quigley, M. E. (1992). Severity of premenstrual symptoms in relation to medical/psychiatric problems and life experiences. *Perceptual and Motor Skills, 74,* 787-799.

Gannon, L., Luchetta, T., Pardie, L., & Rhodes, K. (1989). Perimenstrual symptoms: Relationships with chronic stress and selected lifestyle variables. *Behavioral Medicine, 14,* 149-159.

Garcia v. ELF Atochem N. Am., 28 F.3d 446 (5th Cir. 1994).

Gender, race, and the politics of Supreme Court appointments: The import of the Anita Hill/Clarence Thomas hearings. (1992). *Southern California Law Review, 65*(3), 1279-1582.

General Electric Co. v. Gilbert, 429 U.S. 125 (1976).

Gerdes, E. P., & Garber, D. M. (1983). Sex bias in hiring: Effects of job demands and applicant competence. *Sex Roles, 9,* 307-315.

Gigy, L. L. (1980). Self-concept of single women. *Psychology of Women Quarterly, 5,* 321-340.

Goldberg, P. A. (1968). Are women prejudiced against women? *Transaction, 5,* 28-30.

Goodman, L. A., Koss, M. P., & Russo, N. F. (1993). Violence against women: Physical and mental health effects. Part I: Research findings. *Applied & Preventive Psychology: Current Scientific Perspectives, 2,* 111-121.

Gratch, L. V., Bassett, M. E., & Attra, S. L. (1995). The relationship of gender and ethnicity to self-silencing and depression among college students. *Psychology of Women Quarterly, 19,* 509-515.

Grauerholz, E. (1989). Sexual harassment of women professors by students: Exploring the dynamics of power, authority, and gender in a university setting. *Sex Roles, 21,* 789-801.

Greenhouse, S. (1984, October 31). Former steel workers' income falls by half. *New York Times,* p. A-17.

Gregory, C., Minugh, P. A., Riedford, M., Rocchio, C. D., & Saris, C. (1993, March). *Women against sexual harassment (WASH) unite: Working to eliminate sexual harassment from the academic community.* Workshop presented at the national meeting of the Association for Women in Psychology, Atlanta, GA.

Griggs v. Duke Power Co., 401 U.S. 424 (1971).

Grimsley, K. D., Swoboda, F., & Brown, W. (1996, May 3). Sex harassment: Tales of the assembly line. *International Herald Tribune.*

Gupta, N., Jenkins, G. D., Jr., & Beehr, T. A. (1983). Employee gender, gender similarity, and supervisor-subordinate cross-evaluations. *Psychology of Women Quarterly, 8,* 174-184.

Gutek, B. (1985). *Sex and the workplace.* San Francisco: Jossey-Bass.

Gutek, B. A. (1992, February). *Responses to sexual harassment.* Paper read at Claremont Graduate School Symposium on Applied Social Psychology, chaired by S. Oskamp & M. Costanzo.

Hall, R. M., & Sandler, B. R. (1982). *The classroom climate.* Washington, DC: Association of American Colleges.

Hardin v. Stynchcomb, 691 F.2d 1364 (11th Cir. 1982).

Harris & Associates. (1985, July). Harris poll. *Business Week.*

Harris v. Forklift Systems, Inc., 61 FEP 240 (M.D. Tenn. 1991).

Harris v. Forklift Systems, Inc., 976 F.2d 733 (6th Cir. 1992).

Harris v. Forklift Systems, Inc. 510 U.S. 17 (1993).

Hartstein, B. A. (1995). Weeks v. Baker & McKenzie: A potential "blueprint" for sexual harassment litigation. *Employee Relations Law Journal, 20*(4), 657.

Hawthorne, M. H. (1993). Women's recovery from coronary artery bypass surgery. *Scholarly Inquiry for Nursing Practice: An International Journal, 7,* 223-244.

Hayes v. Shelby Memorial Hospital, 726 F.2d 1543 (11th Cir. 1984).

Hays, W. L. (1981). *Statistics.* New York: Holt.

Heilbrun, A. B., Jr., & Frank, M. E. (1989). Self-preoccupation and general stress level as sensitizing factors in premenstrual and menstrual distress. *Journal of Psychosomatic Research, 33,* 571-577.

Henley, N. M. (1977). *Body politics: Power, sex, and nonverbal communication.* Englewood Cliffs, NJ: Prentice Hall.

Henson v. Dundee, 682 F.2d 897 (11th Cir. 1982).

Herbert, T. B., & Cohen, S. (1993a). Depression and immunity: A meta-analytic review. *Psychological Bulletin, 113,* 1-15.

Herbert, T. B., & Cohen, S. (1993b). Stress and immunity in humans: A meta-analytic review. *Psychosomatic Medicine, 5,* 364-379.

Heston, T. F., & Lewis, L. M. (1992). Gender bias in the evaluation and management of acute nontraumatic chest pain. *Family Practice Research & Journal, 12,* 383-389.

Holahan, C. K., Holahan, C. J., & Belk, S. (1984). Adjustment to aging: The role of life stress, hassles, and self-efficacy. *Health Psychology, 3,* 315-328.

Hopkins v. Baltimore Gas & Elec. Co., 77 F.3d 745 (4th Cir. 1996).

Idson, T. L., & Price, H. F. (1992). An analysis of wage differentials by gender and ethnicity in the public sector. *The Review of Black Political Economy, 20,* 75-97.

Irwin, M., et al. (1986a). Depression and changes in T-cell sub-populations. *Psychosomatic Medicine, 48,* 303-304.

Irwin, M., et al. (1986b). Life events, depression, and natural killer cell activity. *Psychopharmacology Bulletin, 22,* 1093-1096.

Irwin, M., et al. (1987). Life events, depressive symptoms, and immune function. *American Journal of Psychiatry, 144,* 437-441.

Jagacinski, C. M., LeBold, W. K., & Linden, K. W. (1987). The relative career advancement of men and women engineers in the United States. *Work and Stress, 1,* 235-247.

Jessor, R., & Jessor, S. L. (1977). *Problem behavior and psychosocial development: A longitudinal study of youth.* New York: Academic Press.

Jury Verdict Research. (1996). *Tips to tackle wrongful termination.* Horsham, PA: LRP Publications.

Kanner, A. D., Coyne, J. C., Schaeffer, C., & Lazarus, R. S. (1981). Comparison of two modes of stress measurement: Daily hassles and uplifts versus major life events. *Journal of Behavioral Medicine, 4,* 1-39.

Kelly, E. (1995, September 8). Ethics Committee says court fight, scope dragged out Packwood probe. *Gannett News Service.*

Kelly, M. P. F. (1996, July 25). Feminism and the morality police. *Providence Journal Bulletin,* p. B6.

Kessler, R. C., & McLeod, J. D. (1984). Sex differences in vulnerability to undesirable life events. *American Sociological Review, 49,* 620-631.

Kessler, R. C., Price, R. H., & Wortman, C. B. (1985). Social factors in psychopathology: Stress, social support, and coping processes. *Annual Review of Psychology, 36,* 531-572.

Kiecolt-Glaser, J. K., et al. (1984a). Psychosocal modifiers of immocompetence in medical students. *Psychosomatic Medicine, 46,* 7-14.

Kiecolt-Glaser, J. K., et al. (1984b). Stress and the transformation of lympocytes by Epstein-Barr virus. *Journal of Behavioral Medicine, 7,* 1-12.

Kiecolt-Glaser, J. K., et al. (1985). Distress and DNA repair in human lympocytes. *Journal of Behavioral Medicine, 8,* 311-320.

Kiecolt-Glaser, J. K., et al. (1986). Modulation of cellular immunity in medical students. *Journal of Behavioral Medicine, 9,* 5-21.

Kiecolt-Glaser, J. K., et al. (1987). Marital quality, marital disruption, and immune function. *Psychosomatic Medicine, 49,* 13-34.

Kiecolt-Glaser, J. K., et al. (1988a). Marital discord and immunity in males. *Psychosomatic Medicine, 50,* 213-229.

Kiecolt-Glaser, J. K., et al. (1988b). Methodological issues in behavioral immunology research with humans. *Brain, Behavior, and Immunity, 2,* 67-78.

Kiecolt-Glaser, J. K., et al. (1993). Negative behavior during marital conflict is associated with immunological down-regulation. *Psychosomatic Medicine, 55,* 395-409.

Kiecolt-Glaser, J. K., & Glaser, R. (1987). Psychosocial influences on herpesvirus latency. In E. Kurstack, Z. J. Lipowski, & P. V. Morozov (Eds.), *Viruses, immunity, and mental disorders* (pp. 403-412). New York: Plenum.

Killian, M. (1996, November 12). Shalikashvili calls sex scandal a tragedy. *Chicago Tribune,* p. 3.

Klein, E. (1984). *Gender politics.* Cambridge, MA: Harvard University Press.

Kleinman, C. (1983, July 26). Gender gap in educational executive posts. *Providence Evening Bulletin.*

Kleinman, C. (1988, August 29). More women managers being fired than men. *Providence Journal Bulletin,* p. E1.

Kleinman, C. (1991, January 21). Women stopped by "glass ceiling." *Providence Journal Bulletin,* p. A12.

Klonoff, E. A., & Landrine, H. (1992). Sex roles, occupational roles, and symptom reporting: A test of competing hypotheses on sex differences. *Journal of Behavioral Medicine, 15,* 355-364.

Klonoff, E. A., & Landrine, H. (1995). The Schedule of Sexist Events: A measure of lifetime and recent sexist discrimination in women's lives. *Psychology of Women Quarterly, 19* (4), 439-472.

Klonoff, E. A., Landrine, H., & Scott, J. (1995). Double jeopardy: Ethnicity and gender in health research. In H. Landrine (Ed.), *Bringing cultural diversity to feminist psychology* (pp. 335-360). Washington, DC: American Psychological Association.

Kobasa, S. C. (1979). Stressful life events, personality, and health: An inquiry into hardiness. *Journal of Personality and Social Psychology, 37,* 1-11.

Koss, M. P., Koss, P. G., & Woodruff, W. J. (1991). Deleterious effects of criminal victimization on women's health and medical utilization. *Archives of Internal Medicine, 151,* 342-357.

Krieger, N. (1990). Racial and gender discrimination: Risk factors for high blood pressure? *Social Science and Medicine, 30*(12), 1273-1281.

Krieger, N., & Sidney, S. (1996). Racial discrimination and blood pressure: The CARDIA study of young Black and White adults. *American Journal of Public Health, 86*(10), 1370-1378.

Kutner, N. G., & Brogan, D. (1990). Sex stereotypes and health care. *Sex Roles, 24,* 279-290.

Landrine, H. (1992). *The politics of madness.* New York: Peter Lang.

Landrine, H. (1995). *Bringing cultural diversity to feminist psychology: Theory, research, and practice.* Washington, DC: American Psychological Association.

Landrine, H., & Klonoff, E. A. (1996a). *African American acculturation: Deconstructing race and revising culture.* Thousand Oaks, CA: Sage.

Landrine, H., & Klonoff, E. A. (1996b). The Schedule of Racist Events: A measure of racial discrimination and a study of its negative physical and mental health consequences. *Journal of Black Psychology, 22*(2), 136-160.

Landrine, H., Klonoff, E. A., Alcaraz, R., Scott, J., & Wilkins, P. (1995). Multiple variables in discrimination. In B. Lott & D. Maluso (Eds.), *The social psychology of interpersonal discrimination* (pp. 224). New York: Guilford.

Landrine, H., Klonoff, E. A., Gibbs, J., Manning, V., & Lund, M. (1995). Physical and psychiatric correlates of gender discrimination: An application of the Schedule of Sexist Events. *Psychology of Women Quarterly, 19*(4), 473-492.

Lazarus, R. S. (1966). *Psychological stress and the coping process.* New York: McGraw-Hill.

Lazarus, R. S., DeLongis, A., Folkman, S., & Gruen, R. (1985). Stress and adaptational outcomes: The problem of confounded measures. *American Psychologist, 40,* 770-779.

Lazarus, R. S., & Folkman, S. (1986). Reply to Cohen. *American Psychologist, 41,* 718-719.

Lazarus, R. S., & Launier, R. (1978). Stress-related transactions between person and environment. In L. A. Pervin & M. Lewis (Eds.), *Perspectives in interactional psychology* (pp. 287-327). New York: Plenum.

Leader, J. (1991, November 16). For comedienne Diane Ford, unequal pay isn't funny. *Providence Journal Bulletin,* p. A10.

Lee, L., & Heppner, P. P. (1991). The development and evaluation of a sexual harassment inventory. *Journal of Counseling and Development, 69,* 512-517.

Lee, V. E., Marks, H. M., & Byrd, T. (1994). Sexism in single-sex and coeducational independent secondary school classrooms. *Sociology of Education, 67,* 92-120.

Levy, S. M., et al. (1989). Persistently low natural killer cell activity in normal adults. *Natural Immune Cell Growth Regulation, 8,* 173-186.

Lex, B., Teoh, S. K., Lagomasino, I., et al. (1990). Characteristics of women receiving mandated treatment for alcohol or poly-substance dependence in Massachusetts. *Drugs and Alcohol Dependence, 25,* 13-20.

Lipsett v. University of Puerto Rico, 864 F.2d 881 (1st Cir. 1988).

Litt, I. F. (1992). Letter from the director. *Stanford University Institute for Research on Women and Gender Newsletter, 16*(2), 1.

Lott, B. (1987). Sexist discrimination as distancing behavior: I. A laboratory demonstration. *Psychology of Women Quarterly, 11,* 47-58.

Lott, B. (1989). Sexist discrimination as distancing behavior: II. Primetime television. *Psychology of Women Quarterly, 13,* 341-355.

Lott, B. L. (1990). Dual natures or learned behavior: The challenge to feminist psychology. In R. T. Hare-Mustin & J. Marecek (Eds.), *Making a difference: Psychology and the construction of gender* (pp. 65-101). New Haven, CT: Yale University Press.

Lott, B. L. (1994). *Women's lives: Themes and variations in gender learning.* Pacific Grove, CA: Brooks/Cole.

Lott, B. (1995). Distancing from women: Interpersonal sexist discrimination. In B. Lott & D. Maluso (Eds.), *The social psychology of interpersonal discrimination* (pp. 12-49). New York: Guilford.

Lott, B. (1996). Sexual harassment: Consequences and remedies. In B. Lott & M. E. Reilly (Eds.), *Combating sexual harassment in higher education* (pp. 229-244). Washington, DC: National Education Association.

Lott, B., Asquith, K., & Doyon, T. (1997). *Women's responses to personal experiences of sexist discrimination related to ethnicity and age.* Unpublished paper, University of Rhode Island.

Lott, B., Lott, A. J., & Fernald, J. (1990). Individual differences in distancing responses to women on a photo choice task. *Sex Roles, 22,* 97-110.

Lott, B., & Maluso, D. (1995). *The social psychology of interpersonal discrimination.* New York: Guilford.

Lott, B., & Rocchio, L. (in press). Standing up, talking back, and taking charge: Strategies and outcomes in collective action against sexual harassment. In L. H. Collins, J. Chrisler, & K. Quina (Eds.), *Arming Athena: Career strategies for women academics.* Thousand Oaks, CA: Sage.

Magidson, J. (1981). Qualitative variance, entropy, and correlation ratios for nominal dependent variables. *Social Science Research, 10,* 177-194.

Marcus, A. C., & Siegel, J. M. (1982). Sex differences in the use of physician services. *Journal of Health and Social Behavior, 23,* 186-197.

Martin, S. E. (1994). "Outsider within" the stationhouse: The impact of race and gender on
    Black women. *Social Problems, 41,* 383-400.

McGrath, E., Strickland, B. R., Keita, G. P., & Russo, N. F. (1990). *Women and depression:
    Risk factors and treatment issues.* Washington, DC: American Psychological Associa-
    tion.

Meritor Savings Bank v. Vinson, 477 U.S. 57 (1986).

Metzler, C. W., Noell, J., Biglan, A., Ary, D., & Smolkowski, K. (1994). The social context
    for risky sexual behavior among adolescents. *Journal of Behavioral Medicine, 17,*
    419-438.

Monroe, S. M. (1982). Major and minor life events as predictors of psychological distress.
    General Psychiatry, 39, 189-203.

Myers, J. K., Weissman, M. M, Tischler, G. L., Holzer, C. E., Leaf, P. J., Orvaschel, H.,
    Anthony, J. C., Boyd, J. H., Burke, J. D., Kramer, M., & Stoltzman, R. (1984).
    Six-month prevalence of psychiatric disorders in three communities. *Archives of
    General Psychiatry, 41,* 959-967.

Naliboff, B. D., et al. (1991). Immunological changes in young and old adults during brief
    laboratory stress. *Psychosomatic Medicine, 53,* 121-132.

Neal, A. (1995, January 28). Where to draw the line between porn and rights. *The In-
    dianapolis Star.*

Neuborne, E. (1996, May 3). Sex harassment suits soar. *USA Today,* p. A1.

Newmann, J. P. (1986). Gender, life strains, and depression. *Journal of Health and Social
    Behavior, 27,* 161-178.

Newmann, J. P. (1987). Gender differences in vulnerability to depression. *Social Service
    Review, 61,* 447-468.

News from the United Nations. (1991, November). *SPSSI Newsletter,* p. 11.

Nieva, V. F., & Gutek, B. A. (1981). *Women and work: A psychological perspective.* New
    York: Praeger.

Nolen-Hoeksema, S. (1990). *Sex differences in depression.* Stanford, CA: Stanford Univer-
    sity Press.

O'Leary, A. (1990). Stress, emotion, and human immune function. *Psychological Bulletin,
    103,* 363-383.

The Omnibus Crime Control Act, Pub. L. 103-322, Title IV, § 40141(b) (1994).

Oncale v. Sundowner Offshore Servs., 83 F.3d 118 (5th Cir. 1996).

O'Neill, J. (1985). Role differentiation and the gender gap in wage rates. In L. Larwood,
    A. H. Stromberg, & B. A. Guteck (Eds.), *Women and work* (pp. 50-75). Beverly Hills,
    CA: Sage.

Paglia, C. (1994). *Vamps and tramps: New essays.* New York: Vintage.

Paludi, M. A. (1990). *Ivory power: Sexual harassment on campus.* Albany: SUNY Press.

Paludi, M. A., & Bauer, W. D. (1983). Goldberg revisited: What's in an author's name? *Sex
    Roles, 9,* 387-390.

Paludi, M. A., & Strayer, L. A. (1985). What's in an author's name? Differential evaluations
    of performance as a function of author's name. *Sex Roles, 10,* 353-361.

Paludi, M., et al. (1995). Ethnicity and sexual harassment. In H. Landrine (Ed.), *Bringing
    cultural diversity to feminist psychology* (pp. 177-191). Washington, DC: American
    Psychological Association.

Perman, L., & Stevens, B. (1989). Industrial segregation and the gender distribution of fringe
    benefits. *Gender & Society, 3,* 388-404.

Perrone, J. (1991). Sexism far from dead in medicine. *American Medical News,* p. 5.

Physicians' Health Study Group. (1989). Final report on the aspirin component of the ongoing
    physician's health study. *New England Journal of Medicine, 321,* 129-135.

Piper, A. M. S. (1990). Higher-order discrimination. In O. Flanagan & A. O. Rorty (Eds.), *Identity, character, and morality: Essays in moral psychology* (pp. 285-309). Cambridge: MIT Press.

Posner, R. A. (1989, Fall). An economic analysis of sex discrimination laws. *University of Chicago Law Review, 56,* 1311, 1318-1320.

The Pregnancy Discrimination Act, 42 U.S.C. § 701(k) (1978).

Pugliesi, K. (1988). Employment characteristics, social support, and well-being of women. *Women and Health, 14,* 35-58.

Quick v. Donaldson Co., Inc., 90 F.3d 1372 (8th Cir. 1996).

Radloff, L. S. (1977). The CES-D Scale: A self-report depression scale for research in the general population. *Applied Psychological Measurement, 1,* 385-401.

Radtke v. Everett, 501 N.W.2d 155 (Mich. 1993).

Reed v. Shepard, 939 F.2d 484 (7th Cir. 1991).

Reid, R. L., & Yen, S. S. C. (1981). Premenstrual syndrome. *American Journal of Obstetrics and Gynecology, 139,* 85-104.

Reifman, A., Biernat, M., & Lang, E. (1991). Stress, social support, and health in married professional women with small children. *Psychology of Women Quarterly, 15,* 431-445.

Repetti, R. L., Matthews, K. A., & Waldron, I. (1989). Employment and women's health. *American Psychologist, 44,* 1394-1401.

Rickel, A. U., Gerrad, M., & Iscoe, I. (Eds.). (1984). *Social and psychological problems of women.* Washington, DC: Hemisphere.

Riger, S. (1991). Gender dilemmas in sexual harassment policies and procedures. *American Psychologist, 46,* 497-505.

Robins, L. N., Helzer, J. E., Weissman, M. M., Orvaschel, H., Gruenberg, E., Burke, J. D., & Regier, D. A. (1984). Lifetime prevalence of specific psychiatric disorders in three sites. *Archives of General Psychiatry, 41,* 949-958.

Rogers v. EEOC, 454 F.2d 234 (5th Cir. 1971).

Rohter, L. (1991, March 17). Are women directors an endangered species? *New York Times,* pp. H14, H20, H21.

Roiphe, K. (1993). *The morning after: Sex, fear, and feminism on campus.* Boston: Little, Brown.

Root, M. P. P. (1995). The psychology of Asian American women. In H. Landrine (Ed.), *Bringing cultural diversity to feminist psychology* (pp. 265-301). Washington, DC: American Psychological Association.

Rosenberg, J., Perlstadt, H., & Phillips, W. R. F. (1993). Now that we are here: Discrimination, disparagement, and harassment at work and the experience of women lawyers. *Gender & Society, 7,* 415-433.

Rowe, M. P. (1973, December). *The progress of women in educational institutions: The Saturn's rings phenomenon.* Unpublished manuscript, Massachusetts Institute of Technology, Cambridge.

Rowe, M. P. (1990). Barriers to equality: The power of subtle discrimination to maintain unequal opportunity. *Employee Responsibilities and Rights Journal, 3,* 153-163.

Rubin, B. M. (1995, April 9). Ouster of top execs raises sexual harassment issue to new level. *Chicago Tribune.*

Ruble, D. (1977). Premenstrual symptoms: A reinterpretation. *Science, 197,* 291-292.

Russo, N. F. (1995). Women's mental health: Research agenda for the twenty-first century. In B. Brown, B. Kramer, P. Reiker, & C. Willie (Eds.), *Mental health, racism, and sexism* (pp. 373-396). Pittsburgh: University of Pittsburgh Press.

Russo, N. F., Amaro, H., & Winter, M. (1987). The use of inpatient mental health services by Hispanic women. *Psychology of Women Quarterly, 11*(4), 427-442.

Russo, N. F., & Green, B. L. (1993). Women and mental health. In F. L. Denmark & M. A. Paludi (Eds.), *Psychology of women: A handbook of issues and theories* (pp. 379-436). Westport, CT: Greenwood.

Russo, N. F., & Sobel, S. B. (1981). Sex differences in the utilization of mental health facilities. *Professional Psychology, 12*, 7-19.

Saris, R. N., Johnston, I., & Lott, B. (1995). Women as cues for men's approach or distancing behavior: A study of interpersonal sexist discrimination. *Sex Roles, 33*, 289-298.

Schmidt, P. (1985, March 24). For the women, still a long way to go. *New York Times*, sec. 12, pp. 14-15.

Schreiner, T. (1984, May 29). A revolution that has just begun. *USA Today*, p. 40.

Schur, E. M. (1983). *Labeling women deviant*. Philadelphia: Temple University Press.

Selvin, P. (1991). Does the Harrison case reveal sexism in math? *Science, 252*, 1781-1783.

Sexual harassment. (1994, February). Kingston: University of Rhode Island Publications Office.

Smeltzer, C., & Whipple, B. (1991). Women and HIV infection. *Image, 23*(4), 249-256.

Spielberger, C. D., Gorsuch, R. L., & Lushene, R. (1970). *State-trait anxiety inventory manual*. Palo Alto, CA: Consulting Psychologist Press.

Sprogis v. United Air Lines, 444 F.2d 1194 (7th Cir. 1971), *cert. denied*, 404 U.S. 991 (1971).

Stanko, E. A. (1985). *Intimate intrusions: Women's experience of male violence*. London: Routledge & Kegan Paul.

Stead, B. A., & Zinkhan, G. M. (1986). Service priority in department stores: The effect of customer gender and sex. *Sex Roles, 15*, 501-611.

Stolberg, S. (1996, November 11). Army reveals more details of sex inquiry. *Los Angeles Times*, p. A1.

Stombler, M., & Martin, P. Y. (1994). Bringing women in, keeping women down: Fraternity "little sister" organizations. *Journal of Contemporary Ethnography, 23*, 150-184.

Stukey v. United States Air Force, 809 F.Supp. 536 (S.D. Ohio 1992).

Tangri, S. S., Burt, M. R., & Johnson, L. B. (1982). Sexual harassment at work: Three exploratory models. *Journal of Social Issues, 38*(4), 33-54.

Taylor, S. E. (1995). *Health psychology*. New York: McGraw-Hill.

Teamsters v. United States, 431 U.S. 324 (1977).

Thoits, P. A. (1984). Explaining distributions of psychological vulnerability: Lack of social support in the face of life stress. *Social Forces, 63*, 463-481.

Tobin, J. N., Wassertheil-Smoller, S., Wexler, J. P., et al. (1987). Sex bias in considering coronary bypass surgery. *Annals of Internal Medicine, 107*, 19-25.

Torres v. National Precision Blanking, 1996 U.S. Dist. LEXIS 14952 (N.D. Ill. 1996).

Torres v. Wisconsin Department of Health & Social Services, 859 F.2d 1523 (7th Cir. 1988), *cert. denied*, 489 U.S. 1017 (1989).

U.S. Bureau of the Census. (1991). *Current population reports, Series P-60, No. 172: Money income of households, families, and persons in the United States, 1988 and 1989*. Washington, DC: Government Printing Office.

U.S. Merit System Protection Board. (1981). *Sexual harassment in the federal workplace*. Washington, DC: Government Printing Office.

Verbrugge, L. (1980). Sex differences in complaints and diagnoses. *Journal of Behavioral Medicine, 3*, 327-355.

Verbrugge, L. (1985). Gender and health: An update on hypotheses and evidence. *Journal of Health and Social Behavior, 26*, 156-182.

Verbrugge, L. (1986). Role burdens and physical health of women and men. *Women and Health, 11*, 47-77.

Verbrugge, L. (1989). The twain meet: Empirical explanations of sex differences in health and mortality. *Journal of Health and Social Behavior, 30*, 282-304.

Vinson v. Taylor, 753 F.2d 141 (D.C. Cir. 1985).

Volokh, E. (1992). Freedom of speech and workplace harassment. *UCLA Law Review, 39,* 1791.

Waldron, I., & Jacobs, J. A. (1989). Effects of multiple roles on women's health. *Women and Health, 15,* 3-19.

Wassertheil-Smoller, S., Steingart, R. M., Wexler, J. P., et al. (1987). Nuclear scans: A clinical decision-making tool that reduces the need for cardiac catheterization. *Journal of Chronic Disorders, 40,* 385-397.

Weeks v. Baker & McKenzie, No. 943043, 1994 WL 636488 (Cal. Super. Sept. 30, 1994).

Weissman, M. M., & Merikangas, K. R. (1986). The epidemiology of anxiety and panic disorders: An update. *Journal of Clinical Psychiatry, 47* (6 Supplement), 11-17.

Wenger, N. K. (1990). Gender, coronary artery disease, and coronary bypass surgery. *Annals of Internal Medicine, 112,* 557-558.

Williams v. Saxbe, 413 F. Supp. 654 (D.D.C. 1976), *vacated,* 587 F.2d 1240 (D.C. Cir. 1978). (Vacation based on district court's failure to try the case *de novo*)

Willingham v. Macon Telegraph Publishing Co., 507 F.2d 1084 (5th Cir. 1973).

Wohlgemuth, E., & Betz, N. E. (1991). Gender as a mediator of the relationship of stress and social support to physical health in college students. *Journal of Counseling Psychology, 38,* 367-374.

Wolman, C., & Frank, H. (1975). The solo woman in a professional peer group. *American Journal of Orthopsychiatry, 45,* 164-171.

Woods, N. F. (1984). Relationship of socialization and stress to perimenstrual symptoms, disability, and menstrual attitudes. *Nursing Research, 33,* 145-149.

Woods, N. F., Dery, G. K., & Most, A. (1982) Stressful life events and perimenstrual symptoms. *Journal of Human Stress, 8,* 23-30.

Woods, N. F., Lentz, M., & Mitchell, E. (1993). The new woman: Health-promoting and health-damaging behaviors. *Health Care for Women International, 14,* 389-405.

Woods, N. F., Most, A., & Longnecker, G. D. (1985). Major life events, daily stressors, and perimenstrual symptoms. *Nursing Research, 34,* 263-267.

Wright v. Olin Corp., 697 F.2d 1172 (4th Cir. 1982).

Wrightson v. Pizza Hut of America, Inc., 1996 U.S. App. LEXIS 28266 (4th Cir. 1996).

Yarkin, K. L., Town, J. P., & Wallston, B. S. (1982). Blacks and women must try harder: Stimulus persons' race and sex and attributions of causality. *Personality and Social Psychology Bulletin, 8,* 21-24.

Yoder, J. D., & Aniakudo, P. (1995). The responses of African American women firefighters to gender harassment at work. *Sex Roles, 32,* 125-137.

Yount, K. R. (1991). Ladies, flirts, and tomboys: Strategies for managing sexual harassment in an underground coal mine. *Journal of Contemporary Ethnography, 19,* 396-422.

Zinkhan, G. M., & Stoiadan, L. F. (1984). Impact of sex role stereotypes on service priority in department stores. *Journal of Applied Psychology, 69,* 691-693.

Zorn v. Helene Curtis, Inc., 903F Supp. 1266 (N.D. Ill. 1995).

Index

About the Authors

Hope Landrine is a Black clinical and health psychologist. She received her Ph.D. in clinical psychology from the University of Rhode Island, postdoctoral training in social psychology at Stanford University, and postdoctoral training in preventive medicine as a National Cancer Institute Fellow in the Department of Preventive Medicine, University of Southern California Medical School. A Senior Research Scientist at the Public Health Foundation (Los Angeles County), her research focuses on the health of women and of ethnic-cultural minorities. Her outstanding research in both areas has gained her Fellow status in APA Division 35 (Psychology of Women) and future Fellow status in Division 45 (Psychology of Ethnic Minorities), more than $1 million in grants, the 1996 AWP (Association for Women in Psychology) Distinguished Publication Award, and numerous other awards. Her books include *The Politics of Madness, Bringing Cultural Diversity to Feminist Psychology,* and (with Elizabeth Klonoff), *African American Acculturation: Deconstructing Race and Reviving Culture* (Sage, 1996) and *Preventing Misdiagnosis of Women: A Guide to Physical Disorders That Have Psychiatric Symptoms* (Sage, 1997).

Elizabeth A. Klonoff, a clinical and health psychologist, received her Ph.D. in clinical psychology from the University of Oregon. She was the Director of the Behavioral Medicine Clinic at University Hospitals of Cleveland, Case Western Reserve University Medical School, and is currently Professor of Psychology and Executive Director of the Behavioral Health Institute at California State University, San Bernardino. In addition to teaching and acting as director of the Institute, she conducts numerous, grant-supported research projects on sexism, racism, and physical and mental health. She has published widely on culture and gender diversity in clinical psychology, behavioral medicine, and preventive medicine. Her most recent books (with Hope Landrine) are *African American Acculturation: Deconstructing Race and Reviving Culture* (Sage, 1996) and *Preventing Misdiagnosis of Women: A Guide to Physical Disorders That Have Psychiatric Symptoms* (Sage, 1997).

About the Contributors

Phyllis Bronstein received her Ph.D. in psychology from Harvard University and is currently Associate Professor of Clinical Psychology at the University of Vermont. Her research and writing has focused on the long-term effects of parenting on early and late adolescent adjustment, gender role socialization within the family, and the professional advancement of women and people of color in academia. Her books include (with C. P. Cowan) *Fatherhood Today: Men's Changing Role in the Family,* and (with K. Quina) *Teaching a Psychology of People: Resources For Gender and Sociocultural Awareness,* which won the 1989 Distinguished Publication Award from the Association for Women in Psychology.

Robert H. Klonoff received an A.B. from the University of California at Berkeley and a J.D. from Yale University. Subsequently, he clerked for then-Chief Judge John R. Brown of the U.S. Court of Appeals for the Fifth Circuit and then served for a number of years as an Assistant U.S. Attorney for the District of Columbia and as an Assistant to the Solicitor General of the United States, where he briefed and argued many cases before the U.S. Supreme Court. He also was a visiting professor at the University of San Diego School of Law. He is currently a partner with Jones, Day, Reavis & Pogue, where he has worked on a variety of litigation matters, including one of the largest discrimination cases ever brought by the Equal Employment Opportunity Commission. His books include (with Paul L. Colby) *Sponsorship Strategy: Evidentiary Tactics for Winning Jury Trials.*

Bernice Lott received her Ph.D. in social psychology from UCLA and is currently a Professor of Psychology and Women's Studies at the University of Rhode Island. She served as President of Division 35 (Psychology of Women) of the American Psychological Association (1991-1992) and has received numerous awards and honors for her outstanding and distinguished contributions to the study of women. Her books include: *Women's Lives: Themes and Variations in Gender Learning, The Social Psychology of Interpersonal Discrimination* (co-edited with Diane Maluso), and *Combating Sexual Harassment in Higher Education* (co-edited with Mary Ellen Reilly).

Lisa M. Rocchio received her Ph.D. in clinical psychology from the University of Rhode Island. She is currently in private practice in North Kingstown, Rhode Island, and is conducting postdoctoral research at Butler Hospital in Providence. Her primary areas of expertise include violence against women and feminist therapy.

Lynne A. Wurzburg received a B.S. in industrial & labor relations from Cornell University and her J.D. from the University of Michigan. She completed a legal internship with Amnesty International's Secretariat in London and practiced with the law firm of McGuire, Woods, Battle & Boothe in Washington, D.C., before joining Jones, Day, Reavis & Pogue as an associate. She has worked on numerous discrimination cases brought in federal court.

4160